CLOSE TO THE EDGE

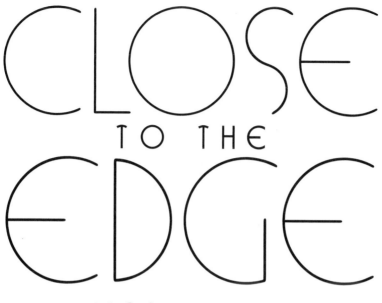

CLOSE
TO THE
EDGE

HOW YES'S MASTERPIECE
DEFINED PROG ROCK

WILL ROMANO

Backbeat
Books

AN IMPRINT OF HAL LEONARD

Published in 2017 by Backbeat Books
An Imprint of Hal Leonard LLC
7777 West Bluemound Road
Milwaukee, WI 53213

Trade Book Division Editorial Offices
33 Plymouth St., Montclair, NJ 07042

Printed in the United States of America

All photos are from the author's collection unless otherwise noted.

Book design by John J. Flannery

Library of Congress Cataloging-in-Publication Data

Names: Romano, Will, 1970- author.
Title: Close to the edge : how Yes's masterpiece defined prog rock / Will
   Romano.
Description: Montclair : Backbeat Books, 2017. | Includes bibliographical
   references and index.
Identifiers: LCCN 2016027534 | ISBN 9781617136177 (pbk.)
Subjects: LCSH: Yes (Musical group). Close to the edge. | Progressive rock
   (Music)--England--History and criticism.
Classification: LCC ML421.Y48 R66 2017 | DDC 782.42166092/2--dc23

LC record available at https://lccn.loc.gov/2016027534

www.backbeatbooks.com

CONTENTS

ACKNOWLEDGMENTS

I would like to thank the following people for their time, input, insight:

Joe Abell, Erin C. Alghandoor (archivist, Kean University), Jon Anderson, David Arkenstone, Victor Atkins, Helena Backman (librarian, special collections, Stockholm University Library), Carl Baldassarre, John Ball (library associate senior, archival services, University of Akron), Peter Banks, Jock Bartley, Clive Bayley, Werner Baumgartner, Jen Beane (records department, Burlington Vermont Police Department), Ian Bell, Jennifer J. Betts (archivist, Brown University), Big Yellow Duck Studios (and Chris Gibney), Jessica Blackwell (librarian, special collections and archives, Dana Porter Library, University of Waterloo), Marshall Blonstein, Jon Brewer, Dave Bryce, Adam Budofsky (*Modern Drummer* magazine), Chris Burns (curator of manuscripts and university archivist, special collections, Bailey/Howe Library, University of Vermont), Colin Carter, Richard Chamberlain, Roy Clair, Andy Clark, Jenny Clark (archivist, Pilkington Library, Loughborough University), Joe Clark, Ed Clift, Cloud 9 Recordings, Bill Cobham, Chad "Chatty" Cooper, Alex Cora, Cove City Studios, Rachel Crane (Wichita State University), Ben Craven, Bob D'Amico, Ken Dashow, Frank Davies, Amanda Dean, Roger Dean, Jack DeJohnette, Claire Deibler, Barry Diament, Bob Dobiesz (assistant library director, Nash Library, Gannon University), Geoff Downes, Brian Draper, Dream Recording Studios, Gary Duncan, Sharron Elkabas, Kim Estlund, Jon Field, Jeff Franklin, Renée Geyer, George Ghiz, Linda Glasser (acquisitions coordinator, Lakeland Community College Library), Bob Gluck, Stewart Goldring, Phillip Goodhand-Tait, Jerry Greenberg, Rayford Griffin, Bob Hagger, James Hammer at Clair Global, Claire Hamill, Thor Harris, Tony Harris and Phil's Book (www.philsbook.com), Tim Hartnett (associate librarian, Feinberg Library, SUNY Plattsburgh), Glyn Havard, Justin Hayward, Lori Hehr, John Helliwell, Celeste Hessler (assistant head of the music library/music cataloger, Stony Brook University), Steve Hoffman, Jason How, Steve Howe, Virgil Howe, Max Hunt, Gregg Jackman, Bob Jackson, Randy Jackson, Al Jacquez, Gary Jansen, Marshall Jefferson, Jerry at J&L Studios, Carol Kaye, Conrad Keely, Stephen Kerber, Chris Kimsey, Debra Kimok, Angela Kindig (assistant archivist, University of Notre Dame Archives), Danny Klein (J. Geils Band), Cynthia Kristof (Kent State), Ray Laidlaw, Elizabeth Lang, Tony La Russa, Mark Lehman, Anne Leighton, Frank Levi, Stephanie Lewin-Lane (coordinator of the music library, University of Houston), Hannu Lintu, John Lodge, Dave Love, Patrick MacDougall, Peter Machajdik, Michael Manring, Stephen Marsh, Jeffrey D. Marshall (director of research collections, Bailey/Howe Library University of Vermont), Pat Mastelotto, Caitlin McCallum, Amy McDonald (assistant archivist, David M. Rubenstein Rare Book and Manuscript Library, Duke University), John McLaughlin, Victoria Paige Meyerink, Mario Millo, Lisa Miranda, Rich Mouser, Dale Newman, the staff of the New York City County Clerk's Office, Kathy Nolan, Phil Naro, Paul Northfield, Kristen J. Nyitray (head of special collections and university archives, associate librarian, Frank Melville, Jr. Memorial Library, Room E-2320, Stony Brook University), Ryo Okumoto, Paul O'Neill, Kathryn Orford, Carl Palmer, Ilka Erren Pardiñas, Brian Parrish, Leonardo Pavkovic, Dale Pelton, Morris Pert, Shawn Phillips, Bruce Pilato, PMA Recording Studios, Olga Potekhina, Jason Prufer (senior library associate, Kent State University Libraries), Aida Räihälä, Les Reed, Father Jason Rendell (The Parish of St. Andrew's, Kingsbury), Tom Rhea, William (Billy) Ritchie, Mark Robertson, Sharon Romano, Tony Romano, Barry Rose, Martin Rushent (RIP), William Sager, David Sancious, Gisele Schierhorst (music librarian, Stony Brook University), John Schlitt, Barry Schrader, Stuart Shapiro, Joyce Shepard (University of Vermont Police Services), Billy Sherwood, Derek Shulman, Thorpe Shuttleworth, Robert Simon at the University of Notre Dame, Michael Solomon, Bob Sparks (librarian, Gannon University), Stephen Speelman, Chris Squire (RIP), Dave Sturt, Mike Tait, Charles Tapp, Geoff Tate, Bruce Thomas, Jody Lloyd Thompson, Mike Tiano, Martin Turner, Ed Unitsky, Steve Vai, Casey Wilcox, Junior Wilson, Mark Wirtz, Dan Wooding, Olav Wyper, Tim Wyskida, Rusty Young.

A special thanks to Eddy Offord, co-producer of *Close to the Edge*; Bill Bruford; Bernadette Malavarca for her patience; Marybeth Keating, John Cerullo, Tom Seabrook, Wes Seeley, and everyone at Backbeat Books for their support.

INTRODUCTION
Independence 101

While putting this book together I experienced some of the most bizarre and treacherous days of the last few years of my life. Aside from intermittent ringing in my ears, fighting a bout of pneumonia, and helping nurse multiple dogs back to health, I'd dealt with numerous other personal issues, which I will not to detail here.

One relatively lighthearted, albeit exceedingly aggravating, incident occurred in Washington, D.C., and seems to sum up the process of getting from A to B for this project.

Although I had gotten a late start heading down to the nation's capital to do research for this project, I was breezing through town after town, flying down I-95 and I-295. I thought I'd arrive in D.C. just in time to conduct a few hours of research and then turn around and take the long drive home.

It'll be a whirlwind day, I thought, *but I can do everything I need to on a budget, all in one shot.*

After six hours or so of driving I made it into the very heart of D.C. and was looking for my destination on Independence Avenue—101 Independence Avenue, the Library of Congress and US Copyright Office, to be exact.

Parking in D.C. in the late morning is murder, so I circle the building a few times without much luck. Finally, as I ricochet around what I thought would be my corner, for the final time of the day, expecting to zip back onto Independence, I step on the gas pedal only to feel the car nearly stall. It barely budges.

At first I think something is caught underneath the pedal and preventing me from pushing it down the entire way. I look. I feel. There doesn't appear to be an obstruction, but I step on it, again. And again. Again, *nothing.* I realize the car is virtually drained of power.

Wonderful, I think. What was supposed to be an easy gig, a breezy ride through the Mid-Atlantic States, is going to turn into a disastrous—and expensive—road trip.

In all the confusion, and as slowly as I am moving, incredibly

I've passed Independence 101. Just then, a Capitol Police car appears in my rearview mirror. I'm sure I'll be pulled over, or even escorted out of the District under suspicion, but mercifully the cop pulls off to the right, and I never see him (or her) again. But now I realize that I need help, and quickly, before the car dies altogether. Spotting another officer down the road, I roll up next to him and ask for assistance with my car troubles.

"Well, you can make a U-turn here," the officer says, pointing off into the distance, "and we can call a tow truck to get you to the station. Or, my advice is, if you can make it, drive up the Hill. There's an Exxon on the right, off Fourth Street."

Rather than wait for a tow truck, I brazenly think I'd have a go at the hill. Why not? I've made it this far. Well, sorta. After two minutes the hill becomes an insurmountable mountain, like something out of Greek Mythology—Sisyphus pushing the stone and all that crap. *Hope this mini-adventure turns out better for me than it did for him.*

A half-hour ticks by but I finally crawl the six blocks to the Exxon station. *Cool.* An attendant waves me in and I feel relieved. After a few minutes I meet with the mechanic. He opens the car door and plugs in a hand-held diagnostic device under the dashboard of my car. He looks up at me and shakes his head.

"Can't fix it," he says. It has something to do with computer chips and such. The car would, ultimately, have to be towed to a dealership . . . in Virginia! Here I am thinking I drove up the hill for nothing . . .

The business day is over and I can't get my research done. I'll have to stay over in D.C. The following day I take the MRT Yellow Line, which is late, back into the heart of D.C. I hop off the train at what I think is the appropriate stop, but for some reason I can't find Independence 101. I ask a few people, but I'm not really comforted that I'm going in the correct direction. Suddenly I'm reminded of the man-on-the-street interviews George Carlin conducted regarding the old joke about getting to Carnegie Hall: *"Can't anyone get me to Independence 101?"*

I did eventually come upon it and I did complete my research with the assistance of the kind and dedicated librarians and archivists there. And, finally, later in the day, I got my car back. I missed it. I paid my bill and I left . . . in a hailstorm. Once I reached Maryland the weather cooperated and the ride back was spectacularly and gratefully uneventful.

I've reflected on my D.C. experience because I think it offers an insight into what it must have been like to put *Close to the Edge* (*CTTE*) together. Yes, it was a never-ending process of creation, deconstruction, and reconstruction, but once completed, the band had a vehicle through which it could reap countless rewards.

The concept of finding "Independence" is especially poignant given that Bill Bruford, the former Yes drummer who appears on *Close to the Edge*, dropped a bombshell on the band, leaving abruptly for rival British progressive-rockers King Crimson even before *CTTE* was released. Looking to improve himself as a drummer and broaden his horizons as an artist, Bruford was searching for freedom as an individual musician and as part of a musical collective.

CTTE is seen by many as a Holy Grail of progressive rock. I tend to agree, and as with any Grail quest, the question and the journey is often more important than that which you seek. To gain greater insight into how painstakingly detailed the recording was (and just why this record is considered the Holy Grail), I've listened to *CTTE* easily over a thousand times for the research portion of this project. I even scribbled a log detailing and breaking down, on a second-by-second basis, the instrumentation of the three-song record. It was sheer madness, but I worked through it.

I've trekked into Manhattan to schedule time at a recording studio (believe it or not, Big Yellow Duck) to listen to the Steven Wilson–mixed surround-sound version of *CTTE* in a proper 5.1 environment. Isolated in a room, playing (and replaying) these tracks at full volume, hearing them like never before—in all their clarity and sonic separation—was simply uncanny. All of these listening experiments were, in their own way, eye- and ear-openers, taking me (pardon the phrase) closer and closer to the edge of full sonic realization.

I've also rented time at a local studio (J&L), here in the sticks, to drum along with the Audio Fidelity hybrid SACD remaster of *Close to the Edge*. I even banged the "skins" in my own living space on an unamplified Simmons SD5K digital drum kit, trying to work out the rhythmic phrasing of the songs.

I guess I felt the need to press sticks to cymbal, hi-hat, and snare to get a better sense of how these songs developed. I needed to truly *feel them* and how they fall under the hands and feet.

Conclusion? Bill Bruford doesn't have to play a lot to express an immense amount. It's not so much his blinding technique but his poise and beat placement that convinces you that he is a master drummer.

Some of Bruford's patterns feel random, until you realize that he's commenting on a guitar line or bass figure or keyboard notes, or some portion thereof, all while economically grooving for the good of the song.

Bruford's playing is like a conceptualized jigsaw puzzle: so concise . . . so precise . . . so sly. Since *Close to the Edge* was recorded in clumps, and he did not write out the drum parts during the sessions, as far as I know, his achievements are, in retrospect, even greater. In essence, Bruford plotted his drumming in his head and managed to maintain a level of continuity in his performances despite a very disjointed recording process.

In responding to a question I had asked him via e-mail, Bruford offered some advice on what sources would be helpful to me for this book. In his inimitable style, he said, "I'll be interested in any new angle or light you can cast on the old warhorse."

I disagree with him about the "warhorse" bit. But if I've succeeded, even in a small way, I will have, hopefully, cast a light on the visionary components of *CTTE*, as well as some of the struggles experienced by both Bruford and the band to find "Independence."

By the same token, I also wanted to champion some of the greats of the genre. Yes bass player Chris Squire was such a tremendous presence that it's difficult to believe he's gone, having died in late June 2015 after being diagnosed with acute erythroid leukemia.

The towering musician once asked me, "How old were you when you started listening to Yes? Were you fifteen?"

I was actually younger, and I told him so, but I understood his point.

"That is a very impressionable age, you know?" he continued. "A very shrewd marketing guy said to me once that the beer a guy drinks in his early teens is the beer he'll probably drink for the rest of his life."

If Jon Anderson was the soul of Yes, then Squire was the motor that kept the band running. Although I've been lured by the taste of imported and exotic draughts many times over the years, I've never really changed my taste in beer, so to speak.

Working on this book, I've gained a greater appreciation of what it means to stretch the boundaries of a musical style and think innovatively. Striving for and achieving such independence does come at a cost, of course, but the result is a work of art that cannot be reproduced, matched, or exceeded.

I dedicate this book to Squire and the surviving members of Yes, who'd honed their craft, and had the vision, the creativity and, let's not deny it, *the balls* to dare create what many deem the perfect progressive-rock album. Thanks for reading.

Salut!

CLOSE TO THE EDGE

CORD OF LIFE
Progressive Rock Begins

The first half of the 1970s was an especially fertile period for British progressive rock, laying claim to classics such as *Tarkus, Selling England by the Pound, Larks' Tongues in Aspic, The Dark Side of the Moon*, and *Thick as a Brick*. Collectively, these and other works represent the best British progressive rock had to offer. Yet it's Yes's 1972 three-track masterpiece, *Close to the Edge*, that presents a snapshot of an adventurous rock band at the peak of its powers, daring to push itself musically, both as individuals and as a unit.

Yes had previously penned epic tracks for *The Yes Album* and *Fragile*, but nothing on the magnitude of the musical gems appearing on *Close to the Edge*. It's something of a small miracle—perhaps even magic—that the virtuoso quintet crafted such a cohesive and compelling album during an often-hectic recording process that very nearly relegated this monumental work to the dustbin of history. So potent was the power of *Close to the Edge* that even before its release it had forever shifted the personal dynamics of the group and the course of progressive-rock history, aftershocks of which are still being felt in the twenty-first century.

Rarely had Yes, or any rock outfit for that matter, been simultaneously so expansive and concise, spiritual and savage, profound and nebulous. Everything that made British progressive rock so brave, so celebrated, is found in *Close to the Edge*. But what was it about the nature of the times and conditions that made this possible?

Tulpas and Technicolor Dreams

Many British artists and musicians I've spoken with over the years have described the UK's sudden transition from the 1950s to the 1960s as being something quite magical, like switching from black-and-white to Technicolor. With an improving economy and the influence of American culture, everything, they've said, changed.

"It took a long time for Britain to recover from the Second World War," says Supertramp sax man/clarinet player John Helliwell.

"Until a new generation came of age, a generation which hadn't experienced the horrors or depravations of those times, a process of building was going on in the 1950s. The musical and artistic explosion was just waiting to happen, and it did with a vengeance."

Clive Bayley, founding member of Mabel Greer's Toyshop, a precursor to Yes, recalls the same period:

> It was exciting. I was a Kingston boy; Kingston-on-Thames where a lot of musicians were hanging about, like Eric Clapton, Yardbirds, Moody Blues. When you were hanging out in the coffee bars, musicians were bumping into one another. There was a big buzz going. I remember at the age of fifteen walking down Kings Road with permed hair and a big sunflower. Being "flower power" days, I had gotten my grandma's dressing gown and turned it into a paisley silk jacket. I will never forget that my parents sent my brother to get me. My brother always said, "You were walking down King's Road with a cowbell around your neck, a huge sunflower, looking completely mad. I just pushed you in the car, kidnapped you and took you back home." It was one of my cherished memories.

"The '60s were an upheaval," songwriter and recording artist Phillip Goodhand-Tait once told me. "So-called baby boomers, like me, renounced not only the music of our parents but our parents' values, too, with the ferocity of adolescent righteousness."

The revolution was happening in Swingin' London circa 1966. Crosspollination may have had some impact on the direction of this cultural and social movement, but scenes in London, New York, Paris, and the Haight-Ashbury District of San Francisco—ground zero for the hippie movement—seemed to have developed independently of one another.

"In that particular time period there was a lot of things happening globally," says Gary Duncan of the Bay Area's Quicksilver Messenger Service. "I think it probably happens in every century. There's a time that you might call a renaissance of sorts. It happened in France, it happened in New York in the '50s, with the Beat generation. It's spontaneously and it simultaneously erupts around the world."

Brits enjoyed the delicacies of a more sensuous, vivid world. The movement was impacting fashion and music (such as with the rise of acid rock), even recreational drug use. Having more free time than generations past, teens and early twenty-something listeners would sit for hours, perhaps dabbling in some extracurricular activities, absorbing music.

The counterculture movement of the 1960s sought to create not only an alternate society, but also an alternate reality. By expanding their minds, exploring their psyches, and treating their bodies like sexual playgrounds, young idealists—or hippies, as they would soon be dubbed—truly believed they could advance to the next plateau in human evolution—something far greater than the Greatest Generation had ever dreamed of, and something miles beyond the drug-addled Beats.

LSD (lysergic acid diethylamide) drifted out of the labs and into the hot little hands of young adults whose recreational use of the drug was on the cutting-edge of chic. The hallucinogen's self-appointed, unofficial spokesperson, Timothy Leary, a former psychology professor at Harvard University, viewed the drug's mind-expanding properties as something that should be experienced by every adult. LSD, it was believed, could help humanity map the largely unexplored regions of the inner space, something Leary was championing. Denying oneself a rare window into the soul was tantamount to surrendering one's basic human rights.

Some believed that hallucinogens were the cure-all for society's ills, reminiscent of the fictional panacea "Soma" from Aldous Huxley's *Brave New World*. It was believed it could unlock the key to madness and send long-repressed feelings bubbling up to the surface for professional psychoanalysis.

At its heart, the underground or hippie culture in both the US and Britain valued experimenting of all sorts, crossing borders—and oftentimes crossing the senses—to create new sensations, emotions, and sound textures, which would often either foster or enhance the psychedelic experience. Live performances were simply an extension of this esthetic.

An admixture of music, a titillation of the senses, and an overload of visuals, dubbed "happenings," became a regular occurrence in London from 1966–1967. Nightclubs hosted these LSD-laced multimedia "happenings," and suddenly indie publications and newspapers, such as the *International Times* (started in 1966), were cropping up to cover them.

The alternative or progressive music scene, buoyed by artists such as AMM, Pink Floyd and its star and LSD *dimensionaut* Syd Barrett, Soft Machine, and Social Deviants, among others, brought color, spice, sex, sound, and infinite possibilities.

Dick Taylor of the psychedelic pop/blues-rock band the Pretty Things once described for me his perspective on these "happenings":

> I know that where I lived in a flat, upstairs from me, were some people who organized happenings at the Marquee Club where they locked the doors, before LSD was made illegal. Everybody took acid, and they'd have loads of light shows and things going on. Bands like Pink Floyd and the Social Deviants and other attractions were there, which were really very far out. I remember once there was a band who had a backing tape, which was the "speaking clock" from the telephone [an automated service giving callers the correct time], and they would improvise around the speaking clock.

London nightclubs such as the Marquee and, in particular, the UFO (Unlimited Freak-Out) employed projectors, which beamed imagery of bodily fluids and acid onto screens and other architectural surfaces as wild musical forays into psychedelic or space rock were launched.

Many such happenings sprung up in Swingin' London and beyond. On January 28 and February 4, 1967, at the Roadhouse Theatre in North London, a multimedia event titled Carnival of Light was staged. In April, a partially televised, acid-laced fundraiser, the 14-Hour Technicolor Dream concert at London's Alexandra Palace, boasted appearances by Pink Floyd, the Move, Yoko Ono, the Pretty Things, Soft Machine, Arthur Brown, and Ron Geesin. The Games for May event in May 1967 at Queen Elizabeth Hall featured Pink Floyd partaking of experimental, improvisational music, inspiring drummer Nick Mason to saw wood and vocalist/ bassist Roger Waters to toss potatoes at a gong. As this performance art, of a sort, was transpiring onstage, daffodils were handed out to the crowd, audio was being pumped through the venue in quad, and "sampled" sounds of nature and pre-recorded noises of all kinds were played.

To observers, Pink Floyd's live performances were hyper-real, almost supernatural. Author Jenny Fabian once remarked to BBC broadcaster John Cavanagh, for his book *The Piper at the Gates of Dawn*, that Floyd may have been dreamed into existence—a concept some might say is similar to the Buddhist notion of a *tulpa* (i.e. a material object that's been brought into the physical world purely through the powers of the mind).

Frank Davies, veteran record industry man and former manager of prog-pop band Klaatu:

> The younger people in the EMI department, who were going to be involved in the careers of new artists, often went to see showcases of artists that the A&R guys were having in the basement of EMI, in Manchester Square. In 1966, I remember getting this memo saying we are looking at this band, we hadn't signed them, but we are looking at this band called Pink Floyd. "Anybody . . . who would like to attend the showcase, just come down to the basement studio and you can see them give a performance." It was my first exposure to what became progressive rock. I was about twenty-one, maybe, at the time.
>
> So, I go down and I see Syd Barrett and the Floyd. It was very psychedelic; the light show was to give the impression that you've been taking drugs. It was about creating swirling colors against their bodies while they were playing that sort of psychedelic music.

Musicians on both sides of the Atlantic—and their tripping, hip-shaking fans—believed they were channeling cosmic vibrations of the Great Universal Pulse. In a way they were. By plying themselves with mind-altering, euphoria-inducing drugs, concert-goers could heighten their awareness of the astral plane and tap into a river of consciousness.

River of Dreams

The Beatles, for one, were well aware of this. Their *Sgt. Pepper's*

Lonely Hearts Club Band was the most anticipated record release not only of 1967's so-called Summer of Love but the entire year and probably the entire decade. It reflected, exploited, and even at turns ignored the hippie subculture germinating in London and beyond. With it, the Fab Four performed an incredible balancing act: they dabbled in and yet were also detached from the far-flung realms of altered consciousness so prevalent to hippie enclaves. Incredibly, they sold a product to a generation that, by and large, rejected the ideas of consumerism and commercialism.

"We listened to every record the Beatles put out," explains Quicksilver Messenger Service's Gary Duncan. "They were the best at that time. It's amazing that it was this long ago, but their last actual show was in 1966 in San Francisco. We all played the Beatles until we wore out the grooves and . . . I'm speaking for myself, but I'm sure every other musician in town was influenced by the Beatles, mainly because of their phenomenal musical aggregation."

Earlier in the year, the single "Penny Lane" b/w "Strawberry Fields Forever" had hinted at a more personal, autobiographical direction for the then-upcoming *Sgt. Pepper's* record via memories of childhood in Liverpool. "I thought it would be nice to lose our identities," Paul McCartney told *Playboy* magazine in 1984, recalling the initial concept that shaped *Sgt. Pepper's.*

It's no secret that the Beatles were in desperate need of escape from their professional lives. Actually, more succinctly, they were sick of each other, and of being the Beatles. McCartney's simple and subversive vision was just the remedy for such doldrums—one he felt would be welcomed with open arms and minds.

Yet not everyone was pleased with the band's new creative direction. John Lennon was seemingly content with opening wounds of his painful childhood and analyzing them through song and lyrics, but guitarist/vocalist George Harrison was so turned off by McCartney's idea that he flat out stated he hated it. Harrison would further turn inward and to the East.

Lennon and Harrison eventually came around and realized the value of the idea. By acting as their own doppelgangers, the Beatles could explore different aspects of their musical personalities and create with a little less pressure. Given the many shifts in pop music since their last release, they could respond to new trends and take chances the Beatles wouldn't or couldn't.

This concept of self-transcendence, of assuming alter egos, of becoming the *Fab Faux* and shedding fame, vaguely recalls the process of "ego loss" that hallucinogen users undergo when in the psychedelic throes of LSD. It's often been speculated that McCartney, who was the last Beatles member to actually take LSD, may have begun to do so around the time "Penny Lane" was being finished and recorded. He admitted to taking the hallucinogen when speaking to a *Life* magazine reporter in 1967.

At the time Lennon had begun to explore the realms of inner space, he turned to *the* handbook for tripping, *The Psychedelic Experience*, co-authored by the so-called Pope of Dope Timothy Leary and based on the *Tibetan Book of the Dead*, a mystical text designed to be spoken to the dying as they transition from one spiritual plane of existence to another.

Tracks such as "When I'm 64," "She's Leaving Home," and "Being for the Benefit of Mr. Kite!" are emblematic of the counterculture's fascination with escapism and romanticism of the past, yet are often interpreted, and dismissed, as retro oddities, out of step with the psychedelic times. By contrast, songs such as "Lucy in the Sky with Diamonds" and "A Day in the Life" *seem to be* informed by, if not speaking directly to, the psychedelic experience. "Lucy" was banned by BBC radio due to its perceived connection to acid (the story goes). The song in fact may not have been a glorification of LSD, as Lennon had said it was inspired by a picture his son Julian drew of his playmate, Lucy. In addition, George Harrison *may* have been exploring the connection between lysergic acid and Hinduism with his song "Within You Without You."

From Indian music to music hall, *Sgt. Pepper's* presents pop art-rock panels in a psychedelic slide show. The postmodernist bent helped to shape the ambition and genre-crossing instincts that gave rise to progressive rock. *Sgt. Pepper's* also threw down the gauntlet, daring competing bands to top the Beatles' latest and perhaps greatest recording effort.

Whether the Beatles (or anyone else for that matter) were aware of it or not, they, Brian Wilson (and the Beach Boys), and Frank Zappa were caught in a bizarre musical triangle of influences/competition, with each artist attempting to prove they were the more creatively audaciousness. (Throw in the Rolling Stones' late-1967 effort, *Their Satanic Majesties Request*, and this *ménage a trio* becomes a kinky, squared-off, quirky musical quadrangle.)

Wilson and the Beach Boys had reportedly held prayer meetings to ask the man upstairs to help them rival, if not more precisely best, the Beatles' 1965 album *Rubber Soul*. The result was Wilson's masterpiece, *Pet Sounds*, one of the most inspired experimental pop records of the '60s—or any decade, for that matter—which turned McCartney into an obsessed musical auteur, bent on creating *Sgt. Pepper's*' semi-conceptual construct. *Sgt. Pepper's* didn't send musical contrarian Frank Zappa into a tailspin as much as a tizzy. Sniffing a whiff of hypocrisy wasn't what set Zappa off; what may have really incensed the maestro was knowing that a rival band, from England no less, had completely, simultaneously, and succinctly promoted and destroyed the hippie culture and drug movement in one fell swoop.

For Zappa, *Sgt. Pepper's* was a parody of the counterculture, a plastic psychedelia, something that he had been aspiring to for years but up to that point had never truly achieved. He would, of course, unleash his *Sgt. Pepper's* parody, *We're Only in It for the Money*, in 1968.

This competition was further fueled by an industry eager to push a more expensive and expansive recorded format, namely the LP. A more sophisticated listening audience—and, dare we say, artistic aspirations to move beyond tried and tested styles of music— inevitably led to the 45rpm single steadily being replaced by the LP as the preferred audio medium of choice. (More about these "size matters" in a moment.) In turn, as the LP became the gold standard, album cover artwork became an essential tool for escapism, drug-induced hypnosis/meditation, and record-label marketing.

In short, the canvas on which an artist could paint was larger. Filling the space with innovative and expansive music was inevitable. Indeed, the length of the medium led to ever-more spacious rock music, which fueled mammoth fan listening sessions.

Fans of new forms of rock in the late 1960s and early 1970s weren't content relaxing on the couch, passing a joint around and simply *vegging* out. Yes, this occurred, too, but if substances blocking some form of clarity of mental vision did not already seduce prog-rock listeners, they could seek to understand clues that were left for them.

They could seek, after being gently urged to do so by the creators of the art in question, secret knowledge embedded in the very texts, chords, scales used to construct the heady and often serpentine compositional structures found in progressive rock, not to mention the visionary artwork of the designers who created the packaging for the records. In some cases, the acts of buying, enjoying, and internalizing obscure material known as prog rock demonstrates a preoccupation with the so-called occult.

Both Kevin Holm-Hudson, author of *Genesis and The Lamb Lies Down on Broadway,* and Allan Moore (*Rock: The Primary Text*) have noted that musicians that produce the more fantastic strains of rock (prog rock), tend to focus on the obscure and the occult (hidden knowledge). Moore went so far as to claim that prog-rockers' tendency to work toward the goal of obscurity was a form of gnosis. If this is the case, wasn't this gnosis the apotheosis of the hippie dream of creating an alternate reality?

Prior to progressive rock's proper rise, some were seeking for genuine spiritual insight and turned their glassy-eyed gaze to the hazy horizons of the East. Walking hand-in-hand with mystical searches were musicians willing to transgress geographical and musical boundaries. Bands such as Jade Warrior, East of Eden, Third Ear Band, Quintessence, and others were part of a larger groundswell fusing rock, jazz, and so-called "world" music styles.

The East held an allure for artists working in a wide range of musical genres, including iconic jazzers the Dave Brubeck Quartet (featuring drummer Joe Morello, whose odd-time figures in "Time Out" and "Blue Rondo à la Turk" inspired Bruford) and saxophonists Yusef Lateef (also an accomplished flute player) and John Coltrane, who had immersed himself in the study of Sufism during what is considered his experimental or spiritual period. Coltrane reportedly studied with Ravi Shankar in the mid-1960s, and the saxophonist's son is named Ravi. Coltrane, who some say single-handedly added a spiritual dimension to jazz, searched for and perhaps found a "time beyond time" with his fluid spontaneous compositions or "sheets of sound." These textures were informed by his use of Indian modalities and his penchant for long-form songs with cyclical patterns, which bear a passing resemblance to Indian ragas.

Coltrane battled the bottle and heroin, but he claimed to have experienced a spiritual awakening in which he "humbly asked to be given the means and privilege to make others happy through music. I feel this has been granted through His grace," Coltrane once wrote. The saxophonist later admitted that he entered into a period of "irresolution" that ran contradictory to his pledge to the Almighty. The groundbreaking 1964 work *A Love Supreme* was one of the manifestations of 'Trane's sort of homecoming, and a deeply personal musical statement. For instance, "Psalm," the final section of *A Love Supreme*, can be interpreted as a kind of tone poem to the higher power—an interpretation of the words printed on the album sleeve, written by Coltrane himself.

"Heck, often the things that hit you immediately don't last very long," former Yes drummer and co-founding member Bill Bruford once told me. "I couldn't understand *Bitches Brew* for one note of it when I first put it on, or *A Love Supreme*, when I was younger. But now, of course, they continue to offer up treasures, and this is a kind of pop music. They were just pointing the direction of the time."

"John had that spiritual quality," says legendary jazz drummer and bandleader Jack DeJohnette, an influence on Bruford, who sat in with Coltrane in Chicago. "John put the *om* back into the music—that spiritual aspect of the music you are perceiving."

Coltrane's *Sun Ship*, *Meditations*, and *Om* were further proof of his spellbinding spirituality. *Om* even contains scattered references to *The Tibetan Book of the Dead* and the *Bhagavad Gita*. Coltrane was never far from spirituality; it helped to shape what some view as his last great work, 1967's *Interstellar Space*, which features only 'Trane and percussionist Rashied Ali.

To paraphrase Ali: *Interstellar Space* was a milestone in Coltrane's search for what some might deem the cosmic pulse—music not measured in beats, notes, and rests. Simply put, the music was a free-flowing river of expression and thought.

The '60s as a whole was a time period for the awakening of a global consciousness, which informed musicians across the board. The folk-rock band the Byrds played what was once described as "raga-rock," a hybrid of Coltrane's tenor sax, Bach's organ music, and Shankar-esque sitar drones.

The Byrds were a seminal band, but for most people in the mainstream of life, on both sides of the Atlantic, the spiritual search for and to the East began with the Beatles and, in particular, George Harrison, who embarked on an intensive study of the sitar with Indian music master Ravi Shankar.

Harrison was introduced to the sitar as far back as 1965, but he did not visit Shankar in India until the fall of 1966, when he was taught music and culture of the Subcontinent. (Harrison, of course, famously used the sitar on "Norwegian Wood (This Bird Has Flown)" from the Beatles' 1965 studio album *Rubber Soul*.) As music scholar John Covach points out, Harrison started a trend that developed into a defining factor for a generation of music makers. The inclusion of Indian music elements in pop became almost a litmus test, a "basic component of the psychedelic movement," Covach writes in his 1997 essay *Progressive Rock, "Close to the Edge,' and the Boundaries of Style*.

Although the *New York Times* later reported that sales of Indian music were down following the Beatles' infamous disillusionment with the Maharishi Mahesh Yogi, father of Transcendental Meditation, the impact of Eastern thought and music was incalculable.

Those who were aroused and lured by the hippie lifestyle also nurtured a hunger for alternative thought, which was quickly invading all aspects of contemporary life. Just as experimenting with LSD challenged traditional notions of reality, the counterculture gazed beyond Western religious dogma straight into the heart of Eastern mysticism.

The extended, cyclical nature of Indian drone music appealed to hippies' sense of the infinite and meditatively hypnotic. "When George played the sitar on *Rubber Soul*, my ear pricked up and from that point on, tens of thousands of guitar players across the US, including me, started playing what was called raga-guitar," says guitarist Jock Bartley of Firefall, who recorded a version of "Within You Without You" for his record *Colorado to Liverpool: A Tribute to the Beatles*. "You'd get into a 'D' tuning, smoke a joint, and play for two hours."

"The Beatles use of the sitar started an interest in Eastern scales amongst rock musicians," says guitarist/vocalist Geoff Nicholson of East of Eden, an early jazz-rock band formed in 1967 that infused its music with "world" influences.

Others as far ranging as Donovan, David Crosby, and Brian Jones of the Rolling Stones can and should be rightly credited with bringing Indian influences to popular rock and folk music of the mid-1960s. (Some have even claimed that it was Crosby who introduced Harrison to the sitar.)

The cover artwork of the Jimi Hendrix Experience's *Axis: Bold as Love* was a visual display of this popular esthetic, although in deference to his Native American ancestral heritage Hendrix proclaimed the cover "the wrong" kind of Indian. And in 1967, Danelectro introduced the Coral Sitar Guitar to the retail market.

Following the Beatles, the likes of Traffic, Pentangle, Donovan (with Shawn Phillips on sitar) with songs such as "Celeste" and the later "Hurdy Gurdy Man," the Rolling Stones' "Paint It Black," the Byrds' "Eight Miles High," and even Robbie Kreiger's guitar flourishes on the Doors' "The End" point to Indian tonal coloring, as does Jeff Beck's "Shapes of Things."

"Somewhere around 1963 I was booked into a club called the Purple Onion in Toronto," Shawn Phillips told me fifty years later, in 2013. "In those days when you were booked into a place you were booked in for about a week. I had a night off and a friend of mine said, 'You have to see this guy Ravi Shankar. He plays with an Indian instrument.' I went to the concert and it absolutely blew me away. I went backstage afterwards and Ravi was very gracious. He spent three hours letting me play his instrument. He taught me how to sit with it, how to put the pick on, the *mezrab*."

Yes's longtime guitarist Steve Howe has said that one of his former bands, the In Crowd, which morphed into the underground cult band Tomorrow, was heavily influenced by the lyrics and the musical interplay of "Eight Miles High."

The ubiquitous '60s sessions great "Big" Jim Sullivan played sitar on Tomorrow's "Real Life Permanent Dream"; Howe's tendency in the track seems to be to mimic the metallic whine of the sitar throughout his electric guitar performance. In addition, to some observers, such as music writer Kieron Tyler of *Mojo*, the drone in the group's underground anthem "My White Bicycle" recalls Indian music. (Howe played a "raga" as a lead-in to "My White Bicycle" on his Steve Howe's Remedy tour in 2004.)

"In those days everybody was tinkering with things," Tomorrow producer Mark Wirtz says. "The sitar was almost like a sound effect. I wouldn't be surprised if Steve had been tinkering and plunking around with a sitar, too. We used Jim Sullivan because we wanted someone with facility on the instrument."

By the end of the decade, many of the so-called hippies were forsaking psychedelic trips in favor of natural highs attained through either music or meditation. "By the end of the '60s I was doing hatha yoga and meditation and looking for other ways to achieve altered states of consciousness," jazz-rock fusion guitarist John McLaughlin once told me.

Even Timothy Leary had to admit that LSD wasn't the end all, be all, noting the psychological potency of drone-based Indian classical music and its relation to hypnotism. "Your consciousness focuses on a band of vibration," Leary told the *New York Times* in 1966. "The needle of your consciousness follows the band of sound and you go into another phase of reality."

Raised on Radio

The rapid growth of radio stations, both in the US and abroad, fostered a climate in which progressive music could flourish.

In the mid-1960s, in the UK, pirate radio offered vital options for a new generation seeking alternative outlets for their rebellious cultural expressions. By and large, those who were coming of age in the 1960s were rejecting and resisting the monopolized, government-controlled noncommercial British Broadcasting Company (BBC).

By 1965 estimates, flagship pirate radio station Radio Caroline was broadcasting music to over twelve million listeners on a weekly basis. "Pirate radio was hugely important, because they were playing the music that the BBC wouldn't," Flash vocalist Colin Carter told me in 2013. "These were like American stations, because they were using American DJs. They opened up the spectrum of music that was heard then."

In the US, a movement toward higher fidelity and underground music was gaining momentum. Frequency Modulation (FM) radio had evolved from what was once called a "soft medium for long-haired music" to a major player whose growing tentacles were reaching a cross-section of listeners, from urban to suburban, by the early 1970s.

The largely static-free transmissions, and FM's ability to broadcast over a wider range of frequencies, meant a larger field of listeners, and potential listeners, gaining access to better quality sound.

Sales of portable radios—those capable of tuning in to both AM and FM frequencies, that is—reached over twenty million units in 1969, according to an Electronic Industries Association report and the *New York Times*. Music, clearly, wasn't just big business; it had become part of people's everyday lives.

Although there were still more AM stations in America, the number of FM broadcasters had ballooned to over 2,400 by 1970. Countless stations seemed to find new life by implementing a "progressive rock" format into their regular programming. In October 1967, *Billboard* reported that WNEW-FM in New York hired pioneering DJ Bill "Rosko" Mercer, an on-air personality for WOR-FM, as a host for a seven-days-a-week "progressive rock show."

Stations in cities ranging from Dallas, Texas; and Cincinnati, Ohio; to Ocean City, New Jersey; Washington, D.C.; and Salt Lake City, Utah, slotted the new sound into their regular programming. Some, like Hy Lit, former head of the progressive-rock station WDAS-FM in Philadelphia, Pennsylvania, called for a network of progressive-rock radio stations, the substance of which seemed to foreshadow the emergence of the successful album-cut, AOR radio format.

"WNEW was merely one example," says New York radio personality Ken Dashow, who, as of this writing, is an on-air talent for Q104.3 FM radio in the Big Apple. "Other stations around the same time period were beginning to have or had similar programming."

Admittedly, the radio industry's definition of "progressive rock" may have been a bit vague and elastic in those days. In addition, we have to take into account the context in which the phrase "progressive rock" was being bandied about: the concept of "progressive-rock radio" was as much an indication of the groundbreaking nature of the innovative rock music that was spun as of the *diversity* of music heard in any given broadcast.

The unclear boundaries could be one source of the confusion we experience today, in the twenty-first century, as to the definition of progressive rock (that is, which artists fall squarely under the banner of progressive rock and which ones do not).

Pinpointing the first appearance of the term "progressive rock" is tricky. As far as I could find—and this was not an exhaustive search by any means—*Billboard* magazine was already referring to the format as "progressive rock" radio as early as October 1967. (Further references appeared in the fall of that same year.) In

December 1967, a former station manager of WNEW-FM New York George Duncan discussed with station president Jack Sullivan the possibility of bringing a "progressive rock" or "meaningful music" format to WNEW in 1966.

WNEW, which hired radio icon Scott Muni, a big supporter of progressive-rock radio, in November 1967, managed to spin all manner of musical pieces that varied in style and length within one time slot, from classical and Sinatra to psychedelic blues and the Beatles.

It's probable, but not certain, that since references to "progressive rock" were appearing in the national media as early as the fall of 1967, the phrase was likely in use, at least in some radio circles, in the summer or spring (even winter) of 1967, or perhaps as early as 1966. Indeed. The liner notes to Caravan's 1969 debut portray the band as a "progressive rock" group. The *New York Times* obit for Jimi Hendrix, from September 1970, under the subheading "Produced Space Music," described Jimi as having "made distinct contributions to progressive rock." And *Rolling Stone* used the term in a November 1972 review of Yes's *Close to the Edge*.

As is the case with most commercial ventures, businessmen can hardly resist the urge to label something, so the term "progressive rock" likely arose due to the industry's need to box this type of music for capital gain.

Just as 45rpm singles and tired old radio stations failed to excite 1960s youth, in increasing numbers the listening masses were looking not just for popular artists, but popular artists who took risks by expanding the boundaries of accepted norms in rock music. "My boss asked me if I wanted to do a Sunday show, and I did," legendary DJ Russ Gibb told me in 2007. "I would do everything opposite to what we were doing on AM. I would slow it down and play [Iron Butterfly's] "In-a-Gadda-Da-Vida," which was a seventeen-and-a-half-minute song. The kids knew about FM."

"Back then, not many people cared so much about commercial radio," says Gary Wright, solo artist and member of Spooky Tooth. "With FM radio they would play anything and mix and match and so you really had that license to do whatever you wanted to do."

For progressive-rock bands, says Dashow, radio "was everything":

It was the doorway. The keeper of that door was my mentor and rabbi and radio dad, Scott Muni. Were there other stations? Yeah, in Philly, and the Mighty Met in L.A., but it started with Scott. It was such a personal business back then. Scott and Ahmet [Ertegun, founder Atlantic Records] were drinking buddies. Scott drank too much, but he never took a nickel to play a record, and never would. But if Ahmet sent him this test pressing and said, "I've got this thing, Scott. I don't know if you are going to play it." "Yeah, I'll play it." If Scott Muni will play it, forget ratings, there were not really ratings like we have today, but if Scott will play it, then the other FMs would play it, and "We can make some money at concerts, and then you call Ron Delsner." When [Emerson, Lake, and Palmer's] *Pictures at an Exhibition* came out, a live interpretation of Mussorgsky, Scott went, "Great. I'm in. We'll promote it." It was the same for Yes. Whenever I've talked with [former Yes vocalist] Jon Anderson about it or [former Yes keyboardist] Rick Wakeman, they would say, "That was everything." The thing was, "Did Scott like it? Would Scott play it?" As I said, radio was the entrance into America.

Eventually, the AOR format was developed to meet the needs of a generation that had largely rejected the commercialism of Top 40. "There was a musical revolution on our hands," says Lee Abrams, recognized as one of the fathers of the AOR radio format. "I remember playing 'The Knife' by Genesis early on. Yes, certainly, was being played. Those early stations, some songs would get immediate reaction and they later turned into album classics."

Following the rise of FM radio, record labels expressed a desire to develop nascent underground talent, either as true believers or simply to benefit from it financially. Majors responded by forming subsidiaries devoted to promoting a new brand of rock music: EMI had Harvest; Philips/Phonogram had Vertigo; Pye had Dawn Records (marketing music by Donovan, Mungo Jerry, Atomic Rooster, and others); and, later, RCA rolled out Neon. While not every artist who appeared on these labels could be considered progressive rock, each entry on their release rosters seemed indicative of a certain musical sensibility that spoke to the ambition to explore rock music outside the normal parameters of popular tastes.

In America, Atlantic Records, once called the world's largest independent label, was no different. By the late 1960s, Atlantic had been sold to Warner Bros.–Seven Arts, although founder Ahmet Ertegun was still running and making decisions for the label. Ertegun was a shrewd businessman as much as he was a great appreciator of jazz and blues. However, he knew that British rock bands were the future of the label, at least for the foreseeable future. English hard-rock power trio Cream signed to Atco, and soon after Led Zeppelin and Yes found a place at the once soul/R&B-dominated label.

Optically, it appeared as though Atlantic was presenting a smooth transition from largely African-American artists to young British rock musicians playing blues-based rock. Tying white British musicians to the established African-American R&B and soul artists was essential. Ertegun even went as far as to describe Yes vocalist Jon Anderson as having "soul."

This may have been the golden age of artist development. You'd expect an artist to take an album (or two, possibly even three) to ramp up commercial success before the big money came rolling in. This meant the label was investing in the artist, and the artist could hone his/her craft, which often led to more ambitious creative projects. Artistic individuality was not only accepted and encouraged, it appeared to be nurtured. As a result, artists continued to experiment by mixing and matching and tinkering with musical genres. Sometimes, the weirder and funkier, the better.

Size Matters

The prog-rock movement in Britain has been described as an arrhythmic event, both an outgrowth of psychedelia and also divorced from it. Author and scholar Paul Stump identifies a certain schism occurring in psychedelia, fracturing the musical form into various strains of what we call progressive rock, from the symphonic rockers to the jazz-oriented Canterbury Scene bands. There was a schism: a separation in sensibility, seriousness, competency, commercial value, even in the type of radio airwaves dedicated to carry a more album-oriented style (namely AOR). By 1969 or so, rock music was no longer simply acid-infused jamming but innovative in its structurally and sonic texture.

Although similarities exist between psychedelia and prog rock, there existed stark differences. In both subgenres, musicians were eager to experiment with and erase musical boundaries, improve their songwriting, and add impressionistic dimension to their lyrical expressions. However, musicians that emerged post–*Sgt. Pepper's*, the so-called first wave of progressive-rockers in Britain, circa 1967–1968, chased a greater facility on their instruments (to become more technically adept), and did, or would eventually, apply classical music compositional strategies to rock.

Expanding boundaries, crashing through them, and allowing seemingly opposing concepts to collide to offer a fresh perspective appealed to a new generation of rock musicians hungry for a different headspace. After rock's magic-carpet-ride dalliances in psychedelia, some musicians from Britain (as well as North America and Continental Europe) looked to bring form and shape to the sometimes-amorphous creations artists pressed to the far-out corners of the musical cosmos.

Initially, the underground sound developed as a creative and artistic sensibility. A few years later, with the success of bands such as Yes, ELP, Jethro Tull, Pink Floyd, Genesis, and King Crimson, a European-style rock music would serve as a template for aspiring bands on both sides of the Atlantic, helping to establish what we know today as the codified style of progressive rock. One could argue that, in the timeframe from roughly 1970 through 1972–1973, bands were still operating under the assumption that what they were doing was fresh.

In 2009, drummer Chris Cutler (Henry Cow/Art Bears) told me:

> As part and parcel of the huge cultural changes that swept through the '60s, music became a primary medium expression for a whole generation of post-war youth. Not just as consumers, but as primary producers. Very quickly they broke with the industry model, exploring first folk forms, and then the blues and R&B, which found their way into Britain through black American servicemen stationed here after the war. The lure was precisely that these forms seemed authentically expressive and transgressive. And from that point on it was the bands and their public that called the shots—and they, at least an influential minority

of them, were interested above all in making or hearing something *new*, something unfamiliar—something that would be *real*, and *theirs*.

So the essence of what I would call progressive music was that it extended the vocabulary of rock; introduced new ideas, and explored the unorthodox possibilities of electrification. It's not a style but an orientation toward innovation: mixing and blending forms and genres; introducing new sounds and new structures and new ways of putting sounds together.

"We were aching to do something a bit more challenging and experimental," says Stewart Goldring of Gnidrolog. "If you could play you wanted to explore composition and seeing what you could do with rock instruments in a more challenging way."

There are a number of other factors responsible for the insurgency of progressive rock in the mainstream, including the popularity of the Beatles and their musical evolutions and the myriad social and cultural revolutions of the 1960s, the emergence of FM radio in the US and pirate radio off the shores of Britain, the increased importance of nightclubs as showcases for talent, the proximity of nightclubs and free exchange of creative ideas (a stream of consciousness or river of dreams), a reliance on keyboard technology, and the length of the LP, all of which helped rock to blossom schematically, thematically, and programmatically.

The feedback and fuzz of Hendrix's guitar, the hard-rock, hot-rodded workouts of Cream and others, as well as the cerebral swing of jazz, could certainly be heard, in varying degrees, in bands such as Yes, Crimson, Tull, and ELP, but the progressives were far more detailed, far more baroque. The progressives appeared to look inward and toward the UK and the European continent (and away from America) for musical inspiration. The European heritage, less so the African-American musical tradition, served as a guide for this variant strain of rock.

As we moved further into the 1970s, rock artists were employing these classical strategies with more frequency. Artists allowed for the appearance of musical motifs, recapitulation of themes and partial themes, sonic and recording-based experimentation, and jagged odd time signatures running for several measures at a time—arrhythmic events within the context of a piece, which virtually symbolized the birth of the entire prog-rock genre.

As would be increasingly apparent, rock literally progressed and evolved through multiple "movements" and different moods, and operated using harmonic, rhythmic, and often melodic complexity. Writer Robert Shelton dubbed the fusion of electronics, jazz, classical, or "conservatory elements" and rock a "totally new genre" called "rockophonic." For some, this meant literally transferring classical symphonic works to the rock setting—attempting to cover classical music as a three- or four-piece rock band, or referencing classical tunes, as Clouds, Mabel Greer's Toyshop, Procol Harum, and Yes had done in the late 1960s and early 1970s. It also meant combining symphonies with the electric buzz, howls, and screams of rock—allowing the sound of the street to intermingle with those emanating from the concert hall, as in experiments conducted by the Nice, Deep Purple, Moody Blues, Procol Harum, Yes, and, in Italy, New Trolls.

Whether it was the Nice or Clouds (or 1-2-3 prior to them), rock bands with a keyboard-led lineup reimagined everything from rock 'n' roll to European classical music and incorporated these styles into their underground art—art that was often rife with technical pyrotechnics and ripe with extended song structures, beyond the accepted three-minute pop-song parameters.

Even when songs were not perceived as being classically influenced, the ambition of newer rock artists was apparent. The following is by no means a comprehensive list, but it does offer the reader a look into the lengthy tracks that helped to lay the groundwork for more classically informed pieces composed by later prog rock artists.

The Los Angeles–based psychedelic pop/rock band Love produced its groundbreaking epic "Revelation" (from *Da Capo*) in late 1966, but by 1968 we saw the release of the title track of the Nice's *Ars Longa Vita Brevis*, Procol Harum's "In Held Twas in I" from *Shine On Brightly*, Iron Butterfly's "In-a-Gadda-Da-Vida" (written by Doug Ingle, son of a church organist), and an edited version of Frank Zappa's *musique concrète* "Lumpy Gravy."

The Nice, led by keyboard pioneer Keith Emerson and fueled by Bach, among other influences, created the multi-sectional "Ars Longa Vita Brevis" for the album of the same title. Bassist/vocalist Keith "Lee" Jackson's lyrics become more philosophical, even vaguely Eastern, as the song progresses. As we'll see, the titles of its movements—"Awakening," "Realisation," "Acceptance," and "Denial"—could have easily been envisioned by Jon Anderson and affixed to those movements of Yes's "Close to the Edge."

"In Held Twas in I," a twisted "Jack and the Beanstalk" fairytale epic, was, along with the Pretty Things' 1968 concept record *S.F. Sorrow*, one of the main inspirations for the Who's monumentally important rock opera, *Tommy*. The title of the piece was, famously, extracted from the first word of each verse of the song. In that sense, it is, essentially, meaningless. "We basically named it after we had written it," lyricist Keith Reid once told me. "We didn't know what to call it, because we just had a working title and went along with it. I think we had a working title of 'Magnum Harum' at the time. I don't know why we didn't stick with that. For whatever reason we didn't."

The twenty-minute musical journey from darkness through to the narrator's ultimate spiritual awakening opens with a spoken word passage, "Glimpses of Nirvana"—a soliloquy recounting the exploits of a spiritual pilgrim beseeching wisdom of the Dalai Lama. "I think a lot of us were into that and the meditation thing," says Reid, "and . . . looking for some inner peace. In common with a lot of people of that time, it was something I was drawn toward."

Despite its ethereal origins, the introspective tone and doomy, funeral dirge–like atmosphere casts a pall on the tune. The following section, the fanciful fairgrounds ditty "Twas Teatime at the Circus," alludes to rock icon Jimi Hendrix. "Basically, the piece took on a life of its own and grew organically," Reid continues. "It was very much like the beanstalk the Dalai Lama speaks of in the song, as one observer noted."

Organic growth occurred through the late 1960s and into the early 1970s. Artists were stretching out like never before.

The Beatles hit us with *Abbey Road*'s multipart suite, Miles Davis's *Bitches Brew* boasted marathon jazz-rock fusion workouts, Frank Zappa and the Mothers traversed musical genres and a few time signatures with "The Little House I Used to Live In" (from *Burnt Weeny Sandwich*), Caravan synthesized the 22-minute-plus epic "Nine Feet Underground" (written largely by keyboardist David Sinclair), Egg offered a perceived reference to Grieg in their sizzling "Symphony No. 2," King Crimson got jazzy and a bit classical for the title track of *Lizard*, and Van der Graaf Generator tinkered with analog tape edits to create "A Plague of Lighthouse Keepers." Clearly, by 1971, the shackles of creative restraint were finally and completely shoved off, as artists would and could not restrain their long-winded expression.

Emerson, Lake, and Palmer stunned with the multi-sectional, twenty-plus-minute sidelong masterwork "Tarkus," an aggressive and toxic stew of thrashing, strange, and odd tempos, heavy-metal Hammond organ dissonance informed by Bartok, and moments of countervailing and near-cathartic vocal-based song fragments.

In the opening section, "Eruption," modal shifts juxtaposed or overlapping with the song's stabbing rhythmic qualities create an almost disturbing listening experience—keyboardist Keith Emerson's most effective work.

"Tarkus" might appear to a degree to mimic the structure of a classical piece, but its architecture was closer to earlier, multi-movement psychedelic works. Compositionally, it *seems* disjointed, but there are a few instances of conscious recapitulation and, studied on a micro level, recurring patterns may emerge. Perhaps that's why such a fragmentary song, or one perceived as a fragmentary song, retains a semblance of coherency, even if it is not immediately recognizable.

There may not be any discernable, overarching concept connecting these song divisions, beyond the meaning we associate with the lyrics, the cover artwork, and the title of each movement. However, there's enough substance here to have us wondering what the thread is linking these movements. Perhaps that's the brilliance of "Tarkus": its vagaries allow us to connect the dots.

Germany-based Can's "Aumgn" and "Halleluwah" operate on both the conscious and unconscious level. There's a perceptible presence in these tracks, even if it's not always identifiable. Liberal use of tape echo (think the varispeed technique applied to "Lovely Rita" from *Sgt. Pepper's*) not to mention the creepy, studio-enhanced chants are less avant-garde experimentation and more guide for the uninitiated to explore darker realms of the soul.

The repetitive rhythmic patterns in "Aumgn" don't appear to grow in intensity or even speed or volume, yet we feel a kind of tension throughout Jaki Liebezeit's almost minimalistic drum solo. It's as if, with "Halleluwah" and "Aumgn," Can had hit upon the correct formula of arrangement of notes, track sequence, and beats per minute to open portals to dimensions often left unexplored.

As for unexplored dimensions, Pink Floyd became the crown prince of the form. Floyd created a bridge between psychedelia and prog rock with "Echoes," from 1971's *Meddle*. Stitched together from various sources ("Nothing Parts 1–36," or "Son of Nothing") "Echoes" was once described as a kind of tone poem by lyricist/bassist/vocalist Roger Waters. It was an artistic approach that clearly expanded and improved upon the near twenty-four-minute title track of *Atom Heart Mother*. Some listeners have drawn a connection between the tenets of '60s flower power and the concept of the connectedness we all feel as human beings.

All of these songs were forerunners to what I see as the pinnacle of the progressive-rock movement. Informed by Eastern mysticism and Hermann Hesse's esoteric concepts of the self, the title track of Yes's 1972 studio album *Close to the Edge* occupies the entire first side of the original LP, and arguably perfected many of the musical traits of the songs mentioned above. Part studio construction, part homage to European art-music, part postmodernist mash-up, "Close to the Edge" it seems was tailor-made for the exploding LP market via the infusion of classical music's long-form composition strategies.

Scholar and author Edward Macan reasons that the title track of *Close to the Edge*, composed in four movements, is beholden to the sonata form. The sonata form generally refers to the first movement of a work, which contains three subsections that boil down to "exposition, development, and recapitulation," centered on or involving key changes. Occasionally, an introduction would be placed before the exposition subsection and a coda might be tacked onto the end of the piece, as well.

Macan suggests that the entirety of the song, as well as its first movement, "The Solid Time of Change," could be viewed as following the sonata form. (With the exception of the final key change in the last movement to F-sharp, instead of a reversion to the D of the opening—an accepted norm in classical music—this could be true.) But let's not get ahead of ourselves. More about this later.

"Close to the Edge," and the other two songs accompanying it on the record ("And You and I," "Siberian Khatru"), are marvels of compositional grandeur, studio production experimentation, band collaboration, creative exuberance without excess, varied and exotic instrumentation (such as electric sitar, Hawaiian steel guitar, pipe organ, and harpsichord, as explored in pop music previously by the Beatles, Donovan, and a host of artists in the so-called psyche-folk movement), and commanding musicianship—all the hallmarks of the burgeoning progressive scene.

By the late 1960s it was accepted that rock could be just about anything the recording artist wanted it to be. Reductive artists need not apply. Although this led to gross self-indulgence on occasion, the exoticism of the subgenre known as prog dictated that rock would be as unfamiliar as and unlike anything else that came before it in popular music.

A partial—partial—definition of progressive rock boils down to European influences being infused into a rock setting. By firmly planting one foot in the Western world with its rich melodic history and formalized structures, and another in the wilds of Eastern mysticism, Yes stood at a musical crossroads in 1972. The group had the rare talent for combining innovativeness and commercialism; insightfulness and esotericism; inclusiveness and a feeling of universal consciousness. It was these opposing forces that defined Yes in the 1970s and reached their apotheosis in *Close to the Edge*.

2

SWEET DREAMS
Early Yes

He was born John Roy Anderson, in Lancashire, in 1944. Most in the music world would come to know him as Jon Anderson, lead singer and chief visionary of the British progressive-rock band Yes.

Little in his bio hints at the cosmic explorations he'd undertake or the mystical stage persona he'd project on his journey with one of the most successful recording and touring acts of the 1970s. Anderson's mother worked in a cotton mill factory, and John/Jon was himself a farmhand on weekends, helping earn money for his family. One of his early aspirations was to play football for Accrington Stanley, but this was cut short by family needs.

The North of England's educational system, agricultural occupations, and the pace of life evidently couldn't satisfy his wanderlust. As a result, the young dreamer's mind wandered to music. He had played in a skiffle group as a preteen, although it is unclear if they ever did any gigs. By seventeen years of age, Anderson joined the blue-eyed soul band the Warriors, which had gone through various permutations in its lifespan. It had at one point featured Jon's brother Tony Anderson on vocals, drummer Ian Wallace (later of King Crimson from 1971 through 1972), keyboardist Brian Chatton (Phil Collins, Boys Don't Cry), and bassist David Foster (Badger), among others.

After a tour of Germany, Anderson broke with the Warriors and stayed on in Munich to play local clubs and spearhead a band, the Gentle Party. He has said he felt as though he had been resurrected through a soul-searching process he underwent after leaving the Warriors. Psychoanalysis followed, and Anderson took stock of his life, himself, and where his career was going. Once he let his apprehensions go, he said, he was reborn.

Although he'd been tempted to get on a train and head back to Accrington and live with his family, Anderson fought this instinct and instead desired to move beyond his hometown . . .

It seems the experience Chris Squire, born 1948, racked up as a young musician helped to propel him to the upper echelons of the rock world. Arguably his first serious introduction to music was through the church, Squire having been a choir singer in St. Andrew's in Kingsbury. (Chris's brother Tony was also in the choir.) He once told me:

> After the end of World War II, and going on from there, I think it seemed to me that every kid I knew, not every one, but pretty much every one, within a couple mile radius from where my house was [Kingsbury], was in the church choir. That was just something you did. Your mother told you to join the church choir and you did [*laughs*] . . .
>
> I really did enjoy those days because I had a very, very good, young, choirmaster [Barry Rose]. He came to my local parish and he had a real great enthusiasm for music and fired everyone up to rehearse a lot. He later conducted the choir at Charles and Diana's wedding and his first gig was at my local church, so he was a rising star in the whole church music system. We were lucky to get the benefit of him when we were just kids.

Squire soon formed a band called the Selfs with Andrew Jackman, whom he knew from St. Andrew's choir, drummer Martin Adelman, and others. Within a year or two, however, things would change.

> I think you had pointed out earlier that one of the main inspirations of every musician of my generation was probably the Beatles. I was fifteen in 1963 when they broke out in the major way. Up until then I really hadn't considered that I wanted to be a professional musician, necessarily. I had other options open to me. I had uncles in the stock market and [they were] thinking I would go that way. Then I started thinking what a good life it was being a Beatle . . .

Then, when I was not much older than that, I saw the
Stones live in a little village, a kind of hole somewhere in
south of England, and I thought that was really exciting. I
just started to watch all the TV shows that were springing
up everywhere, exposing all the new acts. Of course, later
on the Who became a huge influence on me, and they
were local to where I lived, so I saw a lot of their shows.

By this point Squire had left school. He eventually found a job
as a salesman at Boosey & Hawkes in London, which imported
some of the first Rickenbacker basses into England through an af-
filiated retail store. Chris's interest in playing an instrument grew
as his desire to become an accomplished choir singer faded. Keenly
aware that some of his favorite bass players, including the Who's
John Entwistle, had used Rickenbackers, Squire made it his mission
to get his hands on this instrument. Working at Boosey & Hawkes
provided him the opportunity to purchase one at a discounted
price. (More about this in a moment.)

After the collapse of the Selfs, Squire formed the Syn, a soul-
rock band with a predilection for Motown, featuring pre-Yes
multi-part harmonies. He corralled drummer Adelman, who'd later
resurface as a photographer credited on the back sleeve of the original *Close to the Edge* LP packaging.

The Syn played mostly covers but also attempted original material for singles, such as "Created By Clive" and what some consider
a conceptual track, "Flowerman," which was released as a single via
Deram in the U.K., b/w "The 14 Hour Technicolour Dream."

Guitarist Peter Banks, born 1947, met Squire on Denmark
Street, near Charing Cross Road, having been introduced to him
via Martin (a.k.a. Martyn) Adelman. Banks, like Squire, cut short
his education in favor of music and joined bands in the suburbs of
London before gravitating toward the city.

Squire and core Syn members vocalist Steve Nardelli, Banks,
and keyboardist Andrew Jackman, soon became the opening act
for the larger-name artists playing the Marquee in London.

Squire told me:

I was drawn more toward listening to Tamla Motown
then that. I think my [interest in] black music came a lot

more from Detroit than it did from the Deep South. The blues thing, the southern blues thing, was not my strong point. I had listened to those guys, Muddy Waters and Robert Johnson . . . John Lee Hooker . . . Jimmy Reed. And when the Who started, they used to do a lot of songs like that. But then again, the Who were very Tamla Motown–influenced, as well. But I was more Tamla Motown. That was the era, mid-to-late 1960s, that was what was going around the clubs in London—white guys playing the white version of blues and Tamla. Sly and the Family Stone were one of my favorite things, ever, as well. I like that. Larry Graham was, of course, a great bass player in that band. So, I picked up a lot from that area, too.

Despite their hip take on R&B and opening for Jimi Hendrix at the Marquee in spring 1967, the Syn's days were numbered. It seemed as though one horrible incident after another closed the curtains on the act. In one such accident, Banks remembers being electrocuted during a band practice session:

> I've been electrocuted, once really badly, back in the Syn days. I still have a scar on my finger because . . . I touched a microphone and had the guitar around my neck . . . The whole thing short-circuited so the band's power went through me. Apparently I lucked out. It was at a rehearsal. Luckily, I had run forward and the guitar cord snapped. I just remember trying to scream and apparently I went blue. As I moved forward . . . I was moving toward Chris, I think, and nobody wanted to go near me. As I moved forward the cord snapped. I think I passed out.

The Syn was finished by 1968, and Squire had moved on, having replaced bassist Paul Rutledge in a new band, Mabel Greer's Toyshop, featuring vocalist and guitarist Clive Bayley and drummer Bob Hagger (a.k.a. Andrew Bellmont), who had actually auditioned for the Syn. Banks followed Squire into Mabel Greer's Toyshop, making Mabel's a foursome.

"Bob found Chris," says Clive Bayley. "He got hold of Chris and persuaded him to join us. That was his fault [*laughs*]."

"When Chris asked Peter to come down, because we were looking for [a guitarist] to full out the sound a bit more, Peter came down mainly because he enjoyed playing with Chris and he enjoyed the freedom of working with Mabel, in that we were unstructured and it gave him a chance to go off to do all sorts of stuff within the confines of song structures," Hagger says.

Very much like the Syn, Mabel Greer's Toyshop found early success, as Bayley recalls:

> We did some recording with Mike Leander, who is no longer with us, but he was a producer for MCA. We did some recording there, which was for John Peel. I called up John Peel or we got hold of him, Bob [Hagger] and I, and he was hanging out in Lots Road where, subsequently, I opened up a nightclub about twenty years later. John was great: he gave us the whole of *Night Ride* [his Wednesday night program on BBC radio]. We performed four songs. It was broadcast on the eve of my eighteenth birthday, and I remember sitting in the car listening to it because the radio wasn't working at home. He gave us our first real break.

Despite this, trouble was brewing. Having two guitarists in the band was not something the independent Banks was willing to put up with for very long. Either wanting to be the band's sole guitarist or believing he couldn't fully express himself with Bayley in the band, Banks left Mabel Greer's and joined rivals the Neat Change, managed by Billy Gaff (Rod Stewart, Faces). Banks would eventually return to Mabel Greer's Toyshop in July 1968, however.

Hagger told me:

> Clive was something like five years younger than [Banks]. He was seventeen at the time, sixteen when I met him. [Peter] wasn't enjoying some of the more structured songs, which was one reason why he left. One of the things that Peter brought to Clive's compositions was the ability to move into a different piece of music in the middle of one song. We would be busy playing one song and he might move into something

like "Midnight Sleighride," a classical piece, and we
would transform it and then come back to the original
theme. Things like that were what Peter was brilliant
at. It was the reason we used to play songs like "Eleanor
Rigby." . . . Put alongside Chris's bass, of course, you really had something excellent.

While Banks was busy with Neat Change, serious conversation
was occurring about his replacement. "Peter left Mabel Greer's for
Neat Change," Hagger says, "which was totally over-structured. I
suspect Peter didn't enjoy that very much, either, and that's why
he eventually came back. But before this, we were having our ups
and downs with Peter, and I remember the words: 'We're good
enough to attract the best, let's go for the best.' The best guitarist
in town at the time was Steve Howe. We were just blown away by
him. I think he stood out completely from the rest of the band. We
started looking for him and it didn't happen."

Anderson's Return

Howe didn't join Mabel Greer's Toyshop, but another future Yes
member did: Jon Anderson. After his Munich epiphany, Jon had
assumed the pseudonym Hans Christian.

Hans Christian Andersen was, of course, the beloved Danish
author of children's stories and fairy tales, such as *Thumbelina, The
Emperor's New Clothes, The Little Mermaid*, and many others.

Jon (a.k.a. Hans Christian) was in the Netherlands to hook up
with another band when he was called back to the UK by EMI
regarding promotion of his first Parlophone single in March 1968,
the blue-eyed soul number "Never My Love" b/w "All of the Time."
(It should be noted that Anderson had already recorded a single as
a member of the Warriors in 1964.)

Anderson would release another single on EMI's Parlophone in
May, the bubblegum-soul track "(The Autobiography of) Mississippi Hobo" b/w "Sonata of Love." (Interestingly enough, Anderson's
voice was multitracked for the song—a recording technique that
would be used to great effect on later Yes productions.) However,
the launch of "Never My Love" and its follow-up were uneventful, and this failure, ironically enough, set the table for his fateful
meeting with Chris Squire at La Chasse Club.

Jack Barrie, co-owner of the Marquee club and owner of La Chasse, had been looking after Anderson and was hoping to match him with a band in the UK, having hired him as a bottle cleaner at his clubs La Chasse and the Marquee. It was Barrie who more or less brokered the first meeting between Anderson and Squire at La Chasse.

"Chris had met up with us one day and said he wanted to introduce us to someone he met at the pub," Hagger says, "and we said, 'Why?' He said, 'He's a singer, a bit older than us. He's already had a career. He's done the Germany thing, like the Beatles. Had a single or two out already.' We were very skeptical until we asked, 'What's his name?' He said, 'His name is Hans Christian Anderson,' and we said, 'Wow, we must meet him. He will fit with Mabel Greer's Toyshop perfectly.'"

"Chris really brought Jon in," says Bayley, "because we were playing at the Marquee, and Jon was hanging around there. That was fine. Jon came in at that point and we played the Marquee. I remember the first time we played, John Gee, the guy who ran the place, looked at me and said, 'That is great. But you're singing flat. Would you mind singing in tune?' I said, 'Yeah.' But I was more interested in whamming out on the guitar with a fuzz box at 400 watts. It was all about psychedelia."

"There was no vote on Jon joining," Hagger remembers. "Jon was in and that was it."

Squire told me:

> When I first ran into Jon Anderson, we were talking about, you know, what music we liked, and by then I had became a big Simon and Garfunkel fan. I was keen on their vocal harmonies and I was also being influenced by what was going on at London's Marquee club, which had become my local venue for music. I lived in northwest London and I used to take the train into central London and the West End and go to the Marquee club and watch a lot of the blues bands. I saw Graham Bond Organisation, which was essentially the beginnings of Cream, with Jack Bruce and Ginger Baker. And, of course, the Nice were playing there with Keith throwing out his classical approach to Hammond organ. There was a variety

of music that was there for anyone, who was around their late teens, like I was at that time, to absorb.

Squire is often described as Jon's complement: practical and more musical adept (or technical) than his former bandmate. It seemed the two personalities balanced one another and worked together like a well-oiled machine.

Anderson may have been accepted straight away, but he was restless. He had been informed by producer Paul Korda that Adrian and Paul Gurvitz of Gun were looking for a singer. Jon tried his hand at performing, albeit briefly, with Gun at the Marquee, while also testing the waters with Mabel Greer's Toyshop.

Guitarist/singer Brian Parrish, of Parrish and Gurvitz, and Badger, recalls:

> If you look at the Warriors with Ian Wallace, David Foster, Brian Chatton, that's an interesting lineup and interesting what came out of that. I have my own Paul Gurvitz connection. We were together in Hamburg and the Parrish and Gurvitz project morphed into Gun. I did a solo thing and Adrian came in and Jon was with them for a brief time. Very brief. I can't imagine that ever would have worked. Jon has this ethereal thing going on with his vocals . . . But it was more than that. I say this because I know the individuals involved. [Paul] is dogmatic and he is very . . . I can't see him mixing well with Jon. Jon . . . likes to be in command of the situation. . . . I mean, everybody can't drive the car at the same time [*laughs*]. I can't imagine what that would have been like.

Anderson was keeping his options open, but progress had already been made with Mabel Greer's. It's part of Yes lore that after their La Chasse meeting, within a day (perhaps a shorter period of time), Anderson and Squire retired to the bass player's apartment and had written "Sweetness," an edited version of which would become Yes's first single, b/w "Something's Coming" in 1969. (We'll return to the writing credits for this song in just a moment.)

There were similar, semi-related covers circulating at the time.

The Nice did a version of the Bernstein and Sondheim track "America," from *West Side Story*, including within it a twist of Dvořák's *New World Symphony*. (According to authors George Forrester, Martyn Hanson, and Frank Askew, in their book *Emerson, Lake & Palmer: The Show That Never Ends*, this was the song that prompted Keith's infamous knife-wielding technique, which he used to sustain organ notes.) Yes, in turn, covered Bernstein and Sondheim's "Something's Coming."

Dynamics began shifting, alliances were forming, and songwriting teams were collaborating. Mabel Greer's Toyshop was morphing, and Bob Hagger, for one, wasn't too happy about it. For one thing, Hagger was not a great fan of being too rehearsed and overthinking every musical action.

"We were very much a live band and we enjoyed playing and improvising," Hagger says. "We didn't do many shows, but I remember one was at the Marquee and another was playing with a band called the Action [at Middle Earth in London], that had changed their name to Mighty Baby, which is more psychedelic."

"I think that was what psychedelic prog rock was about: getting up onstage and playing in the moment—the Eastern philosophy thing," Bayley says. "It was more of, let's have a 'happening' and let's have the audience and venue create the moment."

Hagger:

> When I find myself in rehearsals, playing the same thing, again, for half a day, I don't enjoy that. I was also incompatible conceptually, I think, with the band. Jon would be listening to a different kind of music we would be listening to. I remember him mentioning the Fifth Dimension, the Young Rascals, and people we didn't listen to at all. He was turning out names we weren't, put it that way. He was very much into the American style of music. Whereas most of the stuff we would listen to would be homegrown, London-style. He'd say, "If we could do it like the Fifth Dimension . . . " and some of us were thinking, "No, that's not what we want to do, Jon. We want to play like Mabel Greer's Toyshop."

Mabel Greer's Toyshop would eventually become Yes, of course, and play originals. But that was down the road, and too long a wait for Hagger:

> I was approached by a band that said their drummer had just left, for what reason I don't remember. "We need someone now, are you interested?" When they showed me the gig schedule, I said, "Where do I sign?" I remember calling up the guys [in Mabel Greer's Toyshop] and saying, "I've had enough, I'm leaving now." They said, "That's great, but we have a gig Saturday night." I said, "Well, I think I'm going to be in Scotland on Saturday night." That didn't go down too well.
>
> I joined a band that was . . . playing every night. We were doing a lot of tours of France. This is where I met my wife. I have been married to her ever since. We met in 1968 and married in 1970 and just celebrated forty-five years of marriage.

Hagger admits that the boys in Mabel's liked his drumming, and his leaving may have come as a complete shock to them. "Well, they loved me while I was there, but weren't very complimentary when I'd left," he says. "That's understandable, because look who replaced me. If you compare anyone to Bill Bruford you're going to be in trouble, right?"

Born in Sevenoaks, Kent in 1949, a young Bill Bruford had placed an ad in *Melody Maker* looking to escape the dreary confines of the pop music scene to find something much more challenging, much more jazzy. Although Bruford had played very briefly with Savoy Brown and a band called Paper Blitz in Rome, Italy, his experience was scant. When the members of Mabel Greer's Toyshop contacted Bruford, they were impressed, mostly, because he had an automobile and owned a Ludwig drum kit. (In reality, he had not a Ludwig kit but a piecemeal setup.)

"When Bob left we had to find a drummer, and Bill came along through an audition," Bayley says. "We didn't know any numbers so we said, 'Let's play "Midnight Hour,"' the R&B/Wilson Pickett song. We were doing a gig, some uni [Rachel Macmillan College] somewhere, and we were doing an hour of 'Midnight Hour,' and that was the interview for Bill Bruford, the audition."

"I'm the last of the untrained guys," Bruford told me in 2001. "Most of my drum knowledge and harmony is picked up off the street. I found what I needed, as I needed it. . . . I'm just working with what I've got—and it *ain't* much."

"I think Jon, or someone, wasn't keen [on Bruford]," Bayley says. "I said, 'Hang on. You've got to get him to join the band.' . . . Jon has very strong ideas, and I think I had to convince Jon that Bill was a good choice."

Bruford has always maintained that he was under the impression he was joining some kind of jazz band. "Ever since I started as musician in '68, I've been on a long journey back to jazz, which is kind of strange because I thought I would be a jazz drummer. But in '68, rock was so strong, with Hendrix and Cream and all the London drummers of the day turning into rock guys. Mitch Mitchell, Ginger Baker . . . I was doing the same thing."

For now, Bruford would have to do his best Max Roach within the context of an arty pop-rock band whose direction seemed to be, with increasing certainty, falling under the purview of the spunky lead singer.

Bayley:

> Jon definitely wanted to control things and he was three or four years older than me. But I got on really well with Jon, although he was "Mr. Bossy Boots" [*laughs*]. I let him be Mr. Bossy Boots, but I quite liked him. Chris was a true musician. "We do it like this . . . " sort of thing. I had all the enthusiasm in the world but I wasn't a great guitarist. I'm a lot better now than I was then, but I probably deferred to them a bit. That's when Mabel Greer started getting quite serious. The thing I remember is practicing in the [basement of the] Lucky Horseshoe [café] in Covent Garden, Salisbury Avenue, which is where Yes started. Those were the first rehearsals.
>
> I think [keyboardist] Tony Kaye came in then, as well. We were practicing there, and that's really how Yes started. It moved from Mabel into Yes. We practiced in Chris's flat for a bit and then that got ridiculous. I remember I

used to hang out with Chris, who used to live in Fulham. He had an attic flat. One funny story was, once when I went there, I saw this wig on a head, and I thought it was his. It was his girlfriend's. I said, "Bloody hell. This is taking it a bit seriously."

By the summer, things were rapidly changing for Mabel. For one thing, Banks, who had left briefly, had returned to the fold. Hagger:

> It was in June that I left and Bill Bruford came in. In July, Tony Kaye arrived. Then in August was the time they changed their name to Yes. It was at that point that Peter came back and Clive left. Peter hated the name Mabel Greer's Toyshop anyway, and said it was absolutely ridiculous, and that a nice, short, three-letter name, like the Who, would be better. He came up with Yes. I think that was really when Clive had realized that his baby had been taken away from him. . . . He was part of the rehearsals. I think he did one gig [with Yes]. He talks about a gig in Kingston, Surrey. He may have done one or two gigs and then he was gone. I know he did one in Kingston, because that was where he used to live, and [he] invited the whole band round to the house to meet his mum and dad. That is what they did after the show.

"I think that was another reason why Bob and then I left," Bayley says. "It was our creation but then it started morphing, which was good, but it morphed into Yes and the sound became different from what we had originally envisioned. A lot of the elements were still what we created—our idea to be a hard rock band with three- or four-part harmonies. That was everyone's idea: Queen was the same. It was clear that that was how it was going to go. Jon was certainly 'Mr. Bossy Boots.' So was Chris, actually. But Jon held sway."

"I remember we sat down and both Clive and Chris were choir boys," Hagger says. "They had this church effect when they were doing harmonies and having Jon there, as well, to do the three-part harmonies. It really was quite amazing. It was beautiful."

Flush with cash from early financial backer John Roberts, Mabel Greer's/Yes's rehearsal space in the basement of the small café at Shaftesbury Avenue could not have been more appropriate. Hairpieces aside, there was something special, serious, even magical, about Yes from the very start.

"Things were meant to happen, and things do happen," Bayley explains. "So, we create our magic, if you like, and we create through choice, you either accept it or not, but things are going to pan out in a certain way, and then luck enters into it."

Yes's multipart vocal sections have drawn comparisons to Simon and Garfunkel; Crosby, Stills, and Nash; and Buffalo Springfield; but in many (not all) cases, what we're hearing is Jon's vocals, multitracked. A similar type of vocal layering was done with Freddie Mercury's voice by Roy Thomas Baker with Queen later in the 1970s for tracks such as "Bohemian Rhapsody," "Bicycle Race," "You're My Best Friend," "Fat Bottomed Girls," and "Killer Queen." Queen also shared the stage with Yes in 1971 in Kingston, England. Baker would of course work with Yes, too, once for the ill-fated "Paris sessions" in the late 1970s, and again in the twenty-first century for *Heaven and Earth*.

Finally, Bayley saw the writing on the wall. The band he helped to form was unrecognizable from its origins:

> When I left, Peter Banks carried on. We had two guitarists, and Peter is a much better guitarist than me. I provided the creative madness, if you like, but Pete could actually play, which was useful. I was very fuzz box loud, violin bow, "Let's go . . . ." My music was a little different, as well. I helped with the arrangement of quite a few songs and I put in some interesting riffs, and I wrote a few of the songs like "Sweetness" and "Beyond and Before," because we used to have those in Mabel Greer's Toyshop. They were later used in Yes. I am not entirely sure whether I could say I was in the band as it was called Yes. But I was there for,

literally, probably for a week, when it changed its name
and off they went.

I think there's a few things brushed under the carpet, me included. The guys didn't want me to leave but
I had a nightclub at the time. There was just too much
going on. I knew the band would make it, but for some
mad reason I didn't like the management and didn't
like what I saw in the music business and I think I liked
to paddle my own canoe quite a bit. I will never forget
that Jon brought a manager in. We were practicing in a
warehouse in Shepherd's Bush, did a week's practicing
there, and the manager came in and said, "Fantastic.
Now I want you to all dye your hair green and that's the
way I want you to look." I said, "You must be joking . . .
what are you on? We're a psychedelic band." I think Jon
said, "Well, I don't know, we may have to do it," and I
just said, "That is not what Mabel Greer's Toyshop is."
I probably thought that the music business was not for
me. I didn't want to be told what to do, because that was
the whole idea of progressive rock—the clue is in the
name. It is a not a pop band. I think that's why I left.
But at the time I think Chris and Jon were saying, "No,
don't leave." I actually felt guilty. I sold all my [gear] and
walked away. I didn't ask for any royalties or anything
because I felt guilty leaving them in the shit. Well, possibly. Obviously, Steve Howe joined later, and he is an
incredible guitarist and I could never play like that, but
possibly I may have contributed some musical ideas and
songs and some early feeling to the band.

Indeed. Bayley is credited with co-writing two Yes songs, but he
may have contributed more to the band. I've seen old Yes contracts, and it does not seem as though Clive's name appears there.
Whether he's actually received royalties, I cannot say for sure.

No, I didn't [receive royalties]. I finally got a hold of
Warner Bros. [Music] about a year ago, and when we
were starting [Mabel Greer's Toyshop] with Bob and
we were going to release the album I said, "If I release

'Sweetness' and 'Beyond and Before,' someone might
say, 'These are not your songs.'" So I did write to Warner
and kicked up a fuss and they are paying me royalties,
about $100 a year or something. I certainly haven't
gotten the royalties for forty-five years or something on
it. I'm not bitter about it because, as I said, I feel guilty
about bowing out. But I have those two songs on there
[Yes's self-titled debut from 1969], which I did co-write.
I think the lyrics are Jon's: I wouldn't have written lyrics
like that. But I certainly wrote the music.

"Beyond and Before," I remember writing that in
Wisley [Common], these woods I used to go to as a kid. I
remember taking my guitar up there in winter and there
was frost and snow on the trees and I sat down and wrote
that song, and I think I wrote most of that, to be honest.
There were a few other bits on the album but, hey ho.

Hagger:

You have to understand that the whole band was formed
around Clive's musical ideas. Before Chris had joined
us in Mabel Greer's, I would venture to say that we were
doing songs such as "Beyond and Before," "Electric
Funeral," "Images," some of those songs that Chris was
credited [on], because he came in and started playing
alongside Clive. That was the difference he brought to it.
He made much more powerful pieces, so it was normal
that he would have co-songwriting credits on there. But,
I mean, Clive is, first of all, a composer and an arranger.
That's his strength as an artist. He is very musically
articulate. I think that was probably the attraction for
Chris, at the time. Chris liked that and that's why he
wanted to be a part of it.

Yes's first lineup had been solidified to include Anderson, Banks,
Bruford, Squire, and keyboardist Tony Kaye (Anthony Selridge),
from Leicester, who'd aspired, at one time, to became a classical
pianist. Having been seduced by more popular music, Kaye turned
on to the joys of the Hammond organ and soon gravitated toward

jazz, even playing in a big band. He also bounced around with the Federals, Bittersweet, and Johnny Taylor's Star Combo before he made his mark with Yes.

Although the abovementioned personnel would be the original Yes band, one practically needed a scorecard to keep up with the revolving door of musicians who entered and exited Mabel Greer's Toyshop/Yes in the early days. For one thing, Bruford, who had been in the band for a short period of time, soon returned to university, having made up his mind, for the moment that, he was done with music.

Drummer Tony O'Riley replaced Bruford when the latter quit to concentrate on his studies. It's believed that O'Riley performed with Yes through most of the fall of 1968; Ian Wallace, a buddy of Anderson's from the old Warrior days, who'd go on to become the drummer for King Crimson, also pitched in during this transitional period, beating the skins for possibly only one performance.

This chapter of Yes's early history closed when Bruford saw his former bandmates blow the doors off of the auditorium at Leeds University in November 1968. Suddenly he was convinced to have another go at Yes.

Mike Tait, who graduated from roadie to lighting designer *par excellence* for Yes, recalls this period:

> I'm Australian, and I got a job at the Speakeasy, the music biz hangout, and someone there said, "I have these guys, can you drive the van for them this weekend." That was Yes. That was a show, and I drove them up to Leeds University. Bill Bruford was not the drummer: there was another drummer then. Bill was at university there, coincidentally, and stopped at the gig, of course. Another time I was with Bill driving . . . in my little Volkswagen, and he was saying, "Should I become a drummer or stay at university and be an accountant?" I think that conversation may have helped sway him to be a musician. He was a fairly logical person. Bill was educated and the other boys were educated.

In retrospect, it's likely Bruford was on the fence about making a career of music, and was struggling with the decision to go at it full-blast. Bruford may have been unsure, but what exactly did Mike say to Bill?

"I have no idea," Tait told me, "but I know we spoke about that subject, and he was from a very good family and they were horrified, of course. He loved the music and [was] totally intense."

Yes's big break would come rather rapidly. As legend has it, in September 1968, when Sly and the Family Stone were not available for their scheduled gig, Tony Stratton-Smith, later the head of Charisma Records and then the manager of the Nice, suggested Yes take the slot.

Yes's own manager, Roy Flynn (who ran the Speakeasy in London), roused and organized the band members and urged them to get down to Blaise's, where history tells us that Yes went down a storm. It must have been a strange sight for the famous musicians on site—some reports said Pete Townshend and Keith Emerson were in attendance, expecting Sly but instead getting Yes. And yet the performance was so legendary that it led to a prestigious residency at the epicenter of the burgeoning progressive-rock movement in London: the Marquee Club. (The band played two sets, forty-five minutes apiece.)

By now, Yes was generating a real buzz around London, having won an opening slot playing at the Royal Albert Hall on Cream's farewell tour, near the end of November 1968. Yes, it seemed, had arrived.

"It was in November that I was playing in a small club in the south of France, down in Papillion or Toulouse or somewhere, and we had about 150 or 200 people come to see us," says Hagger. "I found out that Yes were playing the Albert Hall. I about fell off my drum stool."

After Yes played the Royal Albert Hall supporting Cream, the band opened for Janis Joplin and did a Christmas show. Next, Yes parlayed its growing popularity into a record deal. Although inexperienced at that time, Flynn had managed to hobble together a coalition of the willing at Atlantic Records, which promptly signed the group.

Some in the band would bemoan the Atlantic deal in later years, but we shouldn't lose sight of the fact that Flynn championed Yes and helped to push the group over the first of many hurdles it would encounter on its way to becoming a commercially viable progressive-rock band.

Flynn may be the most underappreciated person in Yes's storied history. Granted, he may have been over his head on some fronts, and it would have become apparent, one thinks, that Yes did indeed need to find a new manager to take it to the next level. If nothing else, Flynn provided: Yes hung out at the Speakeasy during this time, practically living there while playing gigs during the evening.

(In 1973, Yes's management company, Hemdale, settled with Flynn regarding unfinished business. Prior to the settlement, Flynn was supposed to receive five percent of the band's revenues in exchange for Hemdale assuming management of the band. Flynn reportedly said the amount he was eventually awarded went a small way to deferring some of the expenses he had incurred while helping to support the band during the lean years of the late 1960s and early 1970s.)

For the time being, it was a major accomplishment, and Yes's self-titled debut, released in 1969 and co-produced by Paul Clay, included material from the live Mabel sets, including "Beyond and Before" and "I See You." The band also included "Something's Coming" from *West Side Story*, with its reference to "Midnight Sleighride" based on Sergie Prokofiev's *Trioka*. "Something's Coming" was released as a single, b/w "Sweetness," in July 1969. (Interestingly, the main melody of the Prokofiev piece was nicked for Greg Lake's UK #2 holiday-themed single, "I Believe in Father Christmas," released in 1975.)

"That was in the 1970s when he was doing it," Hagger says of the band's inclusion of "Midnight Sleigh Ride" in an original song. "I claim we were doing it first [*laughs*]. I didn't even know that anybody had done that."

We also get the first whiff of the band's creative ambition with the six-and-a-half minute, nearly liturgical, multi-sectional "Survival"; the extended jams in "I See You"; and the epic original song "Looking Around," featuring harmonized voices, a juxtaposition of compositional weirdness, and a hard-rock groove. Nearly as mystical is "Everydays," the band's interpretation of the Stephen Stills composition (recorded by Atlantic Records act Buffalo Springfield), the B-side of Anderson/Squire song "Looking Around." ("Everydays" would appear on the band's next studio record, *Time and a Word*.)

The substance, or the essence rather, is there: all of the attributes that would make Yes great and an unlikely success were present as early as 1969. Securely inside the inner sanctum of the band, Bruford began to flourish. His jazzy style is prominent on these early Yes recordings. Whether it's brushwork in "I See You," Yes's cover of the Byrds' classic, or the crazy, Max Roach–esque hi-hat swing pattern of "Everydays." Hell, even "Harold Land"—a song so dubbed for the jazz saxophonist of the same name—hinted at this direction.

Banks told me:

> Bill and I used to listen to jazz a lot and Bill was more of a die-hard jazzer. I didn't know what bebop was or Charlie Parker and Bill introduced me to some of that stuff, though I was listening to John Coltrane and different kinds of things. . . . I had been in a couple of bands with Chris in Syn and Mabel Greer's Toy Shop. I . . . was more of a rock musician than Bill was. Bill was kind of dismissive about anything that didn't have any swing in it. The thing that Bill and I had in common was that we hated repetition. So, we would like to change things around, which, in Yes, wasn't always a good idea. Of course, if I would do something a little crazy then Bill would follow and vice versa. But our taste in music was closer than let's say with Jon or Chris or Tony. Jon and Chris were more into vocals and Bill was always a bit more dismissive about that. I sang backing vocals. The three of us [Anderson, Squire, Banks], we sounded quite angelic at times. But, Bill and I we would sit up late and listen to dirty jazz stuff.

Listen to Bruford's hi-hat rhythm on "Everydays": it's echoed later by Rush drummer Neil Peart's driving swing pattern in "La Villa Strangiato." (Peart also seems to reference another major progressive-rock drummer, Bruford's predecessor in King Crimson, Michael Giles, whose odd-time swing-feel, over-the-bar-line fills in "21st Century Schizoid Man" were surely an influence on the young Peart.)

Yes was still known for covers, however, and "Every Little Thing" was an odd choice. It's not the most exciting Beatles song,

although Banks does spice it up with a reference to "Day Tripper."
Paul McCartney wrote the song for Jane Asher, in her apartment,
so perhaps something less personal, another choice, would have
worked a bit better here. Certainly, this MOR approach is not something that would come to define Yes—or progressive rock for that
matter—as we moved into the 1970s.

The band toured like mad, playing weeks on end throughout
1969. When musicians of a certain era speak about hopping on
"the treadmill," they must have been referring to a predicament
Yes found itself in during the heady daze of the last year of the
decade. Yes performed the majority of the days in the first seven
months of the year.

Banks remember one fateful story:

> I was the real Who fan, way before Yes. I first saw the Who
> play back in 1964, I think. I'd seen them play many times.
> Later I got to know Pete [Townshend, guitarist/vocalist/
> songwriter]. I used to nod to him at the Marquee. I've
> played at the Marquee with five different bands and had
> supported the Who at the Marquee. It was kind of odd. He
> really was a hero of mine and . . . when Syn got together
> and we supported the Who at the Marquee, Townshend
> to me "I just loved what he was doing. Fantastic rhythm
> player. All the aggression." I used to be a Mod, so I was
> very much into the culture thing and into the drugs. The
> whole Mod thing was about taking uppers, or speed, and
> the whole thing was very exciting. But I only got to meet
> Pete when we played in a real horrible, fashionable London
> club, or discotheque, as they use to call them.
>
> We would be playing "Something's Coming," and,
> you know, the theme from *Big Country*, "No Opportu-
> nity Necessary . . . ." We went down terribly. We ended
> the first set and I just wanted to get out of there. I was
> going downstairs and there was a little bar in the base-
> ment area. As I was walking down the stairs someone
> hit me on the back of the head, quite hard. I turned
> around and was ready to hit the guy and it was Townsh-
> end. He said, "You're a fucking great player. Come have
> a drink." It was kind of odd because I was so depressed

about playing there and I mean in those days, if you did a bad gig it was like the end of the world. So, obviously he cheered me up immensely. I went to the bar, we had a chat and he was talking about my playing and he was very complimentary. This is my hero telling me how good he thinks I am. It gave me a lot more confidence. We've kept in touch over the years. The outcome of that was, Yes supported the Who on some gigs. Pete would come on and announce us, which is kind of odd since we were the support band. You know, "This is a fucking good band and you should listen to them."

In between dates, Yes was recording its second album, *Time and a Word*, at Advision Studios, with producer by Tony Colton and recording engineer Eddy Offord.

In a few short years, Offord had graduated from tea boy to engineer. A few years later, he'd become a production architect, helping to shape albums by the two biggest British progressive-rock bands of the era—Yes, and Emerson, Lake and Palmer. Because of his background, Offord was both a technical guru and a visionary producer.

Just as musicians of the progressive-rock scene were pushing boundaries, so were their cohorts on the other side of the studio glass. Throughout the late 1960s and '70s, names such as Alan Parsons, Tony Clarke, John Anthony, David Hentschel, John Burns, Martin Rushent, Denny Cordell, Dick Plant, the 10cc guys in Strawberry Studios, and Frank Zappa were both creative innovators and skilled studio technicians, feeding off the vibe of the times, producing what the Moody Blues' John Lodge once told me was a "progressive-rock avalanche" of the late 1960s.

Offord would soon be inaugurated as George Martin to the British progressive-rock royalty. "Eddy was, without doubt, naturally gifted as an engineer and his laid-back persona helped get the best out of bands enjoying themselves in his sessions," says former Advision recording engineer Gary Martin. "As Yes and ELP were virtuoso instrumentalists, Eddy was a virtuoso engineer. Of the engineers/producers I came across in my time in recording, Eddy was the most talented."

On the recommendation of Atlantic Records executive Phil Carson and producer Colton, Offord was paired with Yes.

He had begun his musical career in 1967—the year that brought us *Sgt. Pepper's*, the Summer of Love, Monterey, Hendrix's debut album, and Pink Floyd's *Piper at the Gates of Dawn*. Within a year, he had become a tea boy/tape op at Advision, and worked initially with Julie Driscoll and Brian Auger on their Bob Dylan cover, "This Wheel's on Fire."

Offord told me:

> I was born and raised in London. Nothing special to say. I was [from an] upper-middle-class family and went to good schools and went to a couple of boarding schools for a while and played a little bit of guitar at school and was into the whole music thing at a very early age. Later on I almost was in a band that got signed. Terry Brown [Rush producer] produced the demo. I was looking at the paper at a job as some gas pump attendant and I saw this ad for a trainee sound engineer, and went for that. That is how I got into the studio thing. I was only maybe eighteen when I started.
>
> I remember someone booked a recording session and none of the real engineers wanted to do it and they said, "Well, give that to Eddy." It turns out the artist was Brian Auger and Julie Driscoll. The song we did was "This Wheel's on Fire," which was a Bob Dylan thing. They did it really uniquely and it was a big hit in England, and it kind of got me started as an engineer at the right place at the right time. From then on, it grew. I went from tea boy to becoming a pretty good engineer within a year or two.

Brilliant as the band and production crew were, *Time and a Word* was a bridge too far: it presented a proposition that may have been just out of the grasp of a young Yes. The band (Jon Anderson really) wanted to place its music within an orchestral setting. Yes thought it needed to employ an orchestra to achieve a "big" sound, so called on the services of musicians from Royal College of Music.

Having seen the Nice use an orchestra, Yes knew that symphonic rock might help it remain relevant. But jumping from Beatles and Byrds covers to the expansiveness of a classical orchestra was perhaps biting off more than they could chew, even for a group of musicians as unconventional as those in Yes. It was perhaps not the greatest idea for a band that was still finding its feet and finicky about the music they made. Still, the die was cast.

In retrospect, it's not difficult to see why. In the late 1960s and early '70s, symphonic-rock hybrids had reached a fever pitch. Deep Purple released *Concerto for Group and Orchestra* a few months prior to *Time and a Word*, and Uriah Heep had *Salisbury* and Barclay James Harvest released their self-titled debut in 1970, following up with 1971's *Once Again* under the auspices of conductor Robert Godfrey. (Procol Harum followed in 1972 with *Live in Concert with the Edmonton Symphony Orchestra*.) Still, Yes's ultimate realization of its dream of truly fusing classical music with rock was still three albums away . . .

There were some bright spots on *Time and a Word*, of course, including "Astral Traveler," "Time and a Word," and "Sweet Dreams," the last two co-written by Jon Anderson and David Foster, Anderson's former mate in the Warriors.

Despite some decent and even catchy songs, some of the original material never really gelled onstage. (In addition, Yes had never done an extended run of live dates with strings. The group had one performance at Queen Elizabeth Hall, back in March 1970, prior to the release of *Time and a Word*, but was it.)

This could be the case because the music is likely trickier to play than it might have seemed at first blush. Peter Banks told me:

> I think there might be an edit in ["Sweet Dreams"], which is something that I think is the only Yes thing I was on [where] we actually edited a track. I know they went on to do that [edit pieces] on the third album, particularly. That was a very difficult thing. We might have attempted it live a couple of times. It never worked out very well. I can't remember why. Also "Time and a Word," we never did that live because that was . . . I think, for me and Bill, it was too much like a pop song. "Sweet Dreams" might have been that same kind of thing. "Sweet Dreams" never felt very comfortable. It seemed like a bit of a throwback . . . it was more like a

kind of Mabel Greer's Toy Shop [song], because it had that kind of droning guitar thing. I was always interested in kind of moving on, which is what I suppose the term progressive music is supposed to be. I think probably I had the most trouble with that piece. I just couldn't get into it. I wasn't too sure what to play in it.

"Dear Father," the B-side of a single featuring "Sweet Dreams," hints at the material on *Close to the Edge*. Recounting the lyrics to me, Anderson recalled what "Dear Father," which he co-wrote with Squire, meant to him:

"'Dear Father, don't crucify me / What's it all about, dear father,'" Anderson recounted for me. "I wanted to know what the truth of God is. Everything is within you. Each human has the same light, has the same collective knowledge within . . . it is not out there."

Anderson's love of classical music and his ability to lead the band and, let's face it, convince the others to even sign on to the idea, led nonetheless to some very unhappy band personnel. Perhaps this is putting it mildly.

Banks had despised the strings because he felt his contributions and, frankly, his guitar tone, were being lost in the mix, gobbled up by orchestral instruments occupying the same sonic register as his guitar. Interestingly, in 2001, I spoke with Steve Howe for the band's YesSymphonic Tour in support of the studio album *Magnification*, and he was concerned about some of the very same issues that had troubled Banks some thirty years prior:

Initially we cut an album that sounded alright with just the band, but that wasn't going to be what anybody else would be interested in, because the orchestra was the main event. When the orchestra came in, it created a sort of mayhem where nobody knew how loud he should be . . . will it play with me or will it obliterate me or will it be in the background of me? I'm using me as an example because I am the only solo instrument player. We didn't have a keyboardist other than Alan [White, drummer] playing piano on a couple of tracks, which we all did [played piano], and most of them [the

tracks] didn't see the light of day. . . . For the most part
it was a guitar group that had an orchestra added on
to it. I didn't like all the arrangements, I didn't like all
the flattened fifths, and all the sevenths on a six, and
I didn't like lots of musical things that were much too
indulgent for me. I was playing G to E minor and then
Larry [Groupé, conductor] would come along and put
an F across it all. What he was doing was he was putting
a seventh on the G and a flattened ninth on E minor,
which, to my ears, this was a shock . . . I had to do stuff
that I didn't really want to do.

The flatted fifth, diminished fifth, or tritone, also known as the
"Devil's interval," was forbidden by the Catholic Church because
it was believed to have conjured the Evil One. It spans three whole
steps, and has been used by Metallica, Deep Purple, Jimi Hendrix,
Cream, and Black Sabbath, among others.

Not surprisingly, artists on the more metallic edge of the progressive-rock genre—bands such as Rush and King Crimson—have
dabbled in the dark art of the dark interval, to the author's ears,
anyway. (Appropriately, Crimson's "The Devil's Triangle," from
In the Wake of Poseidon, and its cover of Gustav Holst's "Mars, the
Bringer of War," from *The Planets*, completed in 1916, are marked
by the use of tritone; so is Stravinsky's *Petrushka* and another twentieth-century classical piece, Sibelius' Fourth symphony, which
some have speculated may have been colored by the composer's
growing distress regarding his throat cancer.)

Although the band may have fallen short of its expectations
and desires, *Time and a Word* was Yes's first serious attempt at
claiming classical authenticity for its rock music. But the sound
was not really something that could have been realistically reproduced onstage. Yes could have used a Mellotron, although even
that mechanical delight/demonic presence couldn't truly replace
the sound of a small orchestra. Besides, Tony Kaye was never a fan
of the instrument.

"With *Time and a Word*, Jon started with an orchestra, [which]
kind of really didn't work," Offord says. "Then Tony Kaye was in
the band, mostly playing B-3."

"*Time and a Word* was a brilliant record," Howe told me in 2001.

"I was not on it, so I can say that without trying to flatter myself, and there you are. They did an orchestra, too. There was this fusion of possibilities."

Fact is, *Time and a Word* just missed the Top 40 in the UK and did very little on the American charts at a time when breaking the US was, well, everything. With little commercial success, the band's days at Atlantic were numbered.

The tale of how Yes remained on Atlantic is a little hazy, and over the years I've received conflicting information about it. One story involves a conversation Jon Anderson had with Ahmet Ertegun over Yes's lack of commercial success. Legend has it that Ertegun told Anderson, "Jon, America just says, 'No.'" Anderson supposedly replied, "What do I do?" Ertegun said, "You go on and record and tour." Despite the string of bad luck, the story goes, Atlantic backed the band, which was never in any danger of falling out with the label.

But is this plausible?

"Atlantic in America didn't know what kind of music the band played," Mike Tait offers. "I went to the office here [New York] in 1969, 1970, on my way back to Australia, and I stopped by to say, 'Hello, I'm Michael Tait, I work with Yes.' 'Yes, what's Yes?' They had no fucking idea."

"Before they signed us for our first album, Atlantic thought we were a fake band," Peter Banks told me. "This is absolutely true. Ahmet Ertegun had seen us play and there was the perception that we were a fake band. That was a ludicrous thing to think. I don't know how that came about."

Like a lot of bands, Yes was getting the bum's rush; had the group stayed on its current course, it would have been doomed professionally. It's even been said that Yes was actually dropped by Atlantic. Former Atlantic executive Phil Carson told me in 2013:

> Yes was very much my band. They are all my friends and Rick Wakeman played the organ at my wedding. We grew up together. I did not sign Yes. Ahmet Ertegun signed Yes about a few weeks before I joined Atlantic Records . . . in the late 1960s. They also dropped Yes. They dropped [Yes] right after the second album, *Time and a Word*. Some people in America thought the first Yes album is *The Yes Album*. But Atlantic dropped Yes after *Time and a Word*

and I re-signed them to make *The Yes Album* with Eddy Offord producing.

Eddy was a guy I knew for many years and he and I made records together back in the '60s, I regret, for Woolworths. We used to record cover versions of the then-current hits. That's what we did. We would make an album a night, would you believe? I had no budget to produce Yes. No one cared at Atlantic, having already dropped them, when I re-signed them.

Carson's desires clearly ran counter to those of the label masters. "Well, it's a funny thing," he adds. "At that time there was no other company like Atlantic: it was a music company. Ahmet Ertegun had the vision to sign Yes and Genesis and ELP and also had the vision to realize that maybe this kid [Carson] knew what he was talking about. He said, 'Hey, if you feel strongly about it, that is what you should do.' He gave me a shot. We did and they were very supportive."

Whichever version of the story is accurate, or whichever one you believe, Yes remained at Atlantic for the entirety of the 1970s and into the early 1980s through releases such as *Drama*, *Yesshows*, and *Classic Yes*. (According to a December 1972 report in *Billboard* magazine, Yes had signed a five-year deal (with annual options) with Atlantic. Yes returned with Atlantic subsidiary Atco for its 1983 comeback album *90125*.)

Yes has Carson and, to a degree, the culture of Atlantic to thank, in part, for its early success. Atlantic was certainly something special. Ertegun and older brother Nesuhi were the sons of a Turkish ambassador who served in Switzerland, France, and England. Ahmet was thirteen when the family moved to the US, where he had actually seen in live performance the musicians he was hearing on the American jazz and blues records he loved. Funnily enough, Nesuhi was the first to break into the business, with the Crescent label, releasing New Orleans jazz music.

Despite what some critics have written about the band, many of the elements that make up the Yes sound are from roots music and American jazz. (I'll return to this idea later.) Ertegun told *Melody Maker*'s New York reporter Michael Watts that he believed acts such as Led Zeppelin and Yes had success in America because of the fact that the British bands are "generally more cohesive" and "have superior working habits."

There's some credence to this. The hardships that some—some—artists in Britain faced growing up in the 1950s and 1960s before going on to form progressive-rock bands often go underreported. We think of art-rock or prog rock as art-school music created by the bourgeoisie class. There's plenty of examples of that, but then again, some of the pillars of the style did not grow up privileged by any stretch, among them Jon Anderson, Peter Banks, Keith Emerson, and Greg Lake. Even though the early members of Genesis went to Charterhouse, Phil Collins and Steve Hackett did not. In the author's opinion, a working-class determination helped Yes, ELP, and Genesis—all of whom eventually wound up on the Atlantic label—to reach artistic and commercial success.

Peter Banks told me:

> My parents didn't have a refrigerator until the mid-1960s. I'm from a British working-class background. As a kid I used to play on bombsites, sites where buildings had been blitzed during World War II. They were just half-standing houses and called bombsites. I don't have any nostalgia about those days at all. . . . Certainly I wasn't middle class, and Jon wasn't. The other three guys were. There's the difference there. Chris Squire went to public school. When we say public school over here, that's like saying private school in America. I was definitely working class, and as far as I know Jon was as well.

Perhaps it's best to describe the members of Yes, regardless of the timeframe we're discussing, as five tributaries in a larger water network. Where the rivers met, these five members agreed to comingle and perhaps resolve their differences by dissolving a bit of their ego (just a bit) for the greater good. The fact that the individuals were so different in temperament is a testament to how strongly they believed in the collective and its music.

The level of seriousness and reverence for the music Yes created was perhaps unparalleled in rock at that time. While it's overkill to state that these musicians performed as though their lives depended upon it, we can say that Yes and the like had tremendous focus and concentration, and the time they'd spent bouncing around both original and cover bands in London's underground circuit prepared them for the postmodern stew they'd stir and serve the mainstream public—on both sides of the Atlantic. The label was keenly aware of this.

"I remember one Atlantic producer, who used to produce a lot of avant-garde twentieth-century piano-type recordings, İlhan Mimaroğlu," says mastering engineer Barry Diament, who transferred *CTTE* to CD back in the 1980s. "He was a fan of Yes. He used to walk around with an army jacket, army green. I think of him when I think of Yes because he was a producer I respected a great deal and I know he respected Yes."

By the time they arrived on American shores, the British progressives, and in particular Yes, had conceptualized, mapped, and executed complicated rock music that was, in many ways, effortless, far superior, and virtually unknown prior to their appearance. The effect was nearly life-changing for the listener, both inside and outside the UK.

But when things change, they change rather quickly, don't they? Before the year of 1970 was out, both the lead guitarist and the manager would get the boot. Banks intensely disliked the process of making *Time and a Word* and was increasingly falling out with other members of the band over creative differences. Press reports at the time stated he quit in frustration; Banks himself told me:

> It was Jon and Chris who decided I would be out of the band. They told me after a gig in Luton. That's it. The band was going through a difficult period. We . . . were always kind of tough on ourselves and we always wanted to keep doing new material and keep on rehearsing. There was always an impetus for change within the band. We just really didn't have the resources or the money to rehearse as much as we wanted. We had to keep playing. Some of the gigs became kind of repetitive. We were getting into a bit of a formula. Everybody was going, "We should do this," "We should do that." There were so many musical ideas flying around between all of us and we just didn't have the resources to rehearse them. We had to keep on gigging. Some of the gigs we were doing

were pretty miserable. We were playing very odd venues in Europe and in this country and sometimes we would just be playing to thirty or forty people.

Banks's desire to change songs from night to night was increasingly becoming incompatible with the band ethos. Playing the same guitar solo every night "just goes against my whole nature," he told me. "I like to think of myself as an improvising musician, and that really does mean improvising. I just don't see the point of having to do the same old solo over and over and over again."

Some of the old demons were hanging around, too. Banks had intimated that he was not crazy about another guitarist/songwriter hanging around the Yes camp, namely David Foster. It's sheer speculation, but perhaps Banks was correct about someone moving into his territory. (Foster was unavailable for comment.) In addition, Banks strongly disagreed with the band's decision to fire manager Roy Flynn:

> [Flynn] really was financing us out of his own pocket. All of a sudden they wanted to get rid of Roy because of his inexperience with managing, which there was a case for that. But they wanted to just like let him go. I just got very emotional and said, "You can't do that." I wasn't thinking in business terms at all. Roy, for me, was always like an extra member of the band. So, what happened was that when they got rid of me they got rid of him at the same time. I was the only guy who spoke for him. I was the protagonist so I got a lot of flack for that, and it was almost the case where, well, "If he goes, I go." That is exactly what happened. It was a bit of a purge. Whether that was the right thing to do or not. . . . They continued through that and they hadn't actually gotten a replacement player for me.
>
> It wasn't so cold-bloodedly as it seems. It wasn't just musical. But I don't know. I'd lost sleep about that one for years.

After Banks exited Yes, he formed the short-lived Flash, a quartet with humongous potential. Flash was building momentum. The group toured the US; had an American Top 30 hit, "Small

Beginnings"; and was a hot act, led by Banks's wild-man stage persona and mastery of effects gadgetry. Unfortunately for the band, it all fell apart after two years, for reasons too complicated to get into here.

Enter Steve Howe, whose name had been kicking around the Yes and pre-Yes universe for years. It's well known, now, that Steve auditioned for Atomic Rooster (featuring Carl Palmer) and walked away from an offer to play with Keith Emerson in the Nice.

Steve joined Yes in the spring of 1970, bringing with him a considerable amount of influences and a laundry list of viable guitar techniques. As a child, Howe lived with his family in Holloway, North London, and would listen to artists such as rock 'n' roller Bill Haley and later Django Reinhardt, Kenny Burrell, and Roy Clark.

Howe had a taste for jazz and classical as well, and enjoyed the stylings of jazz guitarist and flautist Les Spann (Duke Ellington, Dizzy Gillespie), Tal Farlow (the speed and melodic qualities of his playing), Charlie Christian, classical guitarist and lute player Julian Bream (the Villa-Lobos Preludes), Carlos Montoya, and jazz man Barney Kessel (specifically the *Poll Winners* album with legendary drummer Shelly Manne and bassist Ray Brown from 1957, given to him by his clarinet-playing older brother, who told his younger sibling to stop listening to Haley and his Comets if he wanted to learn how to play guitar). As he listened, he would "jump about the lounge," he told *Guitar Player*, fantasizing about being onstage. "I never dreamed it could affect my life as much as it has done."

Howe looked to the music of Bream and Andrés Segovia for inspiration and ability to play along with the power of a symphony orchestra.

Charlie Christian, who was influenced by jazz saxophonist Lester Young, had a tremendous impact on Kessel and his feel. On *The Poll Winners*, we can spot the influence Kessel has had on Steve, particularly his solo material, whether its *Spectrum* or *Skyline* or Steve Howe Remedy's *Elements* or *Live*.

Also influential was Tennessee Ernie Ford and, in particular, the song "Blackberry Boogie" featuring the stratospheric musical conversation of the western-swing duo of pedal-steel player Wesley Webb West (a.k.a. "Speedy" West) and Jimmy Bryant, "the fastest guitarist on the planet," who was instrumental in the development of the prototype of the Fender Telecaster.

The Beatles held sway, as did Chuck Berry, who was trending at the time due to Dave Berry's and the Beatles' covers of his material. Howe was also inspired by Bill Haley's guitarist "Franny" Beecher—possibly Howe's first true influence as a guitarist when he was growing up—as well as Scotty Moore, James Burton, Duane Eddy (specifically "Rebel Rouser" and "The Avenger"), The Shadows (with Hank Marvin), and William Lee Conley Bradley (a.k.a. Big Bill Broozy), whose ragtime-informed guitar figures can be detected in one or two of Howe's monumental and misconstrued acoustic guitar solo pieces, such as "Clap."

Howe told me in 2005:

> In a way, I'm not that conscious of the styles I'm using. How all these things hang together is somewhat a mystery to me, but they come about in the same way that I write. I usually cite Chet Atkins [as a main influence], because he is the only guitarist I had records of, who, unlike all the others, didn't stay in one style. I listened to so many of his records. It was unbelievable how much I listened to the guy, because I used to go to bed with his records on. I fell asleep to [them]. . . . You couldn't actually say what kind of guitarist he was. He was a guitarist. I guess while I was into the blues, folk, rock, and jazz guitarist—all of these headings—the ones that I actually tried to duck—I think Chet is mainly responsible [for Howe's diversity]. . . .Ducking and diving and darting around the musical possibilities seems to have come from the early musical influences as well.

In the early 1970s, Howe employed an unorthodox fingerpicking approach while using a celluloid-based plectrum. A light touch on the strings allowed him to play chordal figures and lead lines simultaneously.

"Clap," which appears on 1971's *The Yes Album*, and was supposedly inspired by Howe's son, Dylan, was inaccurately listed as "The Clap" on the original LP. (Successive releases and reissues of the album have repeated the title in error, and fans continue to refer to the track as such.) When performing "Clap," Howe would splice in pieces of Mason Williams's "Classical Gas."

By the mid-1970s, Howe was internationally recognized as a leader in the rock guitar field. He won the 1977 *Guitar Player* magazine's readership award for "Best Overall Guitarist," and became known not only for his technique but his genre-defying style.

The funky, country-fried blues-rock opening riff of "Siberian Khatru" is a great—maybe the ultimate—example of how he balances or fuses chordal or partial chordal qualities and lead picking. Not only is the *Yessongs* version of "Khatru" one of Steve's favorite guitar solos, but the studio version of the song marks the first time Steve began mixing and matching steel and regular electric guitars in his solos.

"I enjoy being a multi-guitarist, as opposed to a funk guitarist or jazz guitarist or blues guitarist," Howe told me in 2005. "I play steel guitar, mandolin—I like the whole family."

Indeed. Although he appeared to have started relatively late by pro musician standards: he received his first guitar when he was twelve. Early gigs included the Eden Grove Youth Centre, at which Howe had the opportunity to perform "The Frightened City" by the Shadows. Later, Howe moved on to another group of friends that played, of all places, the Prison Club, adjacent to Pentonville Prison.

After this band broke up, Howe continued to perform with vocalist Kevin Driscoll at a place called the Swan, and over time they morphed into the Syndicats. Innovative British record producer Joe Meek produced the band's version of "Maybellene," the Chuck Berry song, which was released in 1964 on Howe's seventeenth birthday. Another, "Howlin' for My Baby," was a version of "Howlin' for My Darling," the Chester Burnett (a.k.a. Howlin' Wolf) and Willie Dixon song originally recorded in 1959.

After the Syndicats, Howe was recruited for the In Crowd, which featured vocalist Keith West and guitarist (later bassist) John "Junior" Wood, both of whom would become Howe bandmates in the influential psychedelic outfit Tomorrow, which recorded the unofficial anthem for Britain's underground psychedelic movement, "My White Bicycle." (Drummer John Adler, or "Twink," of the Fairies, later the Pink Fairies, and the Pretty Things, joined the In Crowd prior to the name change to Tomorrow.)

"My White Bicycle," produced by Mark Wirtz, was so named

for the public transportation program in Denmark. The song's innovative use of backward audio would be echoed by Eddy Offord's productions with Yes.

"It was fairly simple but very effective," Wirtz told me in late 2013. "Those are our early steps of being creative with backward stuff. There was a lot of backward guitar and that was still original, then. Steve Howe did some great things. It was not just jams accidentally that were put in random. It was structured. Keith and Steve would get together before the session to structure the song and the sound and they would . . . play the song to me so I had an idea of what I was dealing with. Then we would start work."

Wirtz's masterpiece, "Excerpt from a Teenage Opera," was a hit, but some in the band cite it as the song that broke the band in two.

West and Howe remained friendly, but Wood and Alder seemed to be on another wavelength. (The latter two did, indeed, collaborate again after Tomorrow.) Yet, despite being on different sides of the creative aisle, so to speak, the members of Tomorrow, including those I've spoken with, agree on one thing: "Teenage Opera" was the time bomb that exploded any chance Tomorrow ever had at a future in the music business.

Wirtz, however, disputed these claims in an interview I conducted with him, saying "Teenage Opera" has become little more than a scapegoat. "This is often overlooked by even members of Tomorrow, including Keith West, [who claim] that 'Teenage Opera' ruined Tomorrow. That is impossibly ridiculous, because of the fact that EMI didn't even want an album on Tomorrow until 'Excerpt from a Teenage Opera' was Top Two [in the UK in August 1967]."

After Tomorrow, Howe joined Bodast, managed by John Coletta and Tony Edwards and featuring future Elvis Costello bassist Bruce Thomas. Thomas, who had previously been in a band called Bittersweet—"a short-lived, meandering, foppish, sub-Floydian band, managed by the Floyd's then co-managers, Peter Jenner and Andrew King, which boxed itself into a corner by having all their song titles named after a girl's name"—remembers his early days when he played with both Howe and Tony Kaye:

> [Our] only gig of note Bittersweet had was a residency
> in a club in Marseilles, in which we were sacked for be-
> ing too loud and dropping ink from the light show on

clients' heads. We also had a couple of gigs at clubs like Blaise's and the Speakeasy, where the luminaries of the day used to hang out and hold court. That was the only self-consciously prog rock band I was involved with, which was originally to be called—I kid you not—the Yellow Passion Loaf, after the Strawberry Alarm Clock.

Tony Kaye was always on the fringe of things. We didn't really become buddies. I was a northern kid and he was a metropolitan sophisticate. Bodast was an altogether meatier proposition [from Bittersweet]. Steve Howe was at his rockiest. I'm trying to think of a guitar-based band that is in the same spirit—maybe Led Zeppelin. But I reckon that band would still fit right in now. It was exciting guitar-driven pop rock and held the greatest unrealized potential of any band I've been involved with. Of course, Bodast's songwriters, Clive Maldoon and Dave Curtiss, were responsible for writing a song that surfaced decades later as a megahit for Madonna, "Ray of Light."

Steve was obviously a serious musician who, from my point of view, maybe, became too serious. For a few weeks we even thought about starting a band of our own together, and he would keep coming up with these riffs for me to play, but there were too many tempo changes and funny timings for me to get may head round. A lot of these ideas made it on to later Yes albums, by which time Steve had found the ideal foil in Chris Squire. Yes were probably *the* prog-rock band of all prog-rock bands. But by this time the Attractions, who laid an hour set down in forty-five minutes, took a very dim view of all this kind of thing. I would also like to say that I used to do quite a few recording sessions with Rick Wakeman, who was one of the funniest guys I've ever met. His version of Liberace playing "Whole Lotta Love" had to be heard to be believed.

For all the musical talent in Bodast, Howe said that this was the only instance, up to that point in time, when he allowed friendship to "interfere with my musical career."

Bodast did perform with the Who and Chuck Berry, but the

writing was on the wall. Finally, Howe accepted an offer to play guitar for Pat "P. P." Arnold on tour with Delaney and Bonnie Bramlett and Eric Clapton. (George Harrison even appeared on the tour for a handful of dates in the UK.) The tour lasted nearly a month, after which time Howe received a call from Squire, someone he'd dimly recalled from the Syn and the UFO Club.

Howe's versatility couldn't have come at a better time. The band was revitalized, and after a gig in Putney, Howe believed that he'd finally found a home in Yes. Perhaps he was not altogether sure what he'd stepped into, however. The band had (allegedly) been dropped or almost dropped (or whatever), and how long would Atlantic's patience last for what was, essentially, a hitless British progressive-rock band? Well, a progressive-rock band once misidentified as a folk outfit.

Of course, Yes would eventually become the most enduring progressive-rock band on the planet, but back in 1970, the quintet's third studio album was do-or-die. Yes didn't disappoint. Under the supervision of Atlantic's legendary producer Tom Dowd, and with the addition of co-producer and recording engineer Eddy Offord, Phil Carson ensured that Yes would be a success.

As Traffic had done before them, and as later prog-rockers (including Camel) would do, the members of Yes sequestered themselves in the country. In the case of Yes, the destination was a farmhouse that Steve Howe later bought. In Devon, Yes "got it together in the country," and wrote much of the material that appeared on *The Yes Album*.

Ray Laidlaw, drummer for Lindisfarne, shared the stage with Yes for a few shows in the 1970s.

> When we were coming up as a support band . . . because we were very popular in the northeast of England we got to play support to lots of big name bands as they came through, college shows. Not so much concert halls, but college shows, really. How we met Yes? It's a long involved story, but we had some friends who lived in Devon, the other end of the country from us, and the guy who used to book all the bands in Newcastle University actually came from down there. We were looking for somewhere to rehearse. He said, "I've got a

place down here. I can also get you a few gigs to make it pay."

We went down there, one summer—June, July, August—for three weekends. The first place we played was Barnstaple Town Hall, in north Devon, and we were supporting Yes, very early on. I think it was just after *Time and a Word* and before *The Yes Album*. We met them and got on with them really well. They were quite encouraging and they paid us quite a lot of compliments, could see we had something, even though we were pretty raggle-taggle in those days. We had shitty old equipment, but we still made good noise. We got to know them.

It turned out they went to north Devon to rehearse and we were the next people in this big farmhouse, where this lovely couple lived in one end and they rented out the other end. Yes did it and we did it about a couple months later. When we were in New Castle and had a few drinks with them after . . . we got to know them a bit more.

Recorded during the final months of 1970, *The Yes Album* was a turning point, exploring some of the deeper aspects of the soul and the concepts of the natural world reflecting the inner landscape.

Although there's been much talk about "Heart of the Sunrise," from the band's next studio album, 1971's *Fragile*, being the forerunner to the material appearing on *Close to the Edge*, earlier songs, such as "Astral Traveler" from *Time and a Word*, and "Starship Trooper" and "Perpetual Change" from *The Yes Album*, are perhaps just as relevant.

Anderson wrote the lyrics of "Perpetual Change" having been inspired by the 1969 Apollo 11 Moon walk and the deadly and disastrous floods in East Pakistan (now Bangladesh) in November 1970. (The Bhola cyclone has since been recognized as the deadliest cyclone in recorded history.) Anderson got to thinking about man exploring space and possibly fouling up other worlds as we reach further and further out into the solar system, while ignoring the ecology of the Earth. (In 1971, ex-Beatle George Harrison would organize his Concert for Bangladesh, raising money for the refugees of war-torn East Pakistan.)

Composed of three movements—"Life Seeker," "Disillusion,"

and "Würm"—"Starship Trooper," like the multi-sectioned "Close to the Edge," appears to have been designed to explore deep mysteries of self-knowledge. Even if the title references a novel by Robert Heinlein, the perceived sci-fi nature of the song shrouds its true purpose. The concepts discussed here resonate with the occult, ancient mystery, and Eastern religions, if not some form of Gnostic Christianity. At the least, "Starship Trooper" is a spiritual quest wrapped in fantasy and sci-fi allegory.

Some of the same or similar concepts we see in "Close to the Edge" appear in "Starship Trooper," such as the idea of wholeness and oneness, rearranging one's perspective, the appearance of a maternal ("Mother Life") or otherwise feminine figure ("Sister Bluebird"), the sun being a symbol of the soul (perhaps), even the image of summer as some form of perfection.

When interviewing Jon Anderson in the late 1970s, industry consultant Lee Abrams, often dubbed the father of album-oriented rock (AOR), described "Starship Trooper" as doing for rock music what Kubrick's *2001: A Space Odyssey* did for science-fiction cinema. In a way, Abrams was correct. "I was writing about my inner self's vision of myself and interpreting . . . each person as this soul . . . as [having] seen everything that that person is and knows everything about that person," Anderson told Abrams.

The idea was a very "spacey kind of thing," Anderson said. With the assistance, apparently and appropriately, of some form of automatic-writing technique, the lyrics seemed to write themselves. "There is a messenger within you that is always inter-reacting with the life form," Anderson told Abrams. "There's that point within yourself that knows you: we call it God, right?"

When the chorus talks about "sons and daughters," we encounter a strange repetition: these sons and daughters "knew" the knowledge of the terrain. Although Anderson had penned similarly repetitive lyrics before, I believe this doubling of words means to draw our attention to this odd phrasing, conveying that these sons and daughters have wisdom to bestow. (Was Anderson speaking about the inner parts of his own being?)

When the chorus is introduced in double-time feel, chord voicings *seem* to change slightly (Amaj7–C–F–B-flat–A-flat–F), and the lyrics speak of the "land" and the "water," which could be references to the landscape of the soul.

After the country-picking acoustic movement, "Disillusion," the final, instrumental section, "Würm," opens with what can be described as a sonic vortex. The repetitive nature of the chord changes (G–E-flat–C, sent through a flanger) has a medicinal, even meditative, effect. This musical sequence mirrors magical incantation: dual soloes, in a country/blues/rock 'n' roll vein, manifest from a trance-inducing psychedelic soup (that is, Howe's overdubbed additional guitars). The building up to a cathartic grand finale might well symbolize how the speaker experiences some form of spiritual breakthrough or enlightenment.

Howe's playing is somewhat schizophrenic here. In a way, the twin leads predate David Gilmour's double-solo performance in Pink Floyd's "Comfortably Numb." One solo seems to be bluesy and the other a bit of hard rock.

"Würm," might reference a body of water. There are at least two rivers in Germany that bear the name. As Dave Rubin, author of *Guitar Signature Licks: Yes*, points out, the word Wurm, without an umlaut, is the name of yet another river in Germany. "Wurm" is also the basis of the word dragon or fire serpent. (Maybe this is related to the "Firebird" of Slavic mythology?)

Getting back to the lyrics: as is so often the case with Anderson (including his work for *Close to the Edge*), pronouns tend to morph, and it can be difficult to ascertain who he is addressing, why he's addressing them, and, for that matter, what timeframe we're occupying. Maybe all of the people mentioned in the song are different aspects of his own psyche.

This slipping through timeframes is part and parcel of a song that was stitched together in the studio and composed of fresh and older material, such as the acoustic "Disillusion" (straight from the Banks-era "For Everyone") and the "Würm" section, penned by Howe during his stint with Bodast. (Good thing for us he didn't bury it.)

"For Everyone" also seems to contain musical bits, especially drum fills and patterns, that would resurface in "Yours Is No Disgrace." In addition, the first lines of the verses, such as "Love for a new day" and "Inside of your love," are reminiscent in their pacing to vocalized lines such as "Hold down the window" and "Warm side the tower" from "Siberian Khatru," which appeared two years later on *Close to the Edge*.

There are, obviously, some vocal rhythms that Anderson preferred, and to which he returned. This isn't an indictment, merely an observation. More importantly, "For Everyone" is yet another example of how on the Yes records of the early and mid-1970s, in particular *Close to the Edge*, the band perfected its approach to writing, recording, and performing its music.

"For Everyone" first aired in March 1970 on John Peel's Sunday Show and officially surfaced on CD with the 1998 release *Beyond and Before: The BBC Recordings 1969–1970* (containing performances culled from audio tapes Banks says he "literally kept in a shoe box") and then later on the 2005 triple-CD collection *The Word Is Live*.

The timeless motif inherent to "Starship Trooper" is echoed in the strange concoction of odd meters: it drifts through 5/4, 4/4, 7/4, 2/4, and 7/8, yet we don't bat an eye. The song simply flows nicely, like a simple ditty. It's far from this, though, and its esoteric secrets put it miles ahead of "Astral Traveler" and one step closer to the *Edge*.

The second side of the original LP opens with "I've Seen All Good People," another compound track featuring "Your Move." The bass guitar/kick drum throb beginning around 0:31 in "I've Seen All Good People," pulsing under Howe's Portuguese *Vachalia* strumming, maracas, Colin Goldring's recorder, and lilting vocals from Anderson, Squire, and Howe, is (in retrospect) an earlier variant of the later "And You and I" six-beat thump. More about this later.

The nod to the Plastic Ono Band's "Give Peace a Chance" at 2:54 is a cheeky, sneaky inclusion of a recognizable melody. In fact, the song scarcely needed it; "All Good People" was Yes's first truly iconic song, and has been played on the classic-rock radio format for decades.

Stewart Goldring of Gnidrolog remembers the session his twin brother Colin, the band's recorder player, attended for *The Yes Album*. He says it was Rick Wakeman, who was *not* the keyboardist for Yes at the time (Tony Kaye was), that recommended Colin to the band.

I had asked Stewart if he had possibly conflated two different incidents, but he was adamant and, indeed, described "the keyboardist" as "a tall guy with very long fair hair who supposedly knew Yes; there was some kind of connection there. It figures because it was quite a small community of musicians around London at the time, so even though people weren't close, we were aware of each other's work."

All of this seems to suggest Wakeman, not Kaye. In any case, Goldring is correct in one respect. There *was* a connection between Yes and Wakeman prior to the writing and recording of *Fragile*: Wakeman had appeared on the Tamla Motown–style recording sessions Brian Lane had produced for his company, Mum and Dad Music. Lane was, of course, Yes's manager.

According to Goldring, Wakeman "came down to see one of the gigs [Gnidrolog] did and knew of Colin and thought his recorder playing would be good for Yes. I went to the session with Colin, in the afternoon, just to see what was going on. I seem to remember Bill Bruford was there, and he was playing drums."

If this account is accurate, here's what likely happened: Wakeman, as a young and successful London session musician, had Lane's ear, or was speaking with him on a semi-regular basis, keeping him informed of anything or anyone interesting on the scene. Lane then used this little tidbit to benefit Yes, regardless of Wakeman's initial intention.

For a brief moment, Yes was part of the British progressive-folk boom—albeit this having nothing to do with Atlantic Records' mischaracterization or misunderstanding of Yes's style.

The British folk boom of the 1960s may, or may not, be the source of the infusion of traditional music in popular culture, but eclectic art- and progressive-rock artists of the 1970s, from Amazing Blondel and Gryphon to Gentle Giant, Pentangle to Jethro Tull, and to a degree King Crimson, were eager to connect to their European roots and fuse rock with various traditional musical styles such as minstrelsy, renaissance, baroque, and Elizabethan. (Amazing Blondel's *England*, in particular, stretched the definition and boundaries of progressive rock and folk-rock.)

Something similar happened earlier in the twentieth-century within the classical world. Early musician and radio personality David Munrow was partly responsible for arranging music for the six-episode BBC television miniseries from 1970, *The Six Wives of Henry VIII*, which later aired in America on CBS in 1971 and was adapted for the big screen as 1972's *Henry VIII and His Six Wives*. Lutes, crumhorns, and recorders were commonplace, and to a degree Yes appeared to pick up on this vibe as well, with the use of not only church organ but also harpsichord.

People such as Munrow helped to, if not spark, then nurture a mainstream interest in early music. The recorder's use in "All Good People" and Zeppelin's "Stairway to Heaven" helped to solidify the pastoral vibe filling the airwaves of the early 1970s. As a result, *The Yes Album* stands as the first Yes record in which the band truly found its voice, creating music that is still considered among the classics of the progressive-rock genre, four-plus decades on.

Even the cover is iconic. Squire was supposedly driving the band van when the vehicle crashed, costing Kaye a broken foot. As a result, he appears on *The Yes Album* cover in a cast. When I spoke with Mike Tait, he intimated that the filmstrips on either side of the image "may have been my idea."

A British tour supporting Iron Butterfly solidified the band's appeal in England. *The Yes Album* grabbed the #1 album slot in Britain and remained on the charts for months. It also made Top 40 on *Billboard*'s Top Tape Cartridges chart.

"When the record came out there was no denying that there was something very special going on with Yes," Carson says.

Mike Tait told me in 2013:

> That was the time when there was a postal strike in England and the returns from record shops weren't being sent to London, so there were no charts. Virgin Records did the charts through their stores, over the telephone. . . . We had our own posters printed and I went to record shops all around London and giving them a poster and making sure they had heard of the band. The record company wasn't doing it. I did it. Hundreds of stores. I took tape with me. I put it up for the stores, because I knew they wouldn't put it up. . . . It became a fairly big seller because there wasn't competition from these other charts.

Regardless of why Yes was gaining attention, the group was no longer playing regularly in just the UK but branching out into continental Europe and even across the pond, to America, opening for Jethro Tull, whose 1971 record *Aqualung* was a Top 10 album in the US.

Anderson admitted that he was impressed with his namesake in Tull, Ian Anderson, and quite taken with his stage presence. It's not difficult to see why. Ian's phallic flute displays, wild-eyed facial expressions, and flamingo-like one-legged balancing acts gave Tull a strong visual focal point. Still, reports from this time indicate that Tull made a grave mistake by taking Yes with them on an American tour. Many in attendance for these shows in North America remember Tull being great, Yes being greater. Yes made true believers of many in the summer of 1971.

"The first tour I did with Yes was when they opened for Jethro Tull's *Aqualung* tour," says Philip Rauls, who worked radio promotions for Atlantic at the time. "It was an enormous success because Jethro Tull could walk on water with the *Aqualung* record. Yes was just breaking at the time."

"I went off to Seattle, Washington, because I wanted to get away from Indiana at that point," says Dale Newman, a Yes fan who'd later guitar tech for Mike Rutherford and manage Genesis's recording studio, the Farm, in England.

> [My friends and I] knew that Jethro Tull was coming. We got tickets to Jethro Tull down at the arena in Seattle. [The Seattle Center Coliseum] The tickets arrived and we looked at them and underneath Jethro Tull, it read, "Yes." We couldn't believe it. I wasn't sure the guys actually existed. I thought it might be something that was manifested by God. I really thought it was beyond capabilities. I had been a teenage guitarist and I wasn't in the business then, but I went along and went early.
>
> When we got in and we were there in the afternoon, I looked down and I noticed that Jon Anderson was standing down by the barrier. I was never shy. We went up to talk to him. I remember him being in awe. He said, "I don't know what is going to happen. I've never been in a place like this." Now I can understand it [living in England for many years]. A coliseum to an Englishman, back then, must of have seemed like the Mother Ship. He was in awe of it and he was obvious nervous. They came out and it was unbelievable. They really stole the show from Jethro Tull.

Roy Clair of Clair Global, an audio, video, and network-services company, offers a similar recollection of one of Yes's shows at

Cleveland's Allen Theatre in 1971 (either on July 20, near the end of the American leg of the tour to support *The Yes Album,* or on December 15, in support of *Fragile;* it's unclear which show Clair was referencing).

> They were more exciting, and the people who came to see Jethro Tull, I think they realized that Yes were more exciting. I'm just paraphrasing what I've heard. They played Cleveland and that's when we did their show. They bought an American system from the Iron Butterfly, which had "W" boxes [referring to the design of the horn in the speaker bin], and we were using W boxes and had a monitoring system in which you could talk from the front of house to the stage. The monitors were on stage. You didn't have to yell. The entertainer could actually talk to you and then you could talk back to him, for rehearsals. They said that was unique.
>
> Jon and Steve would rely on the compression drivers in the system and . . . the high end. But the low-end accentuated Chris Squire's playing. I can't tell Jon that. I think Chris fooled them into thinking it was a great sound system when, in fact, it favored Chris Squire.

For a show at SUNY Plattsburgh, at the New York university's Memorial Hall, on December 5, 1971, Yes held the unenviable position of playing the opening slot before the better-known Humble Pie. Although young, Tim Harnett, an associate librarian at the Feinberg Library at SUNY Plattsburgh, attended the show, and commented that he could, indeed, "attest to the fact that Yes blew Humble Pie off the stage." (SUNY Plattsburgh University, interestingly enough, is where the guitarist/bandleader Peter Frampton would record parts of his 1976 breakthrough double live album, *Frampton Comes Alive!*)

In 1971, Yes played in the South, Northeast, Midwest, and Canada. The group also performed one show in England, the Crystal Palace Garden Party in July, before returning to Advision for the recording of *Fragile* in August, with a new keyboardist, Rick Wakeman.

Wakeman Enters

Reports conflict regarding the band's next major move. When the band began working on the follow-up to *The Yes Album*, Tony Kaye was either nowhere to be found for the latest recordings or simply hadn't contributed much. Rather than wait, Yes pressed on without him. The timing of these scenarios does seem a bit suspect, however, and the official record indicates that Yes was working on "Heart of the Sunrise" when it became apparent, so the story goes, that Kaye wasn't feeling it.

"We had been touring *The Yes Album* in the States and that had all gone real well, and I guess Steve Howe and Tony Kaye weren't getting along particularly well," Squire told me in 2008. "Maybe I am misquoting, but there was some friction from what I remember."

There are at least three versions of why Tony Kaye left the band, including his lack of desire to use synthesizers and personal differences with at least one band member. Someone close to the keyboardist had told me, off the record, that Kaye had been involved in a romance while the band toured America and wanted to stay in the States with his newfound love.

Anderson has said that, in a roundabout way, if a keyboard player can't give a solid explanation as to why a Mellotron or a Moog can't be used on a song, perhaps suitable answers should be sought elsewhere.

Billy Sherwood has been a member of Yes in two different centuries; he's the replacement for bass player Chris Squire in the current iteration of Yes, and also works with Kaye in Circa, featuring Yes drummer Alan White.

> I've worked with both Tony and Rick, and I think [Kaye] comes from a bluesier, old-school rock 'n' roll Hammond approach to it. They are so different. It is like apples and oranges. It would be like comparing Trevor [Rabin] to Steve Howe. They are both great but they don't play like each other at all.
>
> Tony plays what he feels from the moment he gets on that Hammond. Tony is a genuinely nice guy. He's a real easygoing dude. His motivation is to create new music. He brings his talent and abilities to that place. It's not the

sixteenth-note crazy filler over everything that other keyboard players might desire, but for me he delivers a gutsy turn of raw, earthy approach that I like a lot. Listen to "Starship Trooper." Tony tells me he was more into staying with traditional sounds and, as you said, they wanted to move on with things and synths and he wasn't all that interested. Obviously he came back to the band in the 1980s so there was something going on there.

"Tony was more of a groove player," Banks confirmed. "I had no idea about how to keep a groove going. I enjoyed playing with him tremendously. He used to write things on little pieces of paper and I always used to make fun of him for doing that. There were little parts that he couldn't remember. I would take great delight, about halfway through the set, in just like throwing all of these pieces of paper off the top of his Hammond organ, just to see what would happened. It used to annoy him tremendously."

Kaye himself admitted that the band wanted him to play Moog and Mellotron, but that he wished to remain, for the most part, an organ player. (His successor, Wakeman, had a reputation for playing a variety of keyboards with Strawbs, including Mellotron and Moog on "The Shepherd's Song" from *From the Witchwood*.) In 1972, Bruford commented to *Circus* magazine that Kaye seemed content to "plonk chords on his organ." However, Kaye uses a Moog—the same type of patch-board mutant beast Keith Emerson was famous for using at the time—on *The Yes Album*, and plays synth on Flash's energetic self-titled debut record.

The very title, of the band's next studio record, *Fragile*, hatched during a rehearsal for the record, seems a reference to the precarious nature of the band during this time period. (Alternately, it's been proposed that the title was lifted from the phrase "fragile" stenciled onto monitors and/or the band's flight cases.)

Replacing Kaye was an extension of a musical progression that began with the British Invasion in the early 1960s. Bands such as the Beatles and the Who were not only writing their own material but now wanted a command of their instruments. Point being, there was an explosion of psychedelia and the expansion of rock music by bands on both sides of the Atlantic, whether it be Quicksilver Messenger Service, Jefferson Airplane, Cream,

Jimi Hendrix, or Led Zeppelin. Even the Grateful Dead injected a virtuosity into its playing—the kind that led to an acceptance of a band such as Yes in the first place.

When Howe joined, he upped the ante, making a tight and creative band much more expansive. It only stands to reason, then, that Howe would command more of the sonic foreground and perhaps implicitly demand more of his fellow musicians. In short, there was no foil for him or lead-instrument equivalent to his guitar acrobatics.

The Yes Album holds up, even today. But Kaye, a capable keyboardist, apparently did not feel it was his duty to be a busy player. The band thought otherwise. "Getting Rick Wakeman was transformative," says David Bryce, co-moderator of *Keyboard* magazine's online forum. "Tony Kaye approached everything as a pad kind of guy. You don't hear blazing shit out of Tony Kaye, ever. Wakeman, just the fiery shit that came out of him."

"Yes is a very unique band," says Max Hunt, keyboardist of the Yes tribute band Fragile. "I have the benefit of playing in a Genesis tribute band, and I am working on the difference between Tony Banks and Rick Wakeman. Whereas Banks would go through a lot of different chord modulations in a single octave, Rick Wakeman would do it in multiple octaves and much more florid. Much more florid use of arpeggios and scale patterns, underpinned by similar Mellotron chords, and combine that with Chris's bass pedals and you get an epic sound."

Kaye was/is a great organist, but one can see the band's point. Moog had rejected the concept of a polyphonic synthesizer, at least initially, allowing for a monophonic tool to ascend to the top of the musical instrument technology heap. Progressive-rock keyboardists flocked to the machine, knowing it produced one note at a time, making it perfect for lead lines and totally suitable for a new hybrid breed of rock music.

What synths did was generate, modulate, and filter waveforms, by which a note is ultimately produced via the keyboard. Synthesizers, it was said, had a broad spectrum of sonic frequency, from clunky, garden-variety bleeps and burps to earthshattering thunder to pitches beyond a human's capacity to hear.

Rock musicians began to redefine and reconsider the traditional role of keys as merely a rhythm instrument. Put simply, Moog and the later more portable and affordable Minimoog (as well as the

ARP Soloist and Odyssey), challenged creative rock minds to travel in more innovative musical directions and produce sounds that had scarcely been heard on Earth. Ever since *Switched On Bach* and Keith Emerson's loony solo closing ELP's "Lucky Man," and even more recently, in 1972, on Emerson's riveting solo in "Trilogy," the Moog sounded almost otherworldly.

Emerson had, by the early 1970s, become synonymous with Moog, in particular the huge modular unit using patch cords, the cost of which nearly sent his management into a tizzy. When the Minimoog was introduced, it arguably revolutionized the industry. It was compact and featured front-panel performance controls, as well as pitch and modulation wheels for vibrato and pitch bends, doing away with the bulky patch-board and all the cords.

More About Rick

Rick Wakeman was born in May 1949, in Perivale, a suburb of West London. Early bands included the Concordes; his first electronic instrument was the Pianet. He later attended the Royal College of Music but left without graduating.

"Rick was famous for being kicked out of music college," says Max Hunt. "He was kicked out for taking paid work while at college. He was very much his own man and always rebellious. He did the Mellotron on 'Space Odyssey' by Bowie, and you can hear his unique style of playing, but he was obviously drawing on his classical training."

Former Advision recording engineer and producer, the late Martin Rushent, told me that he was aware of Wakeman from the many jingles and pop sessions he had handled at Advision, of which Wakeman was a part. He had done a number of recording sessions, from David Bowie to Cat Stevens. Everyone on the London sessions scene wanted him for their records.

"He did loads [of sessions]," Rushent told me. "Everybody wanted him on sessions because he was such a nice guy. As well as being a great player he was a nice guy. He was very easy to work with."

Wakeman had joined Strawbs in April 1970 and was dubbed "Pop Find of the Year" by the *Times* of London in a review of the band's performance at Queen Elizabeth Hall in July of that year. The reviewer, Michael Wale, called Wakeman a keyboard "hero" and even compared him to a young Steve Winwood with the Spencer Davis Group.

Wakeman's live solo piece, "Temperament of Mind," a dash of wittiness to entertain the crowds, included snippets of silent movie themes. The basic structure remained consistent from night to night, but he improvised from show to show. This not only demonstrated his mastery of a number of musical styles, but his quick wit. A bit like a modern-day EDM DJ, he took the temperature of the room and improvised accordingly, hence the title. (It was supposedly a power outage that forced him to play it on an acoustic piano, at the behest of Cousins, at Sheffield City Hall in 1970.)

Wakeman used a paint roller in a song called "Sheep" (originally on the album *From the Witchwood*). On *Top of the Pops*, he broke out the roller for "Hangman and the Papist," pissing off bandleader Cousins, who felt Wakeman's stage antics didn't match the serious tone of the song. But that was Wakeman, the showman, who'd later become known for his sequined cape, and had a habit of rocking the Hammond organ to create reverb bombs and placing a block of wood with screws on the keys to hold down notes.

Although he was a member of Strawbs, Wakeman was still doing session dates and performing live with others outside the band, including Elton John. He had also, in essence, formed his own band prior to leaving Strawbs and joining Yes, cutting tracks for the movie *Zee and Co.* (a.k.a. *X, Y, and Zee*), starring Michael Caine and Liz Taylor.

Strawbs was, by and large, Cousins's band, and Wakeman found many of his ideas rejected. Despite the fact that the members were friendly, arguments over what material to record would tear the band apart. Wakeman's growing celebrity, not to mention his heavy drinking, placed a strain on him and his fellow Strawbs. But although Yes was a more financially lucrative prospect—a fact that even Dave Cousins admitted to Wakeman, and to me as well— Wakeman certainly had a closer personal relationship with Cousins and the boys in Strawbs than he ever did with the members of Yes.

In a manner similar to how Steve Howe was courted, some members of Yes had spied virtuoso keyboard player Rick Wakeman when the band shared the stage with Strawbs at various English venues in 1970, including the National Jazz and Blues Festival at Plumpton Racecourse, and at Hull City Hall. Strawbs' Dave Cousins later said something to the effect that he saw the vultures circling, waiting to pounce on Wakeman.

Although Rushent seemed to indicate that it was he who helped make Yes aware of Wakeman, the band was likely swayed by Wakeman's performances with Strawbs. By contrast, Wakeman had watched Yes when Strawbs shared a bill with the band in Hull in 1971. He was impressed by the audio clarity and the unusual instrumentation.

There are a few different versions of how Wakeman joined Yes, and how complicated a process it was. Some sources say it took little than a phone call; others that it was a protracted process. There is, of course, the famous story of Chris Squire offering him the job by calling him at 3 a.m. prior to the keyboardist needing to rise at 7 a.m. for a session later that morning. Wakeman was reportedly miffed at Squire's audacity and curtly turned down the invite.

Squire told me in 2008:

> I just happened to get looking through some of the music magazines and noticed that there was a big buzz on Rick Wakeman and I kind of think I picked up from somewhere that he was going to be leaving the Strawbs or an interview he had done that he wanted to try other things or something. So, I pretty much got in touch with him and asked, "Do you want to play with Yes?" After some haggling and wrangling about the idea, which he didn't immediately grab as being exactly what he was looking for, we talked it over a few times and we eventually pulled it together.

Phil Carson:

> One of the things I really remember was, "Don't sign a band unless there's a virtuoso musician in the band," because virtuoso musicians don't just play with good musicians, they play with great musicians. If you have one virtuoso in a band then . . . you have a real chance of having a great band. If you think about it, Led Zeppelin were four virtuoso musicians. Yes, originally, I have to say that Chris Squire is a virtuoso bass player and Jon Anderson was a virtuoso singer. What happened? Love Tony Kaye, a great B3 player, but he's not the virtuoso that Rick

Wakeman is. So . . . Peter Banks was a great guitar player, actually, but he was not Steve Howe. That's the way that band evolved. That tenet of why you should sign a band remained very strong in my mind.

"Wakeman brought so much more colors and textures to the keyboard sounds, in the same way Steve Howe brought similar things to the guitar," says Offord. "Banks was a good guitarist, but there was something about Steve Howe that he had more to offer. And that was the bottom line with Yes. They wanted musicians who really didn't just play good guitar; they wanted someone who could bring a ton of styles. They were trying to make the band better and, in fact, they made the right decision."

Still, Wakeman found it difficult to adjust to this kind of environment at first. Musically, ironically, Wakeman's academic and technical background helped to meld the many different sections and individually written parts of the songs. He could make songs work and the band members, in essence, play nice together and sound unified. He was layering, playing more symphonically and not as a soloist, all the time, more or less as he had done with Strawbs.

Howe admitted that Yes's members were not all that friendly with one another outside the band setting, but they respected one another's musical ability. There was some good-natured ribbing. The nickname "Rick Wake Up" was bestowed upon Wakeman due to his tendency to nod off on occasion at inopportune times. Anderson introduces him as such on the *Keys to Ascension* DVD, just before Wakeman breaks into the piano intro of "Awaken."

The idea of each individual player contributing and being just as important as the next man was a concept foreign to Wakeman at first. "It's taken two albums and six tours to sort that out," Wakeman told *NME* in November 1972.

Fragile

Once A&M and Atlantic worked out the contractual details of Wakeman joining Yes, it was agreed that the fleet-fingered keyboardist would stay with A&M, but as a solo artist. Despite not being a vocalist and having very limited experience with shouldering the bulk of material for a recording, Wakeman, A&M

speculated, was an artist worth betting on, based on his sheer talent and technique.

His first rehearsal with Yes was in Shepherd's Market, where the band had collaborated on what would become some of its most classic songs (including "Heart of the Sunrise" and "Roundabout"). Legend has it that once Wakeman was brought in, "Heart of the Sunrise" was completed in three days. After the song was finished, he said Yes was approaching "orchestral rock."

With his training, Wakeman employed classical concepts such as the recapitulation of musical ideas, which would go on to become another Yes musical hallmark. "Rick could kind of become an orchestra electronically," Offord says.

Bruford addressed this issue in *Melody Maker* magazine, saying Yes's music was marked less by mechanics and more by "precision." Wakeman added that the music is highly arranged and that every bar "is thought out when the song is formulated." Once the foundation of the song had been set and the arrangement in place, the band members could "play it as you feel it."

If we look at the three *major* keyboardists of the major British progressive-rock bands of the 1970s—Wakeman, Emerson, and Banks (although we should acknowledge the contributions of Mike Ratledge, David Greenslade, Rick Wright, Hugh Banton, Woolly Wolstenholme, Eddie Jobson, Dave Stewart, Alan Gowen, and John Hawken)—Wakeman seemed to reach a balance between Emerson and Banks. Part showman but part studied performer.

Some of the showcase pieces of each of these keyboardists, whether it is Emerson with "Tarkus," Wakeman with the solo in "Roundabout" or "Close to the Edge," or Banks on Genesis's "Firth of Fifth," speak to the personality of the keyboardist at the helm.

"The piano solo at the beginning of 'Firth of Fifth' is a bitch—back, front, and sideways," says Dave Bryce. "They don't do it live. You know why they don't do it live? It's too hard. Seriously. [Banks] was making mistakes here and there. Rick Wakeman wouldn't have given a shit. You know what I mean? He would have made the mistake and blustered right past it without worrying about [the] precision of missing some notes."

This didn't mean Wakeman was careless. While he wasn't quite as innovative and high-profile in the field as Keith Emerson, he did jump in with both feet to play the Minimoog. He even met Robert

Moog, the physicist, electrical engineer, musician, and inventor of the Moog synthesizer, when Yes pulled through Buffalo on one its tours of the States in 1972.

It seems the cerebral qualities of the Moog and Minimoog required an extra bit of attention from users. Wakeman would sit in hotel rooms, and wherever else, shut out the world, don headphones, and fiddle for some time with the Minimoog synthesizer's control knobs, filters, and oscillators. When he arrived at sounds he liked, he wrote them down so he could remember the settings. He operated like this for a while, presumably, because he didn't want to thwart his creativity by obtaining too much knowledge of the inner workings of the machine.

I spoke with Tom Rhea, who wrote the original user's manual for the Model D Minimoog (and, as of this writing, is an associate professor at Berklee College of Music). Rhea had a chat with Wakeman around 1973 or so, and stressed the importance of boning up on the intricacies of the Minimoog and how it created sound—and why:

> Wakeman had six Minimoogs because each one had only one memory. It was the front panel, the read-only memory [*laughs*]. You turn it off it is still there. Anyhow, that was the first ROM memory. We talked at great length. Wakeman showed me his facsimiles—line drawings that were depictions of the front panels. I did a Moog sound chart book, assisted by an intern named Hannah Shapiro, whose father was a big-gun musician at Tufts and friends with David Locke. Wakeman showed me some of his sound charts. He said, "I played with it until I got something I liked." I said, "That's good. But you're a big-time artist, why don't you learn how the instrument works."

Within six months, Rhea says, Wakeman had mastered the instrument. "The next trade show, Wakeman was there, and I was there at the Nordland Moog booth, and he said, running up to me, 'Tom, what you told me about understanding the Minimoog, you were right. Now, if I want to get a sound I know exactly how to do it.' It is awfully helpful if you know how stuff works."

With Wakeman's academic background and thirst for technology, Yes's music was moving in many different directions. Some consider *Fragile* the epitome of the growing field of progressive rock. In some ways, it is: it contains extended songs employing classical music compositional strategies and individuals spotlighting the group's technical prowess and songwriting craftsmanship, practically distilling two major attributes of the genre.

The band comes together as a unit on "Roundabout," "South Side of the Sky," and "Heart of the Sunrise," while "We Have Heaven," "The Fish (Shindleria Praematurus)," "Five Percent for Nothing," "Mood for a Day," and "Cans and Brahms" are individual spotlights for each member's talent.

In 2005, Howe told me he thought this was "what the progressives were good at":

> Floyd was more of a collective noise. Great players, too, and cunningly clever, as well, but I think ELP and Yes were more of the virtuoso side, or trying to show off that side, or our abilities together and at the same time. It was remarkable that *Fragile* does exactly that. But I don't think we'll ever have another record like that, which I think is a terrible waste, because, in fact, I never wanted Yes to get into a mold with making records. To have certain techniques is actually very clever and that technique of featuring the band and the individual all on one record was probably why we were so happy.

There has been widespread rumor as to why the band ditched the idea of individual songs and, for that matter, decided to place so many solo pieces on one album. Speculation has run from time crunch to lack of material. Most observers settle on the idea that the band was in debt due to the exorbitant cost of musical equipment it had invested in prior to the recording of *Fragile*.

"There is no real truth in that," Howe told me in 2007. "Sure, we went out and bought a whole lot of Fender Showmans, but I think we did that with the money with *The Yes Album*. By the time we got to *Fragile* we had a hit album in Europe and a #30 album in America . . . *Fragile* was made just the way we wanted to. When we had space we went in and recorded a few songs and when we had a bit more time we went back and finished them off."

In fact, Bruford had taken credit for the solo track idea, but said that he had initially envisioned for each member to take the reins for his individual piece, leading the band in rousing renditions of an original composition. This concept wasn't exactly fully executed and realized.

"The solo pieces was more a question of the other members of the band saying, 'Look. This is not just Chris Squire and Jon Anderson. We want to do something too,'" Offord offers. "It was a way of letting the rest of the band participate in [songwriting]. In some ways publishing came into it, too, you know? I think, going back to the Beatles, they kind of did the same thing: They gave Ringo his 'Octopus's Garden,' and George always had a track or two on the album, but it was mostly Lennon and McCartney."

Traipsing across the UK, bouncing from gig to gig in the late 1960s and early 1970s at all hours of the day and night, was as adventurous as it was dangerous, and the band's hit, "Roundabout," serves as a kind of ode to the road, one could say, by describing the municipal and geographical terrain over which the band were accustomed to travelling.

Offord:

> I wasn't there in the initial stages, when Jon and Steve had gotten together, but knowing them well enough, Steve had all kinds of riffs and licks and stuff in his head that he had made up, and I think he would just present Jon [these musical ideas]. The riff in "Roundabout" would be all Steve Howe, and then Jon would do his thing over the top of it, and they would develop the middle parts and the changes. They would come to the studio with a basic outline of what they wanted to do. It wasn't all pre-rehearsed and pulled together before they came to the studio. They came to the studio with a skeleton of ideas and it was kind of built in the studio with a lot of input from Chris, as well.

The song's famous opening, with Howe's acoustic guitar riff and string harmonics, is unforgettable. "Talking about those harmonics with Yes, I'll give you an example of how finicky we were about the music," Offord says. "Those harmonics on the beginning of

'Roundabout,' Steve would play every other note on one track. . . . He would leave the middle note out so he would play just the first, third and fifth notes of that little sequence. Then on another track he would do the second, fourth and sixth note."

Howe has, more or less, confirmed that this was the approach in the studio. Was all of this his idea, I wondered? "Yeah, because, he played the first harmonic and in order to get the second harmonic, he'd have to stop the first note, and there would be a slight gap," Offord says. "So, how do we get around that? We'd have do it on separate tracks. You can get away with it [in the studio]. . . . You can do things live . . . by using pedals [to] make things ring, but I guess we couldn't do that in the studio."

The track also features a backward piano note drone. "It was probably a Steinway that was used," Offord says, "really close-miked. It had a lot of EQ and compression. Yeah. We compressed it a lot so the note would last a lot longer than normally. It may not sound labored but it was a lot of labor involved."

What might appear at first glance to be a straightforward song instead contains quite a bit of complexity. Make no mistake: this is no ordinary pop hit.

How to describe it? Do we discuss the snaky, simultaneous lines played by Wakeman and Howe (beginning at 3:21)? The doubling of guitar lines, and the soul-infected organ solo starting at 5:50? The partially muted bass strings of the verses, and the funky-as-hell bass line in the chorus, flipping back and forth between common and 2/4 time? Or maybe Bruford's groovin' and elegant beat displacement, complementing Squire, not to mention the drummer's signature ringing snare sound?

"I heard 'Roundabout' on the radio and what stuck out was that Chris Squire bass," says Marshall Jefferson, house music legend, formerly of Chicago, now living in England. "I thought he was a black dude. I thought it was extremely funky, so I bought the album. People were deep into instrumentation back then and Rick Wakeman was just sick."

Offord:

> In those times, we had no samplers. Nothing. We had a Mellotron, which was like the most advanced thing we had. All during the Yes music, there were loop tapes and

kind of editing. Every song was recorded in thirty-second sections and edited together with just a basic pan. So, it wasn't until after the track was completed that they would have to go away and learn it . . . Jon would come in and say, "I want to hear this kind of 'meeeooohwrr' kind of sound at the opening of the track." We talked about different backwards sound and we finally settled on a backwards piano. We got to go out and record the piano forward, turned the tape over, and then stopped it at exactly the right time so it coincided with the first note of Steve's guitar. It all kind of blended together. It was a real physical tape manipulation.

Then came the solo pieces. Wakeman's solo spotlight, "Cans and Brahms," a punk-like condensation of Brahms's Fourth Symphony in E minor, Third Movement, was another *tour de force* in the studio. (Wakeman was going to use an original composition, "Handle with Care," in this slot, but the details of his contract with A&M prevented this.)

"I've no memory of Rick playing more than one instrument at a time," says engineer Gary Martin. "There wouldn't have been a need to and, given the complexity of many of the keyboard parts, I think it's unlikely he would have done so by choice. 'Cans and Brahms,' I guess the clue is in the title, was created by multiple over-dubs. I understand that Rick now dislikes that track."

Anderson's "We Have Heaven" doesn't sound labored, even though there were likely more than a dozen tracks used for this little folk-esque ditty.

Offord:

> It may not sound labored but it was a lot of labor involved. Vocally, I mean, when the band started Steve could hardly sing and it was mostly Jon and Chris. Jon really encouraged Steve to sing. . . . We spent a lot of time getting his vocals in tune. It was really hard work. When the three of them were [singing] together it was a really unique sound; when it was all three of them. But, then, again, it wasn't like they went out and sang it. It was line by line [over-dubbed]. Vocally, it was constructed in the studio.

Perhaps no song on *Fragile* encapsulates Jon Anderson's mystical appeal more than "We Have Heaven," a folky solo showcase constructed of looped and multitracked vocals. Its references to the "March Hare" could very well be nods to Lewis Carroll's *Alice* books. We'd seen this before, as in Anderson's apparent obsession with Carroll during the writing stages of the equally folky "Your Move," the opening section of "I've Seen All Good People." Other precursors such as "Astral Traveler," "Starship Trooper," and the more cosmic aspects of "Perpetual Change" are just as mystical, making "We Have Heaven" the latest entry on a growing list of Yes titles mystifying fans.

The mystical and childlike qualities—attributes that seemed to come naturally to Pink Floyd's brilliant "crazy diamond" Syd Barrett—are difficult to shake. The song, perhaps, relates to the Gnostic idea of the Inner Christ. Or, as Anderson told *Circus* magazine for its March 1972 issue, "Heaven is in your body. You're in your vehicle." Music journalist and author Chris Welch even went as far as to describe the multi-vocal showcase as "the work of an initiate into magic."

As with so much of Yes's music, the perceived simplicity of the songs is deceiving. For example, Yes juggles polymeters (where part of the band plays in 4/4 and the other in 5/4) in "Long Distance Runaround." This creates a kind of sliding floor or floating feel, and it's one the band would return to for "Close to the Edge." What's surprising is how well it works and how well the overlapping elements contribute to the consistently subtle tension between the various different musical elements we feel when we listen to the song.

Bruford's "Five Percent for Nothing" is barely more than half a minute long, but it makes its point in its allotted running time. This is another example of a rather funky figure in progressive rock, a snaky rhythm that could have easily appeared on a jazz-rock fusion record of the time. In an odd way, it perfectly sets up the jazzy "Long Distance Runaround." The piece was titled something else entirely until Mike Tait spoke up, as he told me in 2013:

> I titled the Bill Bruford song "Five Percent for Nothing."
> That was because their former manager, Roy Flynn, was
> getting five percent, and I didn't think he earned it—"five

percent for nothing." Originally it was titled something like "Suddenly It's Wednesday." The other one [I titled] was Chris's ["The Fish"]. They would call me in the middle of the night: "Mickey. We need the name of a fish." They called Chris "Fish," because he was always in the shower, you know, and I had *The Guinness Book of World Records* at home and I looked up the smallest fish in the world. I did everything in those early days. Everything.

"The Fish (Shindleria Praematurus)" is a strange symphony of multiple bass tracks, written in 7/4 and played in "dropped D" tuning. As on "Roundabout," Bruford overdubs percussion. In this case he uses percussion ranging from tambourine to clinking bottles and such, lending the piece a kind of garage-band flair or tribal feel.

"I was a young bass freak when *Fragile* was released, and I was blown away by Chris Squire's playing," says bassist Michael Manring, best known as the Windham Hill label's house bassist, and also for his work with Michael Hedges. "As you know, 'Roundabout' was a big radio hit, and every time I heard it I had to try to wrap my brain around the fact that the amazing sound I was hearing in the music was actually Chris Squire's bass line. I bought the record and listened to it over and over, relishing its creativity in general and in the bass approach, specifically. The bass feature tune, 'The Fish,' was a revelation, and the first time I heard harmonics on bass."

A common criticism of Squire's bass playing over the years has been that he is able to play lead but not keep a thick bottom end. I don't agree with this assessment, and if you've heard "Close to the Edge" (following Wakeman's majestic keyboard solo at approximately 14:13) you'll know that the bass does, indeed, keep the bottom end. In fact, the thick bass rumble is what propels the song, in my opinion, along with Bruford's famous shuffling.

"That's a common and perhaps facile criticism that's often leveled at folks who play bass in an upfront way," says Manring, whom some might categorize as a "lead bassist." "Personally, I don't feel the need to dismiss someone's playing on some categorical level like that. I don't care so much if someone's playing is busy or simple, thick or thin—it's more about the message of the music as a whole and how the bass fits into that. In my opinion, Chris Squire's sound fit beautifully with what Yes was all about."

Some observers have speculated that Squire's instrument of choice in Yes's earlier days, the Rickenbacker bass, explains his recognizable tone. I remember speaking about this with recording engineer Gregg Jackman, younger brother of Andrew Jackman, who features on *Union*, Squire's solo record *Fish out of Water*, *The Steve Howe Album*, and Howe's *Homebrew 2*. Jackman told me that there might have been more to Squire's unusual sound than previously thought.

Conventional wisdom dictates that Squire's punchy bottom end and the texture of the bassist's soaring lead playing really came down to his use of Rotosound strings, the size of his hands, or his "shaved" bass (due to the removal of wallpaper he pasted onto the body during his "flower power" daze). Jackman intimated that the genesis of the magic sound went beyond the type and make of strings, bass, and amp, but wouldn't elaborate or reveal what that missing element was, although some have further theorized that it was Squire's ability to split his bass signal into low and high frequencies and send the lows to a bass amp and the highs to a guitar amp, resulting in a rich, distinctive, and layered tone.

"This is a mystery that Chris might not want to divulge," Jackman told me. "I do know exactly what the answer is. I should e-mail him to see if he's happy about me spilling the beans. You have one thing right though: he has enormous hands. On the other hand he's not the only player that uses Rotosounds, so that's not really it."

Further complicating matters is the fact that Squire, like one of his heroes, John Entwistle, procured a casual product endorsement deal with Rotosound. Although it's been said that Squire used Rotosound, how forthcoming would he be about changes to this particular aspect of his rig or recording setup while receiving a lifetime supply of strings?

If Jackman was correct, however, then there obviously *was* a secret ingredient, either in the recording process or in the treatment of the bass, bass signal, strings, or amp(s), that has either yet to be reported or has gone underreported.

"He used the regular Swing Bass 66 strings," says Jason How, CEO of Rotosound. "He never changed. He always used the 45105.

That's it really. I just think that through all my years in the business that the strings we produce have a certain sound to them and Chris used a pick or a pick and his finger. I think it was a simple combination of that and the strings. I don't think he overanalyzed it."

In the end, does it matter how Squire arrived at his sound? Would anyone achieve the same Chris Squire tone, even if they were using the exact set up he did? It's unlikely.

Like so many other aspects of the revolution in music from, say, 1966 through 1976, the electric bass guitar seemed to represent free spirit and liberation. Names such as John Entwistle, Jack Bruce, Paul McCartney, Jaco Pastorius, Bootsy Collins, Stanley Clarke, Chris Squire, and later Geddy Lee (and, much later, Flea and Les Claypool) were leading lights of electric bass guitar in rock, funk/soul, and jazz-rock.

There were always good, steady four-stringers in popular music, but the idea of a *lead* bassist was somewhat alien in the early 1970s. By the same token, as musicians needed to challenge themselves to successfully complement complex or complicated musical concepts or specific riffs, they strove to improve their skill level, which they often did—at exponential rates.

Roles were shifting everywhere, actually, and progressive rock seemed to be on the cutting edge. It was inevitable that the electric bass, having only been mass-produced for fewer than twenty years by the early 1970s, would go through a transformation in which talent, woodshedding, the desire to improve one's technical facility on the instrument, the nature of the tricky music being played, and the general excesses of the times shaped the concept of bass—or electric bass—as lead instrument.

"I think the zeitgeist was very compelling, and I remember a fascination in the culture with the concept of liberation," says Manring. "A lot of what was happening with the bass was seen as part of the liberation ethos, and the pioneers you mentioned accomplished some amazing things inspired by that spirit. As it became possible to obtain a clear and articulate sound on the bass, theses folks were at the right place and time with talent, creativity, and enthusiasm."

Squire, speaking with *New Musical Express* in October 1972, seemed to agree. "Once the electric bass guitar came on the scene, things just had to change," he said.

Still, the origins of "The Fish" are a bit murky. It may have been rooted in a Mabel Greer's Toyshop song called "Jeanetta."

"Well, there is a lot of riffs and bits and pieces that got rearranged and got thrown in there," Bob Hagger says. "For example, we realize that 'Jeanetta' was Chris Squire's extension into 'The Fish.' I think somebody pointed it out on the Internet. He had taken 'Jeanetta' and extended it and created that wonderful piece. Somebody made a video, comparing the two. It shows how Jeanette moved into 'The Fish.'"

Regardless of its origins, "The Fish" was all about Squire. "It is not a Christian thing," he once told me. "Bill Bruford nicknamed me 'The Fish' because I used to spend a long time in the bathroom when we used to share hotel rooms together. He would say, 'Get out of the bath. You're like a fish in there.'"

Howe's classical- and Spanish-flavored "Mood for a Day," the collaborative and jazzy/classical "South Side of the Sky," and the fusion-y ten-plus-minute "Heart of the Sunrise" complete a very diverse album. "South Side of the Sky" employs sound effects, such as footsteps, whipping winds, and even thunderclaps—something that would come to define "Close to the Edge" a year later. This was the cherry on the cake, however. The multipart chanting—again a pre-echo of material that would appear on *Close to the Edge*—conjures pagan rites of passage just as Wakeman's icy piano notes tingle with frosty isolationism.

Despite being something of a cosmic love song set to a dizzying amalgam of musical styles, "Heart of the Sunrise" features a rumbling opening bass figure in 6/4, evoking the roar and pulse of major urban centers, cities like London, New York, Birmingham, Paris, and so on. This cross-genre affair conjures the golden-orange sun rising above the horizon, sending rays streaming through canyons of city skyscrapers. The song is brilliant, but the final notes leave one in suspense. It isn't a comforting sensation.

Ray Bennett, bassist and guitarist of Flash and an old friend of Bill Bruford, remembers hearing "Heart of the Sunrise" prior to the release of the *Fragile* album. "Bill used to live around the corner from me when I was doing Flash [with Peter Banks] and he was doing Yes, and I remember he invited me to hear some tracks from *Fragile*," he says. "When they finally got their mixes done, Bill would say, 'Come on over and have a listen.' He was proud of that stuff. Bill was digging it when he played 'Heart of the Sunrise.'"

Some have noted the similarity between "Heart of the Sunrise" and King Crimson's screamin', jazz-inflected psych-out, "21st Century Schizoid Man." *Melody Maker* once asked Robert Fripp whether there was a connection between the classic Yes track and Crimson's paranoid-laced freak-out; he simply shot back at the interviewer, "What do you think?"

According to Fripp, the members of Yes were so amazed by Crimson's early performances that they panicked and, presumably, finally shook off their shock and mustered up the musical chutz-pah to compose something remotely similar to "Schizoid Man."

Anderson noted a Stravinsky influence on the Yes songwriters and even used the word "schizoid" to describe the rhythmic patterns of "Heart of the Sunrise" when speaking with biographer Dan Hedges.

Bruford would, of course, perform "Schizoid Man" onstage with Crimson, and we can hear various Bruford interpretations of the song on releases as far-ranging as *USA*, *The Night Watch: Live at the Amsterdam Concertgebouw November 23rd, 1973*, *The Great Deceiver* boxed set, and the twin-disc live sets *Vroom Vroom (2001)* and *Live at the Shepherds Bush Empire, London, 1996* (2008), for which Bruford was coupled with a second drummer, Pat Mastelotto, for Crim's famous double-trio, unveiled in the mid-1990s.

Interestingly, the pumping and twee sounds of the church or-gan in "Close to the Edge" are reminiscent of the wheezing noises heard during the second ending of "The Court of the Crimson King," which we've already established was an influence on Yes.

"Bill and me and Peter went to see King Crimson in 1969 when they first played London, when Greg Lake and Ian McDonald were there," Bennett told me. "We all went to see them in a big London ballroom and Bill turned around and said, 'This is what I wanted Yes to sound like.' He wanted something more intensely based on music rather than the big harmonies and vocal sections."

There certainly are similarities. A familiar rumbling and escala-tion marks the opening of both tracks. Recurring motifs, partial recapitulation of ideas run through "Heart of the Sunrise," acting as a mini-symphony, setting the stage for "Close to the Edge." The recapitulation was less an exact restating than a recalling of earlier motifs. No matter. The "recall" gives weight, balance and coherence to the piece.

Others would argue, however, that although these two songs operate according to similar key musical devices, their feels are immensely different. For one thing, Michael Giles swings in 12/8 like a *mutha* or a madman in "Schizoid Man." Bruford, on the other hand, *grooves* in 6/8 (as well as 9/8 and 10/8).

It should be noted that "Heart of the Sunrise" does slip into 12/8 more than once, including during the opening verse. For all its aggressiveness and funkiness, the song is equally dynamic: sharp cymbal accents and beat displacements, among other subtleties, break with strict harmonies and instances sonic and rhythmic simultaneity.

Banks told me something similar, in an interview I conducted with him in 2008.

> We thought we were pretty hot stuff until Crimson came along. I saw them play their first ever gig at the Speakeasy in London, which was just amazing. They were so good that we started rehearsing quite intensively because we suddenly realized that there was a band around that was much better than us that kind of was a big shock.
>
> But Fripp used to come and watch us play at the Marquee. I knew he played [guitar], and he said he was putting a band together, but I had no idea of what that band would be. I knew Greg Lake [ELP, Crimson] and Greg had just moved to London, and I remember him asking me, "Where did I get my trousers from?" [*laughs*] I had on a pair of white trousers and he said, "Do you think I should wear white trousers, too?" That kind of mundane conversation, but I didn't know anything about Crimson.

"We felt secretively competitive [with] King Crimson, Genesis," Howe confirmed to me in 2005. "It was like, 'Hang on.' We owned a little bit of acres somewhere in the plot of what was called the English resurgence of, I call it, post-psychedelia. Post-psychedelic is really what it was."

Even still, Crimson stressed improvisation as much as composition, and Yes made studio construction a part of its M.O. As such,

"Heart of the Sunrise," like "Close to the Edge," was pieced together via edits.

"There was a lot of tape splicing, and Eddy was very good at it," says Gary Martin, who worked on *Fragile* with Offord. "As you may know, spicing has to be done at an angle and across a two-inch tape. That means that the join point for each track would be in a slightly different place. If you can detect edit points I'm not surprised—although you weren't meant to be able to. Just listening to it again now I noticed that the drum sound does change when it gets to the faster part about 1:30 in. That would certainly have been two parts edited together."

After the close of "Heart of the Sunrise," the record concludes with a stray audio snippet, a reprise of "We Have Heaven." "I think they kind of got that from the Beatles," says Offord. "Didn't the Beatles do something like that? Didn't they just have a snippet?" They did, most notably on *Sgt. Pepper,* and changed rock history forever.

Within a year the same could be said for Yes. It was all building toward something that would go on to define the very essence of British progressive rock.

3

THE SPIRAL AIM
Inside *CTTE*

On the same page of *Billboard* as the magazine's review of Yes's *Fragile* was a piece on *Pictures at an Exhibition*, which included the claim that ELP's "deftness in adapting serious music into contemporary idiom" had blossomed with the release of this live record. It was, no doubt, a very positive review. But just below it, the entry for *Fragile* would nearly deify Yes, proclaiming the band the "supergroup" of the year for taking what "is good from classical and rock and fusing it to form a sound which is uniquely theirs."

Fans thought so too. The band's breakthrough song of the 1970s, an edited version of the eight-and-a-half-minute "Roundabout," written by Anderson and Howe, was on the *Billboard* Hot 100 chart for ten weeks.

This musical sparkplug soared to #13 in March 1972, three months to the day after Yes's first US hit, "Your Move," broke the Top 40. (Yes did not collect a hit on the singles chart in the UK prior to 1977's "Wonderous Stories." However, *The Yes Album* and *Fragile* both climbed to the #7 slot.)

The Yes Album was still hanging around, and by mid-January 1972, it had been on the charts for twenty-nine weeks. It sat at #41, sharing real estate with such classic releases as the Moody Blues' *Every Good Boy Deserves Favour* and *A Question of Balance*; Tull's *Aqualung*; and Floyd's *Meddle*.

In April, *Billboard* reported that *Fragile* had gone gold, and it was in the Top 10 by the spring of 1972, hitting #4 in early May. By the mid-summer, after nearly seven months on sale, *Fragile* was still in the Top 100.

"America"
How appropriate. As Yes was recording a cover version of the Paul Simon song "America," the band was poised to conquer that vast country's large arenas and diverse music fan base.

Yes had already been playing its version of the song live for years and had targeted it for recording. "We got some really great sounds and we rearranged 'America,'" Clive Bayley told me. "I think Jon was more instrumental in doing 'America,' to be fair."

"America" had been covered, earlier, by the Scottish proto-progressive-rock band 1-2-3, led by keyboardist Billy Ritchie, which had morphed into Clouds. (Interestingly, in 1972, both ELP and Yes released singles—Yes with "America," ELP with "Nutrocker"—that were also performed or recorded in some form by 1-2-3 and Clouds.)

Listening to a recording of 1-2-3 at the Marquee in London reveals that Ritchie slyly slips in different sonic references, most notably Bach's piece in 3/4, "Jesu, Joy of Man's Desiring," written for string quartet and often employed as a wedding processional.

We should point out that B. Bumble and the Stingers recorded "The Nut Rocker," a major British hit, in 1962, as well as an interpretation of Rimsky-Korsakov's "Flight of the Bumble Bee" titled "Bumble Boogie." "When we did ["America"] onstage, Ian [Ellis, bassist] used to come over and light a candle on top of the organ as I sang, taking the piss [out of it], of course," Ritchie says. "It was rather churchy in atmosphere."

When Simon and Garfunkel recorded "America," it seemed to reflect the disillusionment of the boomer generation, which would be echoed in another type of road song written by Jackson Browne, called "Running on Empty." "America," much like "Running on Empty," catches the speaker in moments of uncertainty, unsure what the future holds for him, his loved ones, and his country. It's perhaps no coincidence that the song resurfaced during the 2016 US presidential election campaign cycle.

Jon had alluded to the fact that band had always admired Keith Emerson and the Nice and their, as he put it, "arranged excitement." This was a model for the early Yes to follow. (And, interestingly enough, Howe's guitar solo in "America" was inspired by two musicians: Delaney Bramlett and Duane Eddy.)

"Yes in the beginning were doing cover songs and . . . theoretically they could play anyone's music and make it sound like Yes," says Mike Tait. "They could do the Fifth Dimension and a number of others, and all those types of songs, but they didn't recognize that themselves. They really didn't understand that Yes was a treatment of music, not a music in and of itself."

Yet it was the band's original material that catapulted it into stardom. Whether Yes was keeping up with its rivals or swimming in, partaking of, the "river" of influences as mentioned earlier, it is difficult to say. If Yes was compelled to compete with its rivals in the marketplace by being a high-priced covers band, it may have been the last time the group felt motivated to do so in the 1970s. No covers appear on *Close to the Edge.*

While *Yes, Time and a Word,* and *The Yes Album* contain older material, plus bits and fragments of pieces swiped from other sources, same with *Fragile* with its tongue-in-cheek send-up "Cans and Brahms," *Close to the Edge* appeared at the point at which Yes became a fully fledged symphonic rock band capable of writing extraordinarily original material.

This may seem like an obvious point, but it really strikes at the core of what the band set out to do in the first place. Inclusion of someone else's songs on *CTTE* might have skewed its pure vision and would have certainly been perceived as, and in reality may have been, an artistic step backward into the pre–*Yes Album* psychedelic cover-band daze.

But during the first quarter of 1972, Yes was still operating very much as it had in years prior. The song in its entirety, which clocks in at 10:31, was the last track on the July 1972 sampler *The New Age of Atlantic.*

After one twelve-hour recording session, the band still only had three minutes of what it deemed semi-useable music. This was a sign of the kinds of experimentation and long, drawn-out studio work that would mark the *Close to the Edge* sessions.

At least the band was experimenting. For one thing, Bruford wanted to play congas and have them sent through a wah-wah effect unit. Offord, as he so often did, obliged. "Why not?" he asked rhetorically. This effect can be heard in what I call the "Latin" section of the song, both in the single and on the ten-plus-minute *Yesterdays* compilation version (at approx. 3:28), during Howe's countrified rock 'n' roll guitar solo (circa 6:10), and resurfaces later in the song. The wah-wah effect comes through (to my ears) mainly in the left channel. The gurgling, bubbling sound is so electronic that it can fool you into thinking it's some form of synthesizer or electric stringed instrument plugged into an amp.

For this book I attempted to pinpoint the actual recording dates for "America." Reports indicate that Yes was in the studio on February 1 and 2. Three days after the group's initial go at the track, Yes hit Advision studios again and knocked out the song, according to a report in *Rolling Stone* magazine.

The *Rolling Stone* article, dated March 30, 1972, refers to an unnamed column in an undisclosed music paper, which describes how Yes was beginning to scale the heights of fame, even comparing the experience to something akin to Beatlemania.

I found two articles from the time, both from *NME*, fitting this general description. One of them, which reports that the band was in Advision recording "America," refers to the band's dates in the US happening "next week." (It also indicates that sales of *The Yes Album* and *Fragile* had racked up nearly $1,000,000 each in revenue, while moving 350,000 and 250,000 units, respectively.)

Yes was set to play Bethany College in West Virginia on February 18, the first date in America on that particular leg of the *Fragile* tour. I double-checked with Bethany College, and the date is correct. An article from the Bethany College campus newspaper, *Bethany Tower*, dated February 17, 1972, previewed the show, forecasting that the Yes concert was to take place "tomorrow night" at 8 p.m.

Yes was also scheduled to be filmed by the BBC at Advision for the television program *The Old Grey Whistle Test*, which *RS* claims happened the same day the article would hit the stands. *NME* reported that sessions were taking place in Advision "this week." (Yes was also to be filmed for the first of five concerts at the Rainbow Theatre in November 1973 for the BBC show.)

To make a long story even longer, this would place the second round of recording for "America" in the February 4–5 timeframe. In addition, documentation indicates that Bruford was with Rick Wakeman at Trident on February 10, cutting *The Six Wives of Henry VIII*.

It'd take several months, but by July *Billboard* reported that US radio stations were adding the single, "America," like mad, singling out stations such as WVVS and CHUM. The song joined cuts from ELP's *Trilogy*, King Crimson's unfairly maligned live record *Earthbound*, and Curved Air's *Phantasmagoria*. ("America," b/w an excerpt from the song "Close to the Edge," titled "Total Mass Retain," was issued in the US on July 17, 1972.)

Yes had the situation *covered* for the time being, so to speak, but greater things were yet in store.

Closer to the Edge

For such a classic and coherent record, it's surprising to find that the lives of Yes band members were in bit of disarray, even chaos, during the making of *Close to the Edge*. For one thing, Jon and his then-wife Jenny "moved house" several times around London in the months prior to the recording sessions.

Although the band was riding a wave of success from its British Top 10 album, *Fragile*, and a hit single, "Roundabout," Anderson appeared self-conscious, even dejected, in the wake of the death of a close friend, Stone the Crows co-founder Les Harvey.

The Crows, a blues-rock band once led by vocalist Maggie Bell and managed by Peter Grant, happened to have been using Advision in the summer of 1972, at the same general time frame as Yes was busy finishing *Close to the Edge*.

Names were floated as a replacement for Harvey, including Fleetwood Mac's former guitar wizard Peter Green, who appeared ready to temporarily fit the bill but ultimately declined the invitation. Howe lent a hand and performed with the Crows, helping to scribble one of prog rock's most curious footnotes.

In June, *New Musical Express* wondered if Harvey's death, by electrocution, at the age of twenty-seven (making him another unfortunate member of the "27 Club"), would impact Anderson's outlook on life. As it was, Anderson, who was the same age, was finding it difficult to put pen to paper to create lyrics, so conscious was he of the gravity of the band's newfound success.

Along with grief and shock at the death of his friend, Rick Wakeman was dealing with his own personal issues. He missed his first wife, Ros, and in the early part of the year also missed the birth of his son Oliver, future Yes keyboardist, on February 26, 1972. Unfortunately, Yes was scheduled to play that very night at the Capital Theatre in Passaic, New Jersey.

The lanky keys man had bemoaned life on the road for causing him to miss such paradigm-shifting events, and this may have been the reason for some false reports of his early exit from the band. He had also confessed to suffering from stage fright, thinking observers and ticketholders were waiting for him to screw up. How much this mental disposition impacted Wakeman's performances, and how he battled this condition with outrageous concert productions—while donning flamboyant outfits—is anyone's guess.

Unfortunately for Wakeman, the band started believing some of the rumors circulating about him, causing a bit of unrest amongst the ranks. The story goes that one night onstage, he was finicky about his Mellotron, and it appeared he was fed up with it and refused to play. He wasn't signaling anything other than techno-logical distress, but his actions were misinterpreted as unhappiness with the general direction of the band.

Still, Wakeman may have stoked some of those fires when he told the press, as early as the spring of 1972, that he was record-ing a solo album, which he hoped to release by July of that year. In the end, the instrumental concept album, *The Six Wives of Henry VIII*, wouldn't hit shelves until January 1973. (Only some-one with Wakeman's sardonic humor could have thought up a set of progressive-rock pieces channeling the distinct personalities of Henry's largely unfortunate wives.) In addition, in June, Wake-man was recording with Strawbs' Dave Cousins, for his former bandmate's debut album, *Two Weeks Last Summer*, released in October 1972.

Wakeman wasn't the only Yesman working outside the band unit. On July 9, at the Royal Academy in London, Howe appeared with David Palmer (known predominately in rock circles for his work with Jethro Tull) and played both electric and acoustic guitar (a Ramirez flamenco guitar, to be exact). Howe accompanied the London Philomusica orchestra, with Palmer conducting, and per-formed the Palmer score "Since Wenceslas Looked Out," a tribute to Jan Palach.

In January 1969, Czech student Palach, in an act of self-immo-lation, protested the complacency of his countrymen regarding the invasion of their homeland by Central and Eastern European pow-ers. We can only speculate as to the connection David Palmer (now Dee Palmer, following a gender transition), may have felt with Palach, but the total obliteration of one's self may have held some appeal for the young conductor/arranger.

Interestingly, Palmer would later produce the 1993 BMG/RCA Victor release, the musical crossover album *Symphonic Music of Yes* (which hit #1 on *Billboard*'s crossover classical chart), featuring the London Philharmonic Orchestra as well as the English Chamber Orchestra and London Community Gospel Choir. "Close to the Edge" gets the symphonic treatment, and the band's music, on this release, perhaps approaches what Anderson may have envisioned for the 1972 piece before Yes originally recorded it.

Despite the band members appearing to veer in five different directions, Yes remained focused and determined. Howe explained to Chris Welch in late 1971 that the band had "a lot of ideas" for the next album. "It's hard to say what the new LP will be like, because we are still talking about it," he said.

After Yes came off the road in early spring, fresh from a run of dates in America in support of *Fragile*, Anderson and Howe tweaked material they'd been ironing out during soundchecks, in hotel rooms, and backstage. They would exchange ideas and tape their writing sessions as the band toured America in cities of the Northeast and Midwest. The collaborative and cooperative spirit that began on *Fragile* reached its pinnacle with *Close to the Edge*.

Yes arguably wouldn't be as collaborative again until 1977's *Going for the One*. Interestingly, the basic chords that helped to inspire the breakout hit from that record, "Wonderous Stories," a #7 song in Britain, were written by drummer Alan White—on guitar. The title track went Top 30 in the UK.

Unlike Yes's later records, everyone in the band had a hand in the arranging and writing the songs on *Close to the Edge*. Anderson was the conductor, or a catalyst for ideas, but several disparate musical concepts would be fused, the best bits of each being whittled down until the polished riff or musical passage passed inspection. Often, Howe might add to an existing riff, or have several ideas of his own, Squire would mold a bass line to fit Howe's idea, and Bruford might rejigger the piece to include an odd tempo. Much of *Close to the Edge* was coordinated this way.

Ironically, Howe had ruled out the notion of recording another album like *Fragile*. These songs were not to be solo pieces but would be tightly constructed, unifying compositions that quite possibly would have a "religious feel." He went as far as to claim that the new music was some of the "biggest and purest" the band had ever written. "Long pieces are something I've always wanted to do," Anderson told *NME*. He went on to say that each member brings in different ideas and "we fix them together like a jigsaw puzzle."

Anderson also commented that the band was writing and recording music that could stand the test of time, and that the three songs set to appear on *Close to the Edge* were interrelated. "*Fragile* was the situation of the band at the time. Now we're close to the edge of spiritual awareness within the framework of the group, making music. It could depict crumbling into dust or it could just carry on getting better and better."

Despite the perception that Anderson is solely responsible for the perceived hippie-dippie lyrics on *Close to the Edge*, the phrase "close to the edge" was really generated by Howe; it was extracted from an unused portion of a song about the longest day of the year.

In 2007, I discussed the spiritual aspects of Yes's lyrics with Howe, who told me:

> Jon didn't write all of the lyrics, so some of them did come from me, and there were some ideas from me that were suggestive of what you are talking about, the spirituality, but [were] more day to day. But put into context with Jon's lyrics they would all [carry] a spiritual intent.
>
> Like, Jon developed the idea of "close to the edge, down by the river." But, literally, I lived by a river called the Thames, and I was close to the edge of the river. So, in my terms it was a very literal song. It didn't take long before Jon took that [idea] and made it something that was more abstract. I thought that was great. I had no problem with that. But like I say, Jon winds up getting blamed for my lyrics as much as [I do for his].

Over the years, Anderson hasn't directly contradicted this account but has claimed a certain amount of ownership for the entire concept and even the phrase "close to the edge." "The river leads you to the ocean, all the paths lead you to the divine," he told Sid Smith, for the liner notes of the 2013 reissue of *Close to the Edge*. "So, the idea was that as human beings we are close to the edge—the edge of realization, whatever anybody else might want to think."

Still, Anderson's contributions were vastly significant. One notion—empathy—seemed to define the mood of the times. Anderson had seen what was transpiring around the world, especially in Africa, and the disparity between the rich and poor. There was the super rich and then super poor and not much else in between—an idea that led, in part, to the lyric, "I get up, I get down."

Howe had the line "in her white lace," which he sang to Anderson, who then—in Lennon/McCartney fashion—created the lyric and melody for "Two million people barely satisfy," which became the focal point of "I Get Up, I Get Down," the third section of the epic "Close to the Edge."

Yes had rarely been as democratic. While the title track is credited to Anderson and Howe, the second song, "And You and I" lists Anderson first, with "Themes" composed by Bruford, Howe, and Squire. Part two of the song, "Eclipse," credits Bruford and Squire as its authors. The closing song, "Siberian Khatru," is a similar story, with Anderson taking lead credit and "Themes" credited to Anderson, Howe, and Wakeman. It's believed that Bruford, the drummer, even thought up some of the song titles.

Once it was decided that *Close to the Edge* would contain a long-form composition and two shorter songs ("Close to the Edge" clocks in at nearly nineteen minutes, with "And You and I" 10:09 and "Siberian Khatru" a paltry 8:57 by comparison), it's as if the canvas was both widened and restricted. Tracks one, two, and three flow together like no one's business. It's as if Offord and the boys had the foreseen the "sideless" format indicative of the CD medium—back in 1972.

Listening to the LP, however, is, and was, a different experience in more than just the obvious ways. Once side one ("Close to the Edge") was nearing completion and nature sounds wafting off into infinity, the needle cut its way around the vinyl labyrinth, giving us a moment to contemplate what it was we had just heard.

This kind of reflection can occur when spinning the CD, of course, and even the track-sequence-jumbled mass of eight-track, but *Close to the Edge*, as it originally appeared on LP, was not only a product of self-reflection (as we'll see) but also subtly coaxed the listener to evacuate his normal headspace for the psychological high ground of self-reflection.

Interestingly enough, the aforementioned June 1972 *New Musical Express* article observed that Anderson seemed to be entering a process of "self examination." In the first half of '72, he was on the precipice—the edge, if you will—of what he had wanted to achieve for years: being a musical presence on the world stage.

Anderson began thinking about his success and his beginnings in Accrington. From his perspective, not much had changed in those northern England villages. Nothing was new, and he felt he could not relate to the people or the place.

"When I met [Anderson], he wanted to be a rock star," says Bob Hagger with a laugh. "I think he's cultivated that [image], and I think he's enjoyed his life from that perspective."

This isn't to say Anderson manifested signs of full-blown delusions or inflated self-importance prior to his eventual rock stardom. But it's safe to say that he had his eye on being successful. Yet by the early 1970s, Anderson appeared to be working through some form of spiritual transformation—one that seemed to acknowledge his newfound fame.

When I spoke with Anderson about this time period, I came away with the impression that he had been determined to make something happen in his career. If anything, it seemed as though he believed he was on borrowed time, or running out of time, and that opportunities presented to him were a mere catalyst for greater artistic things to come.

"All of the musicians in Yes had already spent about ten years in other bands," he told me, "and we weren't young, spring chickens when Yes started. . . . We couldn't sit around. This could go tomorrow. This could disappear."

The '60s were gone, but the residue of the psychedelic era and the peace movement clung to the progressives, providing them with a sense of urgency and connectedness for a new day.

Prominent thinkers of the 1960s contributed to the turn away from traditional or Western values and philosophies. In the UK, Canada, and Continental Europe, Colin Wilson, psychologist R. D. Laing, media theorist Herbert Marshall McLuhan, psychiatrist Dr. Eric Berne (author of the pop-psychology book *Games People Play*), French philosopher Michel Tournier, esoteric German novelist Hermann Hesse and his never-ending journey to the East, and many others, were examining the self and our individual and collective powers to change our surroundings. They all had one thing in common: they attempted to get at the root core of who and what we are.

Anderson said he wanted to truly understand what it meant to be a musician and create music for a living. He'd been given a gift, and what was he going to do with this blessing?

"I started reading and Hermann Hesse was a very big experience," he told me. "Then you want to put [what you've learned] into lyrical form and express what you're feeling. You can talk about the love of your life, who ran away, [or that] it's going to be a dark day tomorrow, because I'm lost. But that isn't happening to me. I *ain't* got the blues. I don't have the blues, so what do I write about?"

Anderson decided to look at the human condition, his inner being, instead of interpersonal boy-meets-girl romantic affairs of the heart. Concepts such as universal love and the destructive power of hate captured his imagination. Viewed from this perspective, it's suddenly not difficult to see how the lyrical themes of *Close to the Edge*—concepts of self-realization—developed.

But what of Yes's success? How did Anderson square his ideals with that? Maybe the band was simply lucky or reaping the rewards of four years of tireless work, as Anderson himself had postulated. Or just maybe Yes and Jon Anderson *were* destined for greatness, and Anderson's ability to see the future, or *feel* it—this ability to tap into some form of universal consciousness—is something in the order of magic. Maybe.

Either way, it appears as though Anderson was struggling with who he was and where he fit into the world. So, perhaps, *Close to the Edge* represents Anderson, through the vehicle of Yes, reaching his destiny and the culmination of a journey to realize the "otherness" in him.

This otherness took many forms. Some called it the soul, some the self. There was even talk surrounding Anderson regarding the "cord," something that was alluded to in the lyrics of "And You and I," which might be interpreted as consciousness.

In a *Melody Maker* article featuring Anderson from 1972, we encounter Lobsang Rampa, an English mystic, who claimed to be guided by the spirit of a Tibetan lama. Rampa's concept of the "silver cord" was a metaphysical link between the higher self or astral body and the physical body. Anderson has used similar esoteric jargon in conversation, and in lyrics to Yes songs such as "Starship Trooper."

Rampa also talked about "the third eye," or one's spiritual awakening, or "that special organ of clairvoyance" involving astral traveling and dreaming and semiconscious states. Similar ideas were swimming around Anderson's head at the time he was formulating the big lyrical and mystical concepts for *Close to the Edge*.

But, surely, Anderson didn't just begin writing mystical or spiritual songs overnight? Circa 1970, Anderson seemed to have turned a corner and never looked back in the other direction. By then, Anderson had gotten the *h* out of there—he'd dropped the letter from his first name a few years prior to *Close to the Edge*. (In some legal documents I've seen from around this time, and even after, Jon's name is spelled with an *h*.)

Why is this important? It shows a conscious choice to present a public persona divorced from his personal roots. Anderson was seeking to become a new person.

When I asked Peter Banks about Anderson's spiritual journey, he quipped, "How many hours have you got? Now you've caught me [*laughs*]. I'm trying to be diplomatic. Jon is a unique person. . . . If I were speaking with him, for example, and I am pretty pragmatic, he can be annoyingly digressive. I think that's about all I can say."

Banks told me that Anderson seemed to "always be into" spirituality, but others, including past business associates and friends, say Anderson often wears mysticism as a shield. That when he doesn't want to talk about certain uncomfortable topics, he switches his brain to some alternative reality, zoning out to ponder the nature of the universe and becoming difficult to engage in normal conversation. The author had experienced this once in another lifetime (i.e. career).

For a fresh perspective I questioned Clive Bayley, who first set off on his own spiritual path in the 1960s, discovering Eastern mysticism in his late teens. He would not go on record regarding the details of such, but recalling his experience with Anderson, he told me:

> [Anderson] definitely wasn't into [spirituality] at the time we were playing together, but would have been subconsciously. I think I was picking up on that, which is why I liked him. Later, when I heard Yes's mystical lyrics I thought, "Hang on, that's not Jon." But then I thought about it and I realized it must have been him. He kept it quiet or it simply didn't come through for me when I was seventeen, eighteen, nineteen, or something.
>
> "I think it is all about sincerity. I think Jon is sincere. I think I liked him because we didn't know that the other was into a mystic path and at that point he played it down or whether it came later I'm not exactly sure. But

I have been looking at it recently and thinking, "All his lyrics are moving into that area and I have never really considered that before, because he was Jon—"Mr. Bossy Boots" [*laughs*]. It's strange. One of the reasons I think I liked him was that we have a very subliminal connection on that level, if that explains it.

Other statements helped to contribute to the lead singer's public persona, such as Rick Wakeman's famously funny one-liner about Anderson, captured on *The Legend: Live in Concert 2000*: "He's really the only person I know who's trying to save this planet by living on a totally different one."

Similar tales have crossed the dusty borders of rumor into Yes legend. The timeframe gets a bit fuzzy—as do the details—but a story that's been circulating for decades is Anderson's otherworldly dream, or death dream, of his "passing on from this world to the other."

It's unclear if Anderson actually had a near-death experience (NDE) in the 1970s around the time of *Close to the Edge* or just dreamed one. Says former Yes manager Jon Brewer:

Jon said he once saw an angel, and this story he has told many times, but he really believes it. He was sitting in Vegas, sitting on the bed and the wall opened. . . . He told me, "Jon, I was totally sober. I hadn't taken any drugs. I was clean." I said, "What happened?" He said, "A girl came into my room, from the outside and said, 'Don't worry. Everything is going to be okay.'" He said he was so stunned and it was so remarkable. He just sat there and she disappeared. "I know it happened," he said. "This was an experience that was far bigger than anything."

In 2008, Anderson had been battling health issues, reportedly respiratory failure or a "severe asthma attack" that landed him in the hospital. In *Prog* magazine in 2012, the singer detailed these challenges as a "near death experience," which in part relieved him of his duties as the front man for Yes. According to a press statement released to the media that same year, Anderson was advised by doctors to "spend the coming months resting and recovering. Unfortunately, this means I won't be able to tour with Yes this summer [2008, for the Close to the Edge and Back Tour] as originally planned."

How ironic. Possibly cruel. Anderson's original death dream slips him esoteric knowledge and he uses it as creative fodder, but in the twenty-first century, Anderson experiences an actual medical NDE, but is prevented from joining the Close to the Edge and Back Tour.

Whether in the ensuing years the public conflated the two circulating NDE stories is difficult to discern. Either way, Anderson has dealt with some heavy shit, real or imagined.

"Jon supposedly died for two minutes," Brewer told me in 2013.

"Jon flatlined twice and had to be revived twice," another source told me. "He had to have six major operations in the course of a year."

Not to be callous, but if Anderson did pierce the veil either relatively recently or way back when, what did he see?

"You won't get an answer," Brewer retorts.

For the record, I have not. Depending on when this life-and-death-altering event occurred, it's likely Anderson was already a firm believer in things, dare we say, supernatural. That's why it's not surprising to find that songs appearing on Yes's previous efforts, such as *The Yes Album* and *Fragile*, hint at what could be the culmination Jon's mysticism in Yes.

Don't let the playful lyrics fool you. A song like "Long Distance Runaround," for example, likely has religious connotations—as in, Anderson questioning his faith (or a faith he once had). A similar situation exists with the Lewis Carroll–like wordplay of "We Have Heaven."

Interestingly enough, author and music scholar John Covach interpreted the entirety of "Close to the Edge" as a dream or a vision. Anderson has made comments to this effect over the years, saying that the end section, "Part IV," or "Seasons of Man," was based on the infamous and much misunderstood dream discussed above. (Anderson also claims the same section of the song was inspired by a dream in which he stands atop a mountain and is confronted by a male presence. Is this a different scene from the same phantasmagoric vision?)

Death, Anderson indicated to Lee Abrams, "never frightened me ever since," solidifying his belief that the soul lives forever. The physical body withers, yes, but our consciousness never dies.

In the past I've argued that the rock (or prog rock) epic that most closely resembles Berlioz's *Symphonie fantastique* is Rush's "2112." But, in retrospect, "Close to the Edge," which appeared some four years earlier, is a better example of a progressive/psychedelic rock trip that harkens back to Berlioz's most famous work. Another possible candidate, Tull's expansive and frankly fragmented journey of the soul, *A Passion Play* from 1973, simply does not have the same consistency, coherency, or potency as "Edge."

To gain a better understanding of "Close to the Edge" we do have to examine one of Anderson's biggest influences: Hesse's *Siddhartha*, a novel in which the central character embarks upon a journey of self-discovery, transforming himself from a secular, unenlightened soul to a spiritual one.

The lyrics to "Close to the Edge" speak about "disgrace" and the speaker's liver being "rearranged." To achieve balance, one must listen to the music coming "quickly from afar," a lyrical construct that likely coincides with Siddhartha contemplating suicide at the river's edge. He's prevented from doing this only by the sound of the river—the majestic *om.*

Siddhartha has what could be called an NDE, although not in the clinical sense. He sees his reflection in the river and is reborn, shedding the materialism of the secular world, his old life. (It's easy to see why hippies liked the book: Siddhartha is practically a counterculture hero, forsaking the material world for spiritual matters.)

It's been said that *om*, or *aom*—three sounds, A-U-M—signifies the three Hindu deities, Vishnu, Shiva, Brahma, and is one of the central focuses of *Siddhartha*. In the chapter titled "Om," Hesse writes that the titular character cannot at first hear all that the river offers. Under the guidance of the old ferryman Vasudeva, Siddhartha listens more intently to the rushing sounds of the river and realizes that all the sorrows and joys, pains and ecstasies are one continuous voice emanating from the water.

Past, present, and future exist together in the flowing river; this timeless existence generates the sound of *om*, or a perfect unity of everything. When Siddhartha recognizes the *om* and understands what it means, he no longer experiences internal conflict.

Siddhartha's very essence is constant, having no past or future, only present, and his existence is part of a larger stream. Siddhartha becomes whole (that is, achieves self-realization) and then connects himself with the wholeness or oneness of the universe.

Later, a restless Govinda, Siddhartha's old friend, hears of an old wise man who paddles across the river, and wishes to speak with him. Without knowing that the ferryman is Siddhartha, Govinda, a holy man in his own right, is given advice to stop seeking and take a look at the world around him. If one concentrates too hard and too long on a goal, blind to everything else, the goal is the only thing one sees. Govinda eventually recognizes Siddhartha; it is only when he is set to depart does he see a "stream of faces" and all things, good and bad, in Siddhartha's eyes . . .

In his book *The Novels of Hermann Hesse: A Study in Theme and Structure*, Theodore Ziolkowski describes the "symbolic geography" of *Siddhartha*. The "totality and simultaneity" of the river is stressed throughout the book and the river is symbolic of the unity and the oneness Siddhartha wishes to achieve with the world.

It's been suggested that music—singing, really—originated from humankind's desire to imitate his natural surroundings. "The soundscape is far too complex for human speech to duplicate," R. Murray Schafer writes, in *The Soundscape: Our Sonic Environment and the Tuning of the World*, "and so it is in music alone that man finds that true harmony of the inner and outer world."

And so it is with "Close to the Edge." The drone, the *om*, is key to understanding *CTTE*. The album's nearly nineteen-minute title track opens with these nature sounds, which we interpret as the river, the *om* in *Siddhartha*. The actual noises on record seem so organic they could have been garnered from field recordings captured by Offord and Advision staff, but were "actually all from stock recordings," Offord says.

For most of the *CTTE* sessions, Offord played George Martin to Anderson's John Lennon. Well, Martin, Ken Scott, and Geoff Emerick all rolled up into one to Anderson's John Lennon. Legend has it that the bird sounds are part of a tape loop that had an estimated length of forty feet.

"Jon always had ideas," Offord says. "Even with 'Close to the Edge,' he said, 'I'd like to put a babbling brook at the beginning of this record.' It was crazy. We went through with his ideas and it turned out to be the real signature opening of that song. The birds and babbling brook bubbling up and that's how the whole thing started."

What strikes me when going over these tracks is the constant steam of noise I hear (or *think* I hear), particularly in "Close to the Edge." There seems to be a low pulse that pervades entire sections of the track, giving it a strange, mystical atmosphere. You could say this is the actual *om* in a track meant to symbolize such. It also seems, at times, to interact with the psyche just below the level of conscious awareness, achieving what film editors call subliminal messaging.

Offord:

> Anytime you heard any kind of continuous noise in the background it could very well have been a loop. I know "Close to the Edge" has about four or five different loops all going on. All those little sounds you hear in the background in Yes's music, those are little loop tapes that we kind of . . . manufactured separately. The [sounds] would be on a loop tape running around the tape machine, around and around and around, and we'd fade it in at the right parts. We did a lot of that kind of stuff. That was tough, recording back then. Now all you do is hit a button on a sampler you have and Bob's your uncle.

Contributing to the low hum of the record were Squire's bass pedals. One source reported that Squire was using Hammond organ pedals to fatten the sound. "[Squire] came in one day with bass pedals," Offord remembers, although he remembers them as Moog bass pedals. "We used them in places. But, to be honest, I was a bit scared of how they might affect the vinyl, so I probably mixed them lower than I should."

Offord translated Anderson's ideas to the studio environment and helped create an audio landscape of what the singer was envisioning in his head. Instead of George Martin and EMI engineers taking snippets of tape, tossing them up in the air, and randomly pasting them back together to create the kaleidoscopic sounds heard in "Being for the Benefit of Mr. Kite!," Offord was open to suggestions, creating sound continuums, musical and sonic entities that built on themselves in layers via loops.

Case in point: there's a low roar that begins approximately eighteen or nineteen seconds into "Close to the Edge" that increases in volume, culminating in what could be an organ or an across-the-board effect (0:56). From what I've learned, a lot of this was down to the fact that Offord had applied universal effects to the tracks. "That particular [effect] was created putting everything through a flanger and fading it in quickly," he says.

Former Advision recording engineer Gary Martin recalls Offord's approach:

> Eddy was creative in his approach and always ready to try new ideas. He wasn't really a musician, although he did play the piano a bit, I think, but had a good musical sensibility. He was always pretty relaxed and took his time and that suited Yes, who were, by and large, similar in temperament. Eddy and the band knew each other and studio staff over quite a long time and they trusted him, likewise ELP, which made sessions relaxed and enjoyable. I'd say that it was Eddy's ability to make sessions fun that brought about a spontaneous creative atmosphere that had as much effect as his technical inventiveness, although that was considerable.

As Bill Bruford is fond of saying, the art is in concealing the art. The track is so built-up you may have trouble pinpointing the exact instrumentation being used at any given moment. The genius of Eddy Offord often precludes any search for the truth. It's difficult to discern if one is hearing keyboard, electric guitar, bass, bass synth pedals, reverse audio . . .

"Eddy was an inventive engineer and often came up with novel ideas," Martin says. "He was rather like a mischievous elf and was full of energy and fun, usually fuelled further by smoking dope, which he did much of the time. The Yes sessions weren't as druggy as those with ELP, however. As I recall it, the members of Yes varied in how much they partook. I know that Rick and I abstained and preferred to go off to the local pub."

"A lot of [Jon's] ideas weren't that great," Offord says, "plus Jon wasn't really a musician. Everyone looked down on him a little bit, because he wasn't as advanced musically as the rest of the band was. But in some ways, that is what made him great. He would break all the rules musically and come up with ideas that, sometimes, were different and good but made no sense musically, I guess. . . . A lot of his ideas we had discarded because they didn't do anything [for anybody]. But every one out of five ideas was a gem."

For Wakeman, however, "Jon is a clever guy, and I really think he's very unfair to himself." Anderson downplays his musical abilities, Wakeman said, because he can't read music. But was this lack of formal training a hindrance or a boon to Anderson's creative spirit? It's most assuredly the former. Anderson, who strums away on his guitar, may be more innovative and perceptive because he *doesn't* have a technical background. "It's almost like the blind man who has incredible hearing," Wakeman said.

Rayford Griffin, drummer for the AndersonPonty Band, recalls:

> There were a couple of songs that we did that we started and I did what I would do based on what I was hearing, and Jon wanted something completely and totally different. I equate it with Jon being a rock and roll guy from the 1960s and 1970s. At a time they had big budgets and could take as long as they wanted to take to make the records, and try everything under the sun. I think he comes from that school as opposed to going with the first idea. It's more of, "Hey, let's try it this way. Let's try it upside down. Let's try it sideways. Let's try it upside down and sideways."

"I kind of . . . developed a rule: nine times out of ten, if someone had an idea we would try it," Offord says. "There would be big arguments about this. 'Should we try this?' 'Yes, we should.' 'No, we shouldn't.' My idea was, if anyone has an idea, we should try it, but it has to work in the foreground and not be put it in the background. Rather than argue about it . . . we'll check it out. It was very easy to say with Jon, 'That is a crazy idea. Don't even try it.'"

Details, details . . .

Prior to the extensive sessions at Advision, Yes conducted rehearsals at Una Billings' dance school in Shepherd's Bush. In attempting to gather more background on the Billings, I tried to contact her, but was told by a former student that she had passed a few years ago. Although Bruford had called it a rotten place (he used the word "poxy," actually), the dance school, whether Billings was aware of it or not, played a pivotal role in the development of British progressive rock in the early 1970s.

It's well known that the longest song on *CTTE*, the title track, was pasted together via edits. "In the early days we would record two minutes, three minutes, one minute," Anderson told me. "I mean, 'Close to the Edge' is full of edits, but we knew where we were heading. 'Awaken' was done in five parts, because we knew what it was and when rehearsed it and then performed it. As you get older you get more mature about performance."

But this is where the *CTTE* story becomes a bit sketchy. How do rehearsals dovetail with the process of editing and splicing bits of tape together? If a band bothers to work hard in the rehearsal room, shouldn't the material be worked out well in advance of entering the studio?

Editing pieces may have been part of the plan all along, given the band's previous experiences working on *Fragile* with Offord. It's likely that the band got the basic skeleton of the tracks ready while at the Billings dance school then tinkered with them in the studio, where Offord performed his studio magic/experimentation in collaboration with the band. What followed was overdubbing.

I checked with Offord about the chronology and accuracy of this process, and he told me this: "Jon wrote songs with a limited guitar technique. But I think in some ways that was also a strength, because he didn't stick to any basic musical rules. Chris and Bill spent many hours in the studio arranging the drums and bass on various sections."

The Rhino Records and Steven Wilson–remastered reissues of *CTTE* contain the studio run-through of the third track on the record, "Siberian Khatru," alternately titled "Siberia." At the opening of the track, Bruford keeps time and counts off to enable Howe to enter with his famous funky country-blues-rock riff.

Offord says that he tried to keep the sound as live as possible, because he believed Yes was great onstage. "I liked the live sound a lot, so I had individual wooden stages built for the band and put in [at] Advision," he says. "[I was] trying to get a live sound and getting away from the dead studio sound."

It was once believed by the author that if a studio run-through existed for "Siberian Khatru," it might indicate that "Khatru" is the most "live" track on the entire record. However, Offord has indicated something slightly different in relation to the entire recording process for the album.

"Only the drums and bass were kept on the basic tracks," he says. "A scratch guitar was put down, and the keyboards came later. But the band only rehearsed sections; putting it together and writing reprises . . . was done at the studio. When the recording was complete, they would have to learn how to play it all the way through."

CTTE was not completed in a single burst of activity. Far from it. It took weeks—months—of painstaking studio work to finish. The band members always maintained that they performed concerts throughout the recording process, but according to tour archives, Yes came off the road in late March 1972.

Howe seemed to defend this way of recording in an interview I conducted with him in 2007:

> Some of the best records are made between your life—in the cracks of your life, while your life is going on and while you're doing concerts. Not these exclusive *prima donna* times when you have just got to be recording. As if recording is just one thing to do. That is complete nonsense, really. It had nothing to do with that at all. It was a challenging opportunity for us to push the boundaries further with Eddy Offord, who at the time was magnificent. Really, we were just trying to push the boundaries for Yes. *The Yes Album* came out and that did very well . . . and it encouraged us to be experimental again and just go for it.

I attempted to track down an official Advision log, documenting clients who rented time/space at the studio. Initially I'd queried some English recording studio researchers, one of whom told me that I've been, and I quote, "seduced by various Beatles books. This would have very much been an EMI thing." My guess is that no such log exists for Advision, and former Advision recording engineer Gary Martin confirmed this to be true, as far as he knew.

Records and reports indicate that some recording took place in February 1972 (on the 1st and 2nd), but as I've deduced already, this was likely for the single for "America." On February 10, it appears Bruford and Wakeman went into the Trident Studios to cut material for the latter's upcoming *Six Wives* album. Again, records are a bit unclear, but in April 1972 (5th, 13th, 27th), Bruford was busy recording at Advision or Trident with Wakeman.

On June 1–8 the band did more recording for *Close to the Edge*, including a swipe at "Siberian Khatru." The recording sheet on the box for the master reels of *Close to the Edge* indicates that "Khatru" had been recorded on at least one day—June 3, 1972. On June 11–18, Yes continued to record at Advision, and on June 25–29 they were finishing recording of *Close to the Edge*.

Anderson said that the band had "worked at it" (*Close to the Edge*) for two months, which I take to mean that the band was writing and arranging the material for that time period, dating back to the spring 1972, at the latest. The band had rehearsed every day, or so Anderson said, "then we spent the last month in the studio."

"Yes's albums took so long that they pretty much moved into Studio One for weeks on end," Martin says.

On July 1, *NME* reported that Yes was "keeping the two studios active" at Advision; by July 15 the group was "still in residence." However, by the week of July 22, 1972, Yes was in the mixing stage—at the same time, incidentally, as Gentle Giant moved into Advision to record *Octopus*.

The sessions were not only long but were apparently nerve-racking. As if handling the personalities—or egos—the many different recording needs of each individual weren't enough, Offord and his team were tasked with keeping track of every scrap of tape containing recorded audio.

Bruford saw the construction of the album as being shaped less by a collaborative spirit than by negotiation. More than one individual might have an idea for a single song. The trick was fusing three or four different sections into a whole—and making it sound coherent. This led to bits of analog tape being littered across Advision's control room.

In a *Melody Maker* column that invited readers to ask their favorite musicians questions regarding their lives and music, Anderson admitted that *Fragile* was recorded over the course of five weeks with the band working ten hours a day, five days a week, at a cost of $30,000. If only this was the case for *Close to the Edge*.

Advision's Studio One featured a Scully sixteen-track two-inch recorder and an eight-track one-inch unit with variable speed control functions. Mono recording units were also available to clients. (*Close to the Edge* was recorded on a sixteen-track machine. Yes wouldn't bump up to twenty-four-track machine until *Tales from Topographic Oceans*.)

"The mixing console at Advision was built by Dag Felner, but it was a thirty-channel board going to a twenty-four-track tape machine, which I think was an MCI," Offord remembers, possibly contradicting some other accounts.

"The main Studio One mixing room wasn't very big," remembers Martin. "There was a bank of large JBL speakers in front of the mixing desk and a small back room for the tape decks and editing. There was a large glass panel between the mixing room and a large—sixty-piece-orchestra large—studio, so engineers and producers could see the whole space."

Back in the early 1970s, advertised hourly rates for recording music at Advision was thirty pounds sterling (around seventy-five dollars at the time) for eight-track recording. (It'd cost you two pounds more an hour for sixteen-track.) In 1972, that was nothing to sneeze at.

Martin:

> Yes recorded with many, sometimes very many, over-dubs. Sometimes these were quite short and each track of the tape might have numerous different parts one after the other. Eddy was a wizard at resetting the sound of each channel while mixing. Yes's instruments and kit were good quality and, as you know, they were virtuoso players, so the recorded instrumentation was precise and crisp. All of the above meant that the multitrack tape was clean and the orchestral sound was made as much during the mixing as during the original playing. The mixing on Yes's albums took by far the greater part of the whole studio time. They—especially Chris Squire and Eddy—were meticulous.

Offord's veritable symphony of layered tracks and ability to seamlessly stitch together distinct musical passages became the hallmark of the producer's work. But because there were so many musical bits to choose from, the process was often bogged down with too many options.

The writing may have been more collaborative than ever—and the end result the most glorified record Yes ever committed to tape—but a democratic recording and editing process can take ages.

One story bears repeating, if I can. Yes lore dictates that slices of tape were resting in the trash, presumably to be carted away by the cleaning staff hired by Advision Studios. If it were not for our quick-thinking producer and boy wonder, "Close to the Edge" would not have appeared as we know it.

As is typical regarding the details of any great yarn, the exact time, date, and persons of interest seem to have been obscured by generalities and vagueness. The story goes that the blurry-eyed, half-awake musicians, the leftovers from yet another long, draining session, canvassed the garbage pales, getting their hands (really) dirty in search of the missing piece of tape. Someone, we don't know who, noticed that a missing piece or missing pieces of an integral part of "Close to the Edge" was in the dustbin. The piece or pieces were recovered, saving the day just before trash pick-up.

It's been told a few different ways, and two versions may have been conflated to make one mega-rumor, one thinks. Wakeman told radio DJ Redbeard that the band had entered into the studio one day and tracked the entirety of the last section of the song. "The bin for the scrap tapes that we didn't want was out in the garbage . . . chopped up," Wakeman said. "Eddy had taken the piece that he thought was the right piece, and it was the *wrong* piece."

Wakeman mused that the sliver of tape selected was the best performance, but the sonics didn't match up with what had been edited together prior to the new addition. "We all listened to it and looked at each other and there was nothing we could do about it, short of going in and starting recording again," he told Redbeard.

But achieving a similar sound was virtually impossible. "Now the interesting thing is, after about four or five listens, it sounded perfectly natural," Wakeman said.

Uh-oh. Little red flags are starting to go up. This seems like quite an elaborate story.

Let's take the quality of audio issue first, shall we?

Can the casual listener discern the audio disparity? I had asked, among others, mastering engineer Steve Hoffman and engineer

Stephen Marsh, who'd worked together on Audio Fidelity's 2013 version of *CTTE*, and they didn't seem to indicate that the condition of the tapes was an issue. However, they did, in an indirect way, confirm Wakeman's story.

Marsh:

> The thing about *Close to the Edge* is that the material is pretty coalesced already, in terms of arrangement and orchestration. Sonically, it has a pastiche quality. There was a little bit of wrangling to try to get different sections to sound well together. But . . . the beauty of digital is that we can do it over and over and over again and these tape machines all have rewind on them [laughs]. You can go back and try different things and find what works. But it's usually that way whenever you have a lot of edits on the master tape where they have edited chunks of this mix and pieces of that mix, guitar solo from this version, and they edit them together, which a lot of material is generally like that on the actual master tape. Multitrack tapes were always generally chopped up. Usually they get one master and then get the mix off that.
>
> If you had a book where every chapter was written by a different person, and if you had a different person's voice and a different person's tone and vocabulary, you'd need an editor to go through, at the end, to make sure that everything feels like it came from one pen, even if it obviously didn't. That is quite often what mastering becomes: you are trying to interpret the actions of different mixers and producers and engineers at different times and coalesce that material.

The recording, overdubbing, and mixing processes can be exhausting and confusing, especially when an enormous number of tracks are involved. On "And You and I" alone, Howe plays multiple guitars/stringed instruments, including more than one acoustic. By the time the band reached *Close to the Edge*, layering three guitars was a drop in the bucket. It's easy to see how things can go awry.

But was a missing piece of tape really resting in the dustbin outside on the streets of London? Could one of rock's greatest works have been relegated to the trash heap of history?

Bruford, in his book *The Autobiography*, tells a similar tale. It's such an amazing story I felt compelled to authenticate the veracity of it with Offord, who was there for every minute of the recordings.

"Editing . . . tape was always an adventure," he says. "You'd try it one way, but if it didn't feel natural, you'd have to find the piece that you thought was trash and rethink it. I don't really remember what Rick is talking about, because we never left the studio until everyone was happy. But he could be right."

Did any of the tale of the tape really happen, I wondered?

"It's a good story, anyway," Offord concludes.

There have been those who had encouraged me to just "go with it"—Offord included. "I do remember doing an edit while smoking a cigarette," he says. "The edit was great, but I accidently burned a hole in the tape. That edit had to be re-thought."

Despite all the madness, Atlantic was (largely) hands off during the recording process, aside from the usual label B.S. of wanting some form of single to market. Most of the band admits that the record business was very different than what it would become in the coming decades. Yet, another historical aspect of this story that can't be—and won't be—repeated.

"It was like a blessing to be able to go into the studio and create," Anderson told me, "and not have anybody tell you what to do. And that was what was happening in the early 1970s. In a way we were free to do what we wanted and were capable enough to create a certain kind of music, and at the same time [were] professional enough to know when to stop, because all you wanted to do then was take it on the road and perform it onstage."

Yes Sound

Among the major elements of the Yes sound are the multipart vocals and vocal harmonies, such as we hear in "South Side of the Sky" from *Fragile*, the "I Get Up, I Get Down" section of "Close to the Edge," and the "Disillusion" from "Starship Trooper."

Anderson's voice has been reported as an "alto tenor." He's denied time and time again that he sings falsetto.

Offord:

He was always nervous, and we would always try to find ways for him to relax. One day he came into the studio [Morgan Studios] and said, "When I am at home and singing in my bathroom, it sounds good. But I come into the studio and . . . ." So we built him a bathroom in the studio, with tiles and everything. In general, as time went by he got more relaxed. In the beginning he was more nervous about his lack of musical education, but I think as time went by, and [Jon] built an alliance with Steve, who provided more of the musical things, he become more confident.

Offord compared working with Greg Lake and Jon Anderson as vocalists:

Greg had a really good voice. Maybe not quite the range some singers had but he had a very pleasing voice and I found recording him was a lot easier than recording Jon Anderson, because he could deliver . . . we would go fix lines and parts, but he could deliver a pretty good performance. He could deliver a verse and sing it quite well with maybe one or two little mistakes. Then there were times when he did the multitracking thing, with like twelve tracks of some kind of background thing. Greg was very proficient. I think, bass player for bass player, I think Chris might have been a little bit better. But vocally he was really good. His ideas were always good.

"Yours Is No Disgrace" from *The Yes Album* is an interesting study—and an interesting hybrid. While the first vocal section features Anderson's voice(s) as well as what sound like support vocals from Squire (starting 1:30 through 1:55), later in the song it appears that Anderson goes it alone.

On *Close to the Edge*, Howe and Squire provide backing, support, or counterpoint vocals. A cluster or overlapping vocal effect—not really a "round"—can be heard throughout the record. These are found in each of the three songs and, in particular, in "Siberian Khatru," during the interval from 1:35 through 1:42, as the word river comes into focus.

At other moments, such as at 3:06 in "Siberian Khatru," Anderson's high-pitched voice adds to the atmosphere of the song—a single faint vocal line trailing in background. However, in many cases he performed all of the harmonized vocals himself, his voice having been multitracked.

The concept for multipart harmonies in Yes's music likely originated with Anderson and Squire, as they had such a history of harmonies (even dating back to the Mabel Greer's Toyshop days). Band influences—everyone from Simon and Garfunkel and Clouds to former band members, such as Clive Bayley—were sprinkled over the musical sonic stew and stirred vigorously.

I do not think it's out of line to say that a generation of art-pop bands, such as 10cc, XTC, ELO, Queen, and Klaatu, followed in the footsteps of Yes and its studio wizardry. 10cc achieved three Top 40 hits in the US, having reached #2 with "I'm Not in Love," which locked into that position for three weeks, and #5 with "The Things We Do for Love."

Although we must acknowledge the debt 10cc has to the Beatles, the vocal clusters, the abstract lyrical themes, the tape looping and studio experimentation were part and parcel of Yes's M.O. In fact, without tape looping, 10cc's "I'm Not in Love," written by Eric Stewart, wouldn't exist in the form we all know it.

But props certainly should go to Yes and Offord. As true trailblazers in the early 1970s, Offord and, specifically, Anderson each played off the other's creative ideas and musical strengths.

Martin:

> Jon was—is?—very spontaneous and intuitive as a person, and singing overdubbed vocals against a prerecorded track wouldn't have been as comfortable for him as going with the flow of a live band. I remember one day he told me that he had been to see Miles Davis at Ronnie Scott's club the night before and was appalled that Davis didn't engage with the other members of his band, and no one smiled at each other while they were playing. It would definitely have been Jon's preference to feel and engage with the mood of the rest of the band while playing—not so easy in a studio setting. There was some double track-

ing of vocals too, which meant being precise with inflection—not something he'd have needed to do live.

The combination of wide-ranging instrumentation was another melodic strand of Yes's joyous noise. On *Close to the Edge* in particular, we hear harpsichord, steel guitar, Coral electric sitar, Mellotron, Moog, various percussion objects, bass pedals, and more. Each demanded a certain process and a certain amount of special attention during the recording process.

"Close to the Edge" has a vaguely Eastern bent. Just before the 3:54 mark—the lead-in to the verse—the timbre of Bruford's toms remind me of tabla or a chalice drum. Adding to this Eastern vibe, Howe strums a Coral Sitar electric guitar.

"It was always a question of who was in the band at the time, who was willing to listen to all kinds of music, from gamelan to Indian music to African drum rhythms," Jon Anderson told me.

According to Tom Wheeler's *American Guitars: An Illustrated History*, the Danelectro Coral electric sitar's "Sitarmatic" bridge helps to produce string buzz reminiscent of the traditional Indian instrument. An additional baker's dozen of "drone" strings are tuned in half-steps. (Danelectro also made an electric sitar without drone strings, its neck and body shape closer to that of the traditional instrument.)

Howe expected to use the Coral sitar all the way through *Close to the Edge*. It was not to be. He found he wasn't as comfortable on the sitar guitar as he was on a standard electric guitar, and thought his improvising would suffer.

East certainly meets West on *Close to the Edge*. The most outstanding and unusual instrument employed by Yes was the pipe organ at St. Giles Cripplegate Church in London, heard at approximately 12:12 into the title track. Howe had initially envisioned the organ solo as a guitar part but had a rethink, believing church organ would sound better. (Anderson, too, takes credit for the inclusion of the church organ section of the song.)

The pipe organ solo in "Close to the Edge" has always been one of the most hair-raising moments in Yes's music history. In the broader context of the song, it could represent a moment of clarity—an awakening and exaltation. Interestingly, Hermann Hesse too was enamored of the church pipe organ.

When the music breaks down and Wakeman plays twee notes, dewdrops are heard—as if they've been running through the entire track, buried by the massive sound. There's a dramatic pause at approximately 13:51 as chords are held and then a flurry of church organ and Moog notes flood the sonic foreground. Moog notes blossom out of the church organ foundation and climb to the sky and cascade.

In general, pipe organs both add to the architecture of the room and exploit a venue's architectural detail to produce the overwhelming, exalted sound with which we are so familiar. Steven Wilson, who remixed *CTTE* for 5.1 surround sound, indicated to *Sound and Vision* magazine editor Mike Mettler that "all of the reverberation is natural"—a condition of the church.

Current scholarship hasn't revealed when the organ was installed in St. Giles, although it was certainly prior to the seventeenth century, according to Ann Marsden Thomas, the church's current director of music.

Ian Bell, an acoustician, formerly of Mander Organs, who claims to have been responsible for the "new Cripplegate pipework in 1970, and for supervising the site tonal work matching that to the older work," worked to give the St. Giles organ a "spicy and characterful sound . . . which I guess appealed to Rick."

Wakeman tells of a funny story about booking time at Cripplegate for "Jane Seymour," a song that appeared on his *Six Wives* record, which features the same church organ. The church asked for no money from Wakeman or A&M Records to record there. However, or so the story goes, when he arrived with engineer Paul Tregurtha and Terry O'Neil of A&M, the vicar mentioned an appeal to restore the roof. O'Neil pledged £2,000 (around $5,000) toward the repair.

Once recording of the organ was finished, the engineer positioned microphones in the pews to capture the ambient sound of the church. While he was setting up, the vicar explained that the pews had seen better days, and that there was another fund drive for *their* restoration . . .

"By the time we finished this album, it had became known at A&M as the album that had completely rebuilt St. Giles in Cripplegate," Wakeman told the audience during the filming of the DVD *The Legend: Live in Concert 2000*. (After cleaning the pipe organ in 2008, the church embarked upon a further eight-year fundraising campaign to raise the necessary money to complete the job.)

Despite the costs involved, Wakeman has said that the church organ wasn't recorded the way he really wanted, although it's difficult to argue with the finished results. Offord explains his approach to capturing the organ at St. Giles: "The church organ was recorded with two mikes going to a Revox tape machine inside the chapel. I moved the mikes nearer or further from the pipes to get the right amount of ambiance. I did the same thing with ELP [for 'Infinite Space']."

When the church organ is used in its proper setting (the service) it can be devastating effective and psychically transformative. The ceremony itself becomes a psychedelic and mystical experience to enhance scripture and its meanings. As some have correctly observed, at a certain point in the service, the church as a resonant building becomes a factory for the psychedelic: Incense are burned, smoke rises to the sky and dissipates; light streaming through stained-glass windows prints swathes of red, blue and yellow on the floor. The mind wanders as a recitation of prayer reaches the psychic borders of the near hypnotic.

During "Close to the Edge," Wakeman claims his position as the master of ceremonies—at the nexus of the psychedelic experience and liturgical music. The mechanics of the machinery is futuristic, and its sounds are majestic, heavenly. "Close to the Edge," then, has been rightly elevated to the level of the liturgical.

In his study *Progressive Rock, "Close to the Edge," and the Boundaries of the Style*, author and scholar John Covach does a great job of describing some of the similarities of "Close to the Edge" and European art-music and liturgy. "While the use of church organ in itself creates a reference to art music," he writes, "the harmonic progression and voice leading are almost stereotypically 'classical.'"

We're aware of the baroque or classical qualities of Yes's music prior to *Close to the Edge*, from the classical stylings of Howe's "Mood for the Day" to Wakeman's chilly piano passage in "South Side of the Sky" and the keyboardist's interpretation of "Cans and Brahms." We're also aware that Wakeman uses harpsichord in "Siberian Khatru," and of the liturgical chants heard throughout "Siberian Khatru" and "Close to the Edge."

Like many classical symphonies, "Close to the Edge" was composed in four movements (discounting the "sounds of nature" intro), with the final section, "Seasons of Man," containing a recapitulation of sorts of main melody of the first verses.

Earlier, I talked about Edward Macan and his theory about the "Close to the Edge" and the sonata form. As Cedric Thorpe Davie writes in his book *Musical Structure and Design*, "The contrast of two tonalities, and their ultimate reconciliation, is the fundamental basis of the sonata form."

There's really only one question to ask: does "The Solid Time of Change" meet the requirements for a theoretical sonata form? To be fair, it kinda does and kinda doesn't.

"The Solid Time of Change" does perform some of the functions of the sonata form in that it presents themes but also juxtaposes differing moods. In a very simplistic sense, we jump from the jazz-rock opening to the vocal chorus (the "ahhh's" at 1:59 and 2:10, respectively), which ultimately give way to the main theme, just as the song experiences an upshift to the key of D.

The main theme is stated in both D major and D minor in the early parts of "The Solid Time of Change." The tension between and the shifts from major to minor and back again—a device employed in many classical works—generate great emotional impact in "Close to the Edge."

Furthermore, Yes—and specifically Anderson—was influenced by Jean Sibelius's Symphony No. 5. While it is dangerous to compare Sibelius's Fifth to "Close to the Edge," if we just scratch the surface a tiny bit, we may make some unintended discoveries. For one thing, the Fifth is legendary for having had a long creation process, much like "Close to the Edge," and is considered one of the greatest classical works of the twentieth century. "Close to the Edge" is arguably rock's "classical music" and one of its most epic works.

Secondly, Sibelius employed the common tactic of recapitulation of themes, connecting the first and the third (and final) movements. Also, Symphony No. 5 begins in 12/8, but by the second movement it slips into 3/2—just as "Close to the Edge" does in its second section, "Total Mass Retain."

In addition, the first movement has musicologists in knots over whether it's a traditional sonata. At the least, Sibelius broke with form. The consensus among the sources I consulted about this issue was that Symphony No. 5 dispenses with the traditional sonata form, although some seem to indicate otherwise.

These may be sketchy details in the grand scheme, but the perceived links between Yes, Sibelius, Symphony No. 5, and "Close to the Edge," which we may find suspect at first blush, grow stronger the longer we linger on these once-believed tenuous ties.

What's fascinating is that Sibelius and Yes both looked to nature for inspiration. For Yes, the "river" of *Siddhartha* represented a metaphor for spiritual journey; Symphony No. 5 is famous for the "swan theme" of its third movement.

Hannu Lintu, chief conductor of the Finnish Radio Symphony orchestra, conducted the complete cycle of Sibelius's symphonies in 2015. He says:

> The Fifth is certainly the most obvious example of [Sibelius's] intense relationship with nature, but Sibelius was not really "a man of wilds" who spent his time roaming the vast forests of Karelia. Most often, the countryside was a place where he could work in peace; it wasn't necessarily a starting point for composing. The sixteen swans of the Fifth Symphony are a rare exception. It's one of those occasions in which Sibelius was inspired by a specific "natural wonder." He had a profoundly spiritual attitude to nature: he did not actually describe it. He concentrated on the links between our inner world and nature. For Sibelius, man, artist, and nature were the same thing.

Does "rock's classical music" merely boil down to musicians using Romantic classical music strategies for their own original material? After Howe had begun sketching a few different pieces of music, it became apparent that the band would go for broke with its next studio record. Yes would compose a long-form piece, a kind of rock symphony—*its* Symphony No. 1, if you will.

One of the most important lessons in Yes's evolution as songwriters "was the idea of structure," Anderson told me. "That came from me listening to a lot of Dvorak and Holst and Tchaikovsky. [I was asking] 'How did they put all of this music together? How did it work?'"

In one case, the band formulated an entire subsection based

on one line of lyrics, as in "I Get Up, I Get Down." Vocals lines are stated earlier in the song and evolve to become more elaborate and harmonized when they reappear. In addition, the band does a great job of extracting a portion or a lick or a melodic line, expanding upon it, and "blowing it up," elevating the part to a main theme.

The main theme is presented in the first delineated subsection of the song, "The Solid Time of Change." Melodic ideas are developed until we come to the "I Get Up, I Get Down" section, which is unlike nearly everything that has preceded it. A recapitulation of sorts occurs in "Seasons of Man," albeit in a different key.

The development of these themes, or even variation of themes, is a page straight out of the classical music composition playbook—and it appears in all three songs on *CTTE*. All of this may sound very detailed, but it underscores how Yes gradually grew into its symphonic aspirations and tendencies.

Certainly the big sound the band achieves starting at 8:14 in "Close to the Edge," with two electric guitars, Moog, organ, grinding and deep bass, layered vocals, and jazz-inflected drums, is symphonic, and perhaps more so than the orchestrated, keyboard-laden sound the group had on its previous two records.

Much of the same instrumentation found in the first movement can be detected in the final section, "Seasons of Man" (including Mellotron wisps, funky Coral Sitar guitar, bass, piano, guitar, and drums, with Bruford pounding out a variation of the pattern he played during the earlier verses of the song). Anderson's voice is multitracked for a brief chant, beginning 16:13.

The second verse of "Seasons of Man" contains Anderson's excessively high vocal-cluster harmony. Howe and Squire sing support vocals (circa 16:35–17:02), with Howe generally in left channel and Squire generally in the right.

The music comes to a virtual halt from 17:10 through 17:12, as Anderson's multitracked vocals carry the day. Howe has said that to perform this section of the song live, the band needed to drop the key of the final section from G minor down to F. It seems the section was just too difficult for Anderson to sing properly without his vocal cords straining and cracking, night after night.

"They couldn't sustain performing it in that key," says Mike Tiano, editor of *Notes from the Edge.* "It doesn't have that same impact, though. Whereas on the album it just floors you. I remember listening to this with friends and it was very emotional."

As we near the end of the track, Wakeman's repetitive and minimalistic keys spiral in, opening a new "vortex." He plays a line starting around 17:21 that sounds as though it's being performed on a piano—at first blush, anyway.

The main melodic element (beginning at 17:40) fades, and the sounds of nature recover the sonic foreground. For a twenty-second window, the piano, or whatever it is, becomes more and more orchestral. I had asked Offord what this misty, layered sound was; he told me: it "might have been organ, and maybe Mellotron."

Fading keys eventually give way to bird chirpings and the sound of water movement—and that constant background hum, which is reminiscent of the opening *om*. The sonic masterpiece evaporates, and there ends "Close to the Edge."

The minimalistic aspects of the ending hint at Wakeman's later (largely) solo piano works of the mid- and late 1980s, 1990s, and 2000s, such as *Country Airs, Nights Airs, Sea Airs, Preludes to a Century, Visions* (a.k.a. *Visions of Paradise*), *Chronicles of Man*, and *Amazing Grace*, among others.

Howe has made an interesting connection between the band's dedication to eating organic foods, the natural sounds, and the self-reflection inherent to the record. Relying on the bounty of the earth, of not being carnivorous, may have had a hand in the creation of the more new age-y aspects of *CTTE*.

Furthermore, if we categorize the nature sounds heard in "Close to the Edge" as "new age" or "ambient," then Yes was certainly following in the footsteps of Walter Carlos's *Sonic Seasonings*, a major Yes influence around the time of *CTTE*, ahead of Kitaro, Brian Eno, Tangerine Dream, the Windham Hill records catalog, and Mike Oldfield.

Sonic Seasonings features field recordings of birdsong and wind and insect noises, as well as drones and ambient music, or what would become known as "ambient music," produced by synthesizer. This visionary and immersive sound was something Yes wanted to—and did—achieve with "Close to the Edge." Yes was obviously taken with the structure of Carlos's music (one song per side), a model the group would adopt for *Tales from Topographic Oceans*.

By the Numbers

The number three is crucial to understanding the title track and the entire album. Consider this: there are, of course, three songs on the record. But beyond that, there is what author Joseph Mileck in his book *Hermann Hesse: Life and Art* identifies as a "triple rhythm" that shapes the *Siddhartha* narrative.

Throughout the course of the novel, Siddhartha explores the realms of the mind, flesh, and soul in twelve chapters, four dedicated to each realm. In a similar way, Siddhartha, Govinda, and Gotama Buddha represent the different sides of Hesse's idealized self. (We've also discussed the three deities associated with *om*.)

As if picking up on the pulse of the novel, much of the music on *Close to the Edge* was written and performed in "3," or some multiple thereof. Three occurs in different variations and forms throughout the record. Squire's dropped-D bass line in "And You and I," for instance, opens in 3/4, providing the root, the very heartbeat, of the song. It does switch to common time, even half-time throughout, but it later returns to 3/4 and finishes in this time signature.

The bass line of the opening and many of the instrumental passages of "Siberian Khatru" flip back and forth between 4/4 and 3/4, while "Close to the Edge" is all over the map—12/8, 15/8, 9/8, 6/4, 3/4, 3/2.

The polymetric tension created by Squire playing 3/2 against Bruford's 4/2 at the opening of the second movement of "Close to the Edge," "Total Mass Retain," stretches time and creates a kind of sliding sensation. And, for good measure, Howe blasts out notes in triplet fashion; as Rubin surmises, he even employs bluesy/jazzy triple stops (playing three notes simultaneously across three strings), in the crazed, partially spontaneous Mahavishnu Orchestra–like opening section of "Close to the Edge."

Anderson's multitracked vocal harmony parts in the introduction of "Close to the Edge"—the "ahh's" or the "*om*'s"—occur three times, at 1:59, 2:10, and 2:54. (These chants were said to be Anderson's idea.)

Drummer Jack DeJohnette, an influence on Bruford, once described to *Modern Drummer* magazine the out-of-body experience he feels when performing a certain style of jazz. He was referring to the contact he had with John Coltrane in the 1960s and the spiritual nature of 'Trane's music and its ability to transport one into another mental state, an altered state.

DeJohnette admitted that the weightlessness he feels when he's in the zone directly relates to cyclical, repetitive rhythms. The three-beat jazz pulse has a lot to do with this, he indicated. Some have called this three-beat pattern the heartbeat of jazz. It is related to an African 6/8 rhythm, an ancient rhythm, said to have spiritual and healing qualities, that eventually led to the 6/4 swing feel.

In "Close to the Edge," both the bass and guitar begin in 12/8—a variant, you could say, of 6/8 and 6/4. The song does dip, briefly, into common time and also 3/4, and the bass slips into 6/4 during the appearance of the song's main theme. With a few exceptions, including a twist around a 15/8 rhythm for one measure, the verse of the song stays in 6/4 until the chorus (which, for the bass, is largely in 3/2).

The cyclical rhythms and odd tempos induce a hypnotic experience, helping to create what author and Rock and Roll Hall of Fame musician Gary Lachman dubbed the "magical effects of music." These effects, says Lachman, can "alter consciousness and create psychic openings to other worlds."

"'Close to the Edge' put you in a trance, especially when it got quiet and then there was this water dripping in the background," says William Sager, an Internet maven who's done work for Night Flight programming.

If music is a form of meditation induced by chords and rhythms, then the actual recording of Close to the Edge not only centers on self-realization but guides the listener on a path toward gnosis, spiritual healing, and self-discovery . . .

Mahavishnu Orchestra Influence

At the opening of "Close to the Edge," the *om* gives way to a Mahavishnu Orchestra–like jazz-rock craziness, led by the guitar acrobatics of Steve Howe. This is Howe at his most wild—all over the map and playing with a fierceness and abandon that implies atonality. (Bruford keeps pace with his best Elvin Jones/Max Roach/Jack DeJohnette cymbal work.) This jazz-rock or "Mahavishnu" section of "Close to the Edge" seems to reflect the turbulence and churning waters of the river mentioned in *Siddhartha*.

Much later in the song, we see a kind of recurrence of this Mahavishnu section, with a furious organ solo by Wakeman. These two solos bookend the song. Yes revered the Mahavishnu Orchestra, not only for the texture of its music and the technical dexterity of its members but also for their improvisational chops.

The opening improv section of "Close to the Edge" provided a wonderful jumping off point for the rest of the song. Howe loved to improvise and indicated that he had not bothered learning how to read musical notation, and that sheet music and tablature left him somewhat cold. It might be astounding for some to think that a piece such as "Close to the Edge," with all its complexity and "outside" sonic qualities, was written without many of the main songwriters even knowing how to read music very well, if at all.

Rock musicians have always had circuitous routes around the more technical or academic aspects of song creation. Howe would often come up with ideas and record them, at home, on a Revox tape machine or a cassette recorder when the band was on the road. Without a background in reading musical notation, he had to memorize his parts (as did Anderson).

The irony in all of this is that the Mahavishnu Orchestra—the band that inspired Yes—didn't always adhere to the improvisational model that was the very basis of the band's mission statement. Tracks on 1971's *The Inner Mounting Flame* such as "Meeting of the Spirits," "Dawn," "The Noonward Race," "Vital Transformation," and "The Dance of Maya" appear to be at least partly rehearsed. "One Word," from 1973's *Birds of Fire*, presents obvious improvisational elements as well as a recapitulation of musical motifs. A theme, or more precisely a partial theme, is stated at the beginning of the song and then reprised and expanded upon during the Indo-jazz-rock closing section, which contains unison lead lines.

The protagonists (or were they competitors?)—guitarist John "Mahavishnu" McLaughlin, keyboardist Jan Hammer, and electric violinist Jerry Goodman—"trade fours" throughout the middle section of the song as bassist Rick Laird and drummer Billy Cobham hold down the funky groove. Even when the music is at its loosest, there appears to been some forethought and attention to band unity.

As McLaughlin, Hammer, and Goodman converse, the time elapsing between each cycle of "fours" shortens, until the individual riffs overlap and intertwine. When the musical interplay reaches a fever pitch, lead lines are played in both simultaneity and harmony. After the intensity of this section, Cobham's drum solo

Chris Squire (*back row center*) with fellow choristers in St. Andrew's Church, Kingsbury, northwest London. "[Squire] sang treble with the choir for over four years," says his former choirmaster, Barry Rose. Andrew Pryce Jackman (*back row, far right*) was a member of Squire's bands the Selfs and the Syn.

Time and a Word was released in the wake of Peter Banks's exit from Yes. Pictured here are two versions of the cover art: the British edition (*right*), and its North American counterpart (*left*) featuring Steve Howe (*standing, far right*), who did not appear on the album.

Steve Howe with his Portuguese Vachalia guitar at the University of Vermont, February 1972.
(Photo from Ariel vol. 85, *1972, Special Collections, University of Vermont Libraries.)*

Close to the Edge: the pinnacle of the 1970s British prog-rock movement?

As the LP label denotes, the *Close of the Edge* album was a collaborative effort. All arrangements "by Yes."

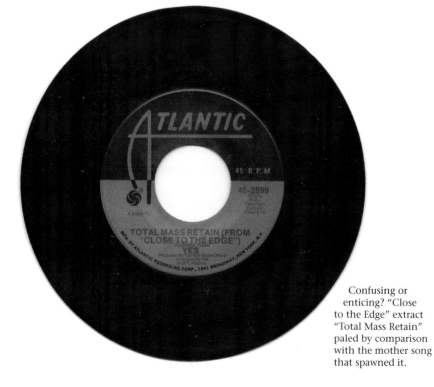

Confusing or enticing? "Close to the Edge" extract "Total Mass Retain" paled by comparison with the mother song that spawned it.

Gold Records for 1972

Singles

DAY DREAMING · Aretha Franklin
Atlantic

THE LION SLEEPS TONIGHT · Robert John
Atlantic

SUNSHINE · Jonathan Edwards
Atco

FIRST TIME EVER I SAW YOUR FACE · Roberta Flack
Atlantic

WHERE IS THE LOVE · Donny Hathaway/Roberta Flack
Atlantic

I'LL BE AROUND · The Spinners
Atlantic

Albums

EXILE ON MAIN STREET · Rolling Stones
Rolling Stones

YOUNG, GIFTED & BLACK · Aretha Franklin
Atlantic

AMAZING GRACE · Aretha Franklin
Atlantic

FIRST TAKE · Roberta Flack
Atlantic

QUIET FIRE · Roberta Flack
Atlantic

FRAGILE · Yes
Atlantic

CLOSE TO THE EDGE · Yes
Atlantic

PICTURES AT AN EXHIBITION · Emerson, Lake & Palmer
Cotillion

TRILOGY · Emerson, Lake & Palmer
Cotillion

ROBERTA FLACK/DONNY HATHAWAY · Roberta Flack/Donny Hathaway
Atlantic

HISTORY OF ERIC CLAPTON · Eric Clapton
Atco

LIVE · Donny Hathaway
Atco

GRAHAM NASH/DAVID CROSBY · Graham Nash/David Crosby
Atlantic

MANASSAS · Stephen Stills
Atlantic

FM & AM · George Carlin
Little David

FOR THE ROSES · Joni Mitchell
Asylum

It's Been a Great Year For Atlantic!

Close to the Edge goes gold, topping off a great year for Atlantic Records.

Howe working the steel guitar during a show at Kent State University, November 19, 1972.
(Photo from the 1973 Chestnut Burr, *Kent State University Archives.)*

Squire's bass lines and Bruford's drums provided the foundation for the material on Close to the Edge.
(Photo from the 1973 Chestnut Burr, *Kent State University Archives.)*

Alan White with Yes at Kent State University, November 19, 1972.
(Photo from the 1973 Chestnut Burr, Kent State University Archives.)

Wakeman navigates a stack of keyboards onstage with Yes.
(Photo from the 1973 Chestnut Burr, Kent State University Archives.)

Wakeman returned to Australia to support his solo works, such as *The Myths and Legends of King Arthur and the Knights of the Round Table*, earning the undying support of loyal rock fans in Oz. *(Photo by Philip Morris.)*

Legendary: Yes's technically proficient and visionary concerts Down Under have since been elevated to near mythic proportions. *Left to right*: Howe, Anderson, White.
(Photo by Philip Morris.)

Into the Lens: they may have faced intense scrutiny from the press in the early goings, but members of Yes now remember their Sydney concerts as "peak performances." *Left to right*: Howe, Anderson, White, Wakeman, Squire. *(Photo by Philip Morris.)*

Sydney's Hordern Pavilion, a major stop on the Australian leg of Yes's *CTTE* tour, played host to packed crowds for two nights in 1973. *Left to right*: Howe, Anderson, Squire. *(Photo by Philip Morris.)*

Wakeman's classic sequined cape created an almost supernatural shine.
(Photo by STUDIO G/REX/Shutterstock.)

Astral Travellers: this early Yes lineup included (*clockwise from left*) guitarist Peter Banks, keyboardist Tony Kaye, lead vocalist Jon Anderson, bassist Chris Squire, percussionist/drummer Bill Bruford.
(Photo by REX/Shutterstock.)

By the mid-1970s, Yes was a creative and commercial force to be reckoned with. Pictured: Jon Anderson at Reading Festival, 1975.
(Photo by Andre Csillag/REX/Shutterstock.)

Bruford and the beat: Bill's love of jazz injected rhythmic complexity into Yes's music.
(Photo by Peter Sanders/REX/Shutterstock.)

is less an opportunity for the drummer to flash his chops than an opportunity for revelatory composition.

"Mahavishnu Orchestra, from the '70s—they were the ones that really pushed the envelope, Billy Cobham especially," Jon Anderson told me.

What's interesting is that as early as autumn 1971's *Fragile*, we find the album closer, "Heart of the Sunrise," displays something that resembles Mahavishnu's template, beginning approximately 6:52. The choreographed chaos carried over into live performance, as well, as heard on *Yessongs* and in particular the *Progeny* boxed set, the latter boasting versions recorded nearly a year to the day after *Fragile* was unleashed. (Check the Knoxville show for relatively clear separation of instrumentation and driving energy, starting at approximately 7:10.) Harmonizing and riff-jousting occurs, involving bass and multiple guitar and keyboard tracks.

And "Heart of the Sunrise" isn't alone. The lead track on *Fragile*, "Roundabout," is marked by this compositional technique as well. At first blush, this might seem like mere jamming. But beginning at approximately 5:50, at Wakeman's organ solo, there's more than just vamping going on. Of course, Howe plays chords or partial chords under Wakeman's showcase, but it's followed, again, by bass and overdubbed guitar tracks, as organ blends into the background.

Wakeman returns to the fore at 6:30, and a strange serpentine ascending/descending guitar riff weaves itself around the fabric of the song. Howe's twisting notes (6:50) diverge from the bass line, until guitar and bass synchronize via harmonization.

Granted, the action on *Fragile* is tamer than what we hear from the Mahavishnu Orchestra, but the end result places Yes (historically, anyway) ahead of the material on *Birds of Fire*. If nothing else, all of this underscores that *Birds of Fire* doesn't and didn't exist in a vacuum.

"And You and I"

When the phrase "symphonic prog rock" and Yes are mentioned in the same breath, it's usually "And You and I" we recall.

There are a few very distinctive qualities about "And You and I": the twelve-string acoustic guitar intro, Wakeman's absolutely devastating use of Mellotron, the elegant rhythmic pulse, and the mere fact that the band decided to compose the music in four movements. In fact, for a song that feels so transparent, it's amazing to discover how much went into creating the track.

I've broken down the first few moments of the song, essentially the "Cord of Life" section, to illustrate how complex, synchronized, and layered the song really is. (See *table below*)

Howe himself once described "And You and I" to me as "beautiful" and indicated that the song may have written itself, in the sense that there appeared to be a blueprint for it prior to the band ever setting foot in the studio. "This is going to be written and sound just like that," Howe told me, describing the band's compositional process.

As mind-bogglingly fluid and creative as the acoustic showcase "Mood for a Day" is, something much more resonant occurs regarding the twelve-string acoustic opening of "And You and I." Space and time collapse amid slurred neck slides, chiming tones, pregnant pauses, and faint keyboard notes spiraling toward infinity. In totality, it slightly recalls the drone of Indian music.

I have, for some time, made a connection between the hypnotic one-chord Delta blues music (and even some of the electric Chicago blues), classical Indian, Celtic music, and prog rock. Yet another shade of that infinite hum that was heard throughout "Close to the Edge."

"And You and I" (total time: 10:03)
(Total time on original LP, SD 19 133: 10:09)

Section I: "Cord of Life"

TIMING	THEME	BASIC INSTRUMENTATION	BASELINE / MELODY PITCH	WORDS
0:00-0:31		**Spoken words:** Either Offord or Mike Dunne or another engineer speaks to Howe, saying something barely audible, which is difficult to decipher—possibly "rolling tape" or something involving the "take." Howe retorts, "Okay"; **Twelve-string acoustic** ("tune-up" with harmonics); **Spiraling keys** faint in background.	E	

0:31- 1:12	"And You and I" acoustic guitar theme	Twelve-string guitar; Keys faint in background.	D	
Approx. 1:13–2:50	Verse	Bass (dropped D); Kick drum locked in with bass in 3/4 time for six-beat pattern, followed by triangle (a looped bit of audio recurs every four–five seconds, beginning around 1:13 and continuing through 2:51 (reprises at 3:17); Bass; Twelve-string (strum); Six-string acoustic; Vocals (Anderson); Anderson multitracked, harmonized voices at 2:51; Lead Moog synth intro at 1:24; Electric guitar (in right channel) at approximately 1:29 (continues every four–five seconds through 2:47); Piano at 1:41 (notes in sync with twelve-string acoustic guitar strum); "Echo" electric guitar at 2:15, intermittently through 2:51.	D	"A man conceived . . ." at approximately 1:39.
2:52–3:16		Possible EDIT; Crash cymbal; Anderson vocals multitracked high harmony shadowing lead vocal line through 3:21; Secondary lead vocal line (2:52–3:09), Anderson's voice multitracked with Howe's and Squire's sent through a Leslie (Anderson's voice in distant echo); Bass; Drums (snare, hi-hat, hi-hat accent at 2:56; kick, crash, and snare at 3:02); Electric guitar; Acoustic guitar; Organ (mimics tone and general rhythmic pattern of the deep background vocals).	F/G	"Coins and crosses . . ."

The song seems simplistic on the surface, but dig into it and it's anything but. For example, after Howe plays the acoustic opening, a polyrhythmic pattern sprouts up to accompany him. A six-beat rhythmic pattern is introduced, based on sixteen notes/beats stated on the kick drum and bass guitar. An eighth-note rest produces a slight pause in between the fourth and fifth notes Squire plays on bass.

"The kick and bass pattern in the start of 'And You and I,' and also a bit later, were recorded first then put on a loop tape," says Offord.

Indeed. Every four-to-five seconds or so, beginning at approximately 1:13 and continuing through 2:51, the bass and drums interlock. Bruford then follows this by striking a triangle. The six-beat pattern is reprised briefly at 3:17 and then disappears from the song.

The triangle's first appearance in the song "And You and I" shatters the silent gap in between the kick/bass riff pattern and Howe's strumming of the twelve-string guitar (the D–G–A–G chord structure pattern in the first movement, "Cord of Life").

The triangle, like the church pipe organ, was "designed to make the deity listen," writes R. Murray Schafer in *The Soundscape: Our Sonic Environment and the Tuning of the World*. The triangle is in the same percussion family as the bell. A church bell, writes Schafer, "evoke[s] some deep and mysterious response in the psyche, which finds its visual correspondence in the integrity of the circle or mandala." Church bells are communal and "centripetal," drawing "man and God together."

The actual dictionary definition of centripetal is "directed toward the center," or a body set in motion along a curved path. If we extrapolate this concept, than the metaphysical path is a spiral. So, the chime of Bruford's triangle doesn't just break the silence when it is first rung; it elegantly and quite impossibly provides one of the more meditative and spiritual aspects of the record.

"And You and I" hovers around 80 beats per minute. (Some sheet music I checked registers the tempo as at 78 or 79bpm.) By contrast, "Siberian Khatru" spikes along a kind of sliding scale, in the range of 120 to 130-plus, meaning moderately fast.

Admittedly, the bpm does dip below this level (to the high 50s), but generally speaking, the pulse of the song is anywhere from, approximately, 60–80bpm, which fits squarely within the normal range of the human heartbeat. No wonder the song breathes so freely and evenly.

Drum Sound

Engineers and producers of the time seemed to like a "dead" drum sound, but apparently Bruford and Offord wanted something a bit more "live." A massive echo was likely added to the drums, probably via an EMT echo plate, in particular for "And You and I" and "Siberian Khatru" (on the tambourine hits), to give the track more presence. ("Right on all accounts," Offord offers.)

To my ears, anyway, the classic "Bruford snare" really didn't happen (in relation to studio recordings) until *The Yes Album*. It probably reached its zenith (with Yes) with *Fragile* and later *CTTE*—a meaty, echo-y sound predating Phil Collins's gated-tom gut punch.

Bruford's ringing snare was the result of two forces: what he terms his weak left-hand grip on the sticks and the need to be heard over electrified and amplified instruments in club settings. "People always say to me, 'I love your snare sound—how do you get it?'" Bruford once told me, "and actually I think what they mean is, 'I love where you place the snare notes—in unusual places in the measure.'"

"It was the fashion in London studios at the time to have a very dead snare sound, often taping the top skin with gaffer tape, and to close-mike," says Gary Martin. "Both Bill and Eddy preferred a more live snare sound—although they did stick with a pretty dead bass drum sound."

Other effects help to create a detailed sonic portrait for "And You and I." Anderson's multitracked voice maintains the vocal lead in the opening movement, "Cord of Life," but a counterpoint vocal section sung by Howe and Squire, commencing with the phrase "Turn around," is sent through a Leslie cabinet (beginning 2:52). Anderson can be heard in a distant echo as organ notes mimic the tone and general rhythmic pattern of the backing vocals.

Those counterpoint vocals were always difficult to discern, but upon hearing the 5.1 surround sound version of *CTTE*, I could clearly pick out words. In addition, the *Progeny* boxed set and the classic live triple-album *Yessongs* offer clearer sonic images than what's presented on the original LP, in my opinion.

Offord:

> All the choral vocals were double tracked with whoever was singing, and, yes, sometimes Jon would add an extra harmony. We were always looking for new sounds and we were usually the first to try out new products. When we got the stereo mike, I tried it on Jon's voice, and the label asked me for a rough mix for radio. I did not know that someone had accidentally wired the two sides of the mike out of phase. When it was played on the radio, which was then in mono, the voice canceled

out and left just the backing. I didn't use it again. I always used a Neumann U 64 for vocals.

"That wasn't spotted until after the track was mixed and pressed and required going back into the studio to remix," Gary Martin adds.

Howe's chiming partial acoustic guitar chord marks both the end of the first movement and the opening of the second, "Eclipse." Slowly, a rising swell of Mellotron strings, beginning at approximately 3:38 and continuing through nearly the five-minute mark (4:54), elevates and carries us across caverns of symphonic sound and rolling sonic wilderness.

Amid Moog, Mellotron, bass, bass pedals, and electric guitar, Howe plays a second steel guitar; his dramatic sonic nosedives begin at approximately 3:48. Howe creates similar sonic dive bombs with the pedal steel in "Siberian Khatru," although here they are more sorrowful, almost like the distant calls of a whale. Later (around 5:14), Howe's steel soars, skyrocketing out of Anderson's vocal section.

Throughout the instrumental section, steel guitar and keyboards play off one another, not really jousting but harmonizing, supporting, overlapping, or working in tandem.

Interestingly, in closing out the second movement, Howe restates the series of picked notes on acoustic we heard in "Cord of Life" (A–D–Em). However, he doesn't recall the earlier twelve-string strumming patterns, instead playing a series of E5, suspended B, and A chords until he breaks with this pattern when the vocals are introduced in the first verse of the section.

The acoustic opening of the third movement, "The Preacher, The Teacher," supposedly written in an afternoon, is injected with uplifting Moog lines complementing the pastoral feel of the section. Wakeman's Moog tone hints at something "wood-y"—an orchestral woodwind or a primitive fife or pipe—which almost instantaneously transports our mind to a grove or a country pasture, suggesting the work of classical masters, Berlioz, Sibelius, Beethoven.

At 7:45, Moog enters again, with a second, bleeping Moog playing a supporting role, largely coming through in the left channel. We once again hear the keys and electric guitar operating in sympathy. Howe's wavering electric guitar tone may have been sent through a Leslie for its effect, and its sonic signature is a good match for the tone Wakeman generates on Moog.

Despite the electronic, almost metallic nature of the instrumentation here, the pastoral qualities shine. (Bruford's tambourine strikes, coordinated with his snare hits, add to the metallic brightness of the section.)

At approximately 8:36 we hear Anderson's vocals (likely doubled) as well as Squire and Howe's harmony vocals virtually melding into the plastering noise of double Mellotrons. In addition, we hear what could be a doubling organ line and a Moog bass line (not to mention a piano sent through an effect). Near the end of the track, Howe creates a beautiful cascading effect on steel, as if the band is itself entering a kind of free-fall.

There were a few steel players in those days, from B. J. Cole to "Sneaky" Pete Kleinow of the Flying Burrito Brothers. Rusty Young, master steel guitar player in Poco—which toured with Yes across the West, Midwest, and South in April 1973—offers his insight on Howe:

> I started playing guitar in 1952. I love Tennessee Ernie Ford because he had these two guys from California who played on all of his records: "Speedy" West and Jimmy Bryant. "Speedy" West was a steel player and I learned every note he played.
>
> "So we're on the road with Yes and we're at a Holiday Inn, and we had the entire floor. I think we had a day off. I was walking down the hallway and one of the doors of the hotel rooms was open and . . . I started hearing Tennessee Ernie Ford music. I'm thinking, *Who in the world is playing Tennessee Ernie Ford?*

That person was, of course, Steve Howe.

> I put my head in the room and he was listening to this little tape recorder. He said he grew up listening to Jimmy Bryant and Speedy West. He was a good guitar player and he could do the jazzy things that Jimmy Bryant could but he was a lousy steel player. He tried to do the "Speedy" West stuff. It was bizarre he was doing it with Yes. The lead

music part for the guitar was a throwback to the Tennessee Ernie Ford records. They not only did Tennessee Ernie guitar parts, but were following in the footsteps of someone like Ford because they were doing theme records, too.

That is one view. Another? The progressives, particularly those of the British persuasion, made the traditional exotic by stamping their signature on American roots music. Yes, there were steel players who remained solidly within certain parameters and genres, and thus were more "authentic." But, generally speaking, few attacked the kind of music Yes did, and did so with a steel guitar. It wasn't about being a country-and-western guitarist but a *progressive* one.

At the time, Howe confessed that he had only been seriously practicing with the steel for nine months, likely since the early days of 1972, and indicated that he was using only a Hawaiian, not an actual pedal steel. Howe indicated that he had two Gibson steel guitars, but it's unclear if these were used on *CTTE*. He tried to introduce new stringed instruments with every Yes release, and *CTTE* was no exception.

As we enter the fourth and final stage of "And You and I," titled "Apocalypse," the bass provides the murky bottom end as the aural properties of the track seem to congeal into a kind of primordial sonic soup. Using the steel guitar, Howe climbs a ladder of ascending notes, creating something of a ghostly whistling effect, a running up the ladder, leading out the song. This is heard earlier, at 5:14, as well. (It certainly appears that Howe uses the steel guitar to create this sound, and this can be verified by listening to *Yessongs* and watching the concert video of the same title.)

"And You and I" was chosen for release as a double-sided single for the album, but it didn't do much in the charts, entering the Hot 100 at #83. It eventually stalled at #42, according to the issue of *Billboard* magazine dated December 16, 1972.

Perhaps, in retrospect, this was no surprise. Maybe looking at chart positions misses the entire point of *CTTE*. The edited version of "Close to the Edge" (the "Total Mass Retain" section) and the two-part "And You and I" don't truly do the full songs justice. In fact, they chop the shit out of masterworks and don't really offer listeners a proper view into the cinematic scope of their respective mother pieces.

Extracting a few minutes from a nineteen-minute song goes beyond being out of context. The single has not context. (The edited version of "America" may be a different story, as it is essentially a pop song elongated by an instrumental middle section.) Furthermore, attempting to distill these symphonic elements practically negates everything the band wanted to achieve in the first place with *Close to the Edge*. In short, the payoff was not in the three-minute snapshot, the cheap Top 40 hit, but in the gradual resolution of musical concepts developed during these classical-rock masterpieces.

Through the failure of singles associated with *Close to the Edge*, Yes's reputation as an album-oriented band was bolstered and clearly defined. Avoiding blatantly commercial musical choices became a Yes hallmark through most of the 1970s. This ethos not only reflected and underscored the ambition of the progressive-rock movement, but also signified all that was good and righteous about the emerging genre.

"Siberian Khatru"

Despite being the shortest song on the record (8:53), "Siberian Khatru" is one of the busiest. The opening riff (what I call "Country-blues Riff #1") has Howe at his most twangin', scratchin' country-blues best. The guitar figure at the top of the song is composed of scalar voicings in the Em–Am–Bm sequence. It eventually ends with a suspended E chord.

Although the guitar playing in "Perpetual Change" captures the essence of Steve's country-picking style, the deliberate and rhythmic scratching of strings in the opening measures of "Khatru" are not unlike the "train" feel Johnny Cash achieved with muted guitar strings on some of his Sun recordings. Howe uses muting later in the song, too, in the bridge, to great funkified effect.

Around 0:24, Howe breaks into the "Main Khatru Guitar Riff," as yet another theme is stated on keyboards: a "Jazzy Motif," one that will later be reprised. At 0:53, still another theme is introduced, "Khatru Riff #2," with organ harmonizing.

What's so effective about the early portions of the song, whether it's the verses, chorus, or bridge, are the multitracked voices and the way the bass challenges the supremacy of the compound vocal melody.

"Obviously, I had learned a lot about being in a choir and harmony," Squire told me. "This is before I could even play bass, you know. I was aware of how musical structure very often had a lot to do with how the top-line melody interacted with the bass line. . . . I learned a lot about that from my church background. Undoubtedly, when I started playing and becoming a young rock player all of those influences were still with me and probably used some of them, if not a lot of them. A lot."

For anyone who says that Squire couldn't hold down the bottom end *and* be a lead player, take a listen to these measures. Bruford gives Squire a wide berth. (The drums are relatively straight forward here, Bruford's almost disco-esque poundings helping to build the song's driving feel.) But in the bridge, Squire hangs back, allowing Howe's busy, funky phrases and famous scratching (in G) work its magic.

As a nice touch, in the song's first interlude (1:46–2:00) Squire plays harmonics as the Main Khatru Guitar Riff is softly reintroduced by Howe on electric guitar.

At the opening of the second verse, Squire thumps and then runs up the ladder of ascending notes, emphasizing the words "ring" and "coming." Something interesting happens here, as well, when Khatru Riff #2 is reactivated. In tandem, Howe, Squire, and Wakeman partake of yet another Mahavishnu-like tradeoff. When Howe and Wakeman are busy riffing on Khatru #2, Squire restrains himself, and vice versa. These fast runs fit together like pieces of a three-tiered puzzle.

Despite the geographically specific title, the song has global, even Eastern, implications that border on "world music." (Excuse the generic labeling.) We even catch a whiff of traditional African-American music, what with the lyric "blue tail/tail fly" conjuring the song "Blue Tail Fly" (or "Jimmy Crack Corn"), as once recorded by Burl Ives. The chorus of vocals at the climax of the song creates a kind of Negro gospel-esque chant, picking up an American roots influence. Anderson has said that he believes musical styles from around the global community bear connections to one another, be it Chinese melodies with Irish ones or Arabic music with Celtic harmonies.

The harmonized "Chant motif" (3:02), likely Jon's voice multitracked (Howe and Squire don't accompany him), flavors an already busy track. Yes will reprise this motif in the staccato Stravinsky / "Flying Brick" section later in the song. It is reminiscent of the Balinese monkey chant, or Ramayana monkey chant, recalling "Roundabout." It's later echoed in "Sound Chaser," from 1974's *Relayer*, featuring Swiss keyboardist Patrick Moraz.

"I remember hearing the monkey chant . . . and was mesmerized by what it was," Anderson said in an interview that aired on SiriusXM satellite radio and was uploaded to JonAnderson.com and SoundCloud.com in 2015. He intimated that he didn't think the Balinese chant was much older than the early twentieth century, but said he'd heard a recording of this vocalized form as early as 1968.

In Christian tradition, chants can either be unaccompanied and monophonic or, as in the Anglican Church, feature four-part harmonies to represent and give glory to God. "Siberian Khatru" qualifies on this basis. Anderson's voice, via overdubbed vocal tracks, captures a liturgical, hymn-like effect, in addition to the ethnic music I've described.

"Chanting brings a state of ecstasy," said Allen Ginsberg, and the placement of such in "Siberian Khatru" sends the music, already jammed packed with ideas, to new euphotic heights.

Coming out of the chant (3:04), we hear Howe's Coral sitar and then a "baroque" section of the song played by Wakeman on harpsichord; bass provides counterpoint to his runs. Wakeman used a Goff harpsichord, which had to be specifically miked for the occasion. More East meets West action . . .

Genre fusion occurs in abundance in "Siberian Khatru." Howe's guitar antics are all over the map, stylistically, compositionally, and schematically. In the interlude, the guitar is in 4/4 (as is the bass guitar) but slips briefly, for a measure, into 3/4. (The triple factor in effect, again.)

With the assistance of multitracking, we hear (at 3:30) Howe entering with his steel guitar solo and what could be ghostly wails on a second steel guitar. We get a visual image from his weepy steel tones, like a bird spreading its wings and floating on the wind.

We also hear a twelve-string electric, the Coral (in the interlude, prior to the harpsichord and guitar solo proper), and two six-string electrics going on at different points—one harmonizing with Wakeman's organ. The solo effectively moves through Indian music, then "cosmic country-blues" and blues-rock. The bass vamps for some of the final twelve measures, dovetailing nicely with a slight recall of the funky Country-blues Riff #1.

The arc of pedal steel in the guitar solo around the 3:31 mark decelerates the pace of the song. More than one steel guitar is being played around 3:37; ghostly pedal-steel work echoes in the background from 4:05 to 4:32.

Mellotron flute—part and parcel of the Egyptian/Arabian/Russian/Indian hybrid Eastern theme—winds through the song as a second Mellotron (on the strings setting) becomes more pronounced at 5:54. Bruford plays what might be a paradiddle variant on snare, fading in at 5:36.

This percussive tract harks back to military/fife-and-drums motifs; it could be straight double-stroke rolls or alternating sticking patterns involving both single- and double-stroke patterns. In addition, Bruford's figures here are similar to the patterns he plays on King Crimson's "Exiles," from 1973. (For that matter, the Mellotron strings recall Crimson's earlier efforts, *In the Court of the Crimson King* and *In the Wake of Poseidon*.)

If it's some form of alternate sticking patterns involving double strokes, we hear this throughout Bruford's playing in Yes, from "Yours Is No Disgrace" to "Perpetual Change," "Heart of the Sunrise," even "Themes" and the climax of "Brother of Mine," years later, on Anderson Bruford Wakeman Howe's debut.

As we return to another verse, the song feels increasingly heavy and dense, even *mean*. By the time we reach the seven-minute mark, or thereabouts, we've entered no-man's-land in terms of the rock world. This section falls somewhere between symphonic rock, blues-rock, ethno-rock, and classical music.

The sound texture of the guitar is remarkable, one of the more distinctive tones on the entire record. At the climax of the track, Howe achieves a kind of Doppler effect. It's been speculated that this was created by having a microphone swung in a circle by an engineer (maybe Mike Dunne). There may be additional effects or manipulation on the track, such as manipulating the tape machine, warping the sound via the Varipseed function, but this remains to be seen.

In 1997, Offord indicated to *Studio Sound* magazine that Howe's guitar solo in "Siberian Khatru" was captured via two mikes, one close and one about twenty feet away. When I asked him about all of this, he surprised me with his response. "I think the effects you're hearing were made with an auto-panner with a bit of pitch change. This is not the track with the swinging mike, by the way."

This staccato pattern—as the Leslie-like guitar effect swirls around the listener's ears—may have been inspired by the ominous and angular rhythms of Stravinsky's *The Rite of Spring*. Preceded by what sounds like some form of exotic cymbal, such as a Chinese gong, the Stravinsky section / chant passage is reminiscent of the opening for "Yours Is No Disgrace," which was itself inspired by the music from a TV show, *Fabian of the Yard*. (We could be hearing a hard edit both coming in, at 7:01, and out, at 7:32, of this section, the harshness of the join masked by a gong or cymbal crash.)

Incidentally, this "flying brick" feel is something the band Rush had fully developed by the early 1980s. The phrase "flying bricks" is one I have borrowed from Rush terminology, a colloquialism for seemingly random staccato rhythms the boys often wrote into their music. Like flying bricks, no one is quite sure where they'll land. (You'll hear bricks fly in "Jacob's Ladder," from 1980's *Permanent Waves*, and "Show Don't Tell," from *Presto*, 1989.)

Yes knew exactly where all of this was going. It's the rest of us who have to figure it out. As such, the phrasing of the flying-brick measures is a bit tricky. Drums play in virtual unison with the chanting voices, hinting at beat- and note-displacement, as the driving bass notes occasionally coincide with the pulse of the chant. (The vocal and bass parts flip back and forth between 6/8 and 4/4 time.)

It may be further sacrilege to some Rush fans, but the smashes heard at 4:48 forward (tambourine sent through an effect) evoke a sound that would later turn up on the Canadian progressive rock/power trio's fusion-esque instrumental "YYZ." With the help of producer Terry Brown, Rush drummer Neil Peart swatted a chair or possibly a stool with a sheet of plywood, something that, to this day, sounds like shattering glass.

"Siberian Khatru" closes with another guitar workout from Howe as Wakeman's jazzy motif (reprised from earlier in the song) and Squire's scalar runs maintain excitement as the song fades.

As with "America," we see multiple sides of Howe's playing. He performs in a slippery feel reminiscent of the jazzy, "quiet" interlude of "Perpetual Change," accompanied by bass, drums, and Tony Kaye on acoustic piano. Although jazzier than the earlier solo, the outro solo for "Siberian Khatru" is still very much of the blues, country, and rock styles that root the song.

4
WHAT'S A KHATRU?
Wordplay

on Anderson has always said that he values the sound of words as much as their dictionary definition. I'll get into what the lyrics *might* mean in a bit, but for right now let's examine the various musical and even phonetic devices employed for "Close to the Edge."

Internal rhymes, alliteration, consonance, and even repetition of vowel sounds occur throughout the lyrics of the work, giving credence to Anderson's remark stressing the importance of texture, rather than textbook definition, of phrases. We encounter rhymes for the words "move," "choose" "dewdrop," as well as "down" and "round." In addition, the rhyme ending in "hour" of the first verse is picked up by "nowhere," the last word of the first line of the second verse.

In "Close to the Edge" we encounter perfect rhymes, such as "disgrace" with "grace," and close rhymes, such as "one" and "sun." Many of these verses employ tricky wordplays, as well as the use of consonance and vowel repetition—what Laurence Perrine calls "sound recurrence" in his book *Sound and Sense: An Introduction to Poetry.*

Sometimes it takes a repetition of a word, or variation of the word, for the lyrics to resonate with the listener. In any case, if the band saw fit to reintroduce certain sound forms, perhaps it's better we pay attention to them.

Some other words and phrases, such as man, woman, and human, appear in all three tracks. Interestingly, "eclipse," used in "Total Mass Retain" of "Close to the Edge," also appears as a subheading in "And You and I." (See *table* below for most common word frequencies.)

The lyrics have a mellifluous quality that escapes labeling and sometimes *feels* like stream of consciousness. It also hints at *scriptura continua*. Ancient scribes wrote the way humans spoke, with no spaces between words. It must be said that the lyric sheet does not feature words that run together, but the manner in which the words are arranged suggests that they should be sounded out and spoken aloud.

I made a list of over two dozen attention-grabbing words that don't seem to match any other in their respective stanzas, but do rhyme or closely rhyme with phrases that appear later in the song.

Is there an encrypted code embedded in the lyrics? If there is, it's a sophisticated one. I have not been able to crack it, or detect what it is, with the naked eye.

Word Frequency

WORD	SONG		
	"Close to the Edge"	"And You and I"	"Siberian Khatru"
"Call" or variant	5	2	1
"Climb" or variant	1	4	1
"Cross" or variant	2	2	--
"Move" or variant	3	3	2
"River"	6	1	7
"Sun" or variant	2	2	1
"Valley" or variant	1	2	--

The second movement, "Total Mass Retain," provides more evocative phonetic and grammatical properties. Vowel sounds are clumped together in "my eyes," "convinced eclipsed," and "I crucified my," for example.

Partial anagrams can also be found. "Since" appears in "license," and the word "or," of course, is right at the heart of "cord." Based purely on phonetics, the phrase "there since" closely resembles "the license."

In three short stanzas opening the third movement, "I Get Up, I Get Down," there are eight occurrences of a "ch" sound. These instances seem to appear in numbers greater than would be expected if they occurred merely by chance. Also consider the words "lady" and "sadly": with the exception of the letter s, "lady" is comprised of the same letters.

This is to say nothing of the tongue twisting Anderson must perform when sliding around similar words in "I Get Up, I Get Down," such as "lace," "she," "clearly," "lady," "sadly," "looking," and "saying."

We're also aware of word shakeups in "The Solid Time of Change." "Assessing" seems to be a rejiggering of the phrase "A seasoned." All of this contributes to the sense of continuity, even familiarity, we perceive in the abstract lyrics.

Further Wordplay

Some of the first lines of each stanza contain at least two s's and often exactly two, calling attention to the word or those specific letters in the word. Like runic inscription, it's as if the lyric-writer has drawn attention to certain letters via important markings. When properly arranged, they could tell their own story, but this would need further investigation.

I attempted to examine the meaning of the letter s in a few different and ancient languages, and found some vague connections, but nothing definitive, from my perspective. However, in *Isis Unveiled*, a book written by Madame Blavatsky, the co-founder of theosophical movement, it was noted that the double s not only denotes black magic, but strangely enough also the presence of the "Holy Spirit" and "pure wisdom," as these letters sometimes appear on chalice cups used in the Catholic mass.

According to Blavatsky, good and evil are interchangeable, anyway, and in Hermann Hesse's novel *Demian*, the concept of the godlike figure Abraxas is an amalgam of opposites—a god neither good nor evil, but a combination of both. In his book *C. G. Jung and Hermann Hesse: A Record of Two Friendships*, Miguel Serrano writes that the "pure archetype" of Abraxas represents "the god which is within ourselves." Serrano describes a drawing Hesse was given before his death of a bird flying toward heaven. When Hesse's widow, Ninon, showed Serrano this artwork, he immediately recalled *Demian* and Sinclair's drawing of a bird. In the novel, the bird flies to god—Abraxas.

"Demian is Sinclair, himself, his deepest self, a kind of archetypal hero who exists in the depths of all of us," Serrano writes. "In a word, Demian is the essential Self."

Bringing this full-circle, with every instance in which a double s appears in the lyrics, we see a literal and grammatical double image. The double *s* could be code for the "god within" or a *Demian*-styled, Abraxas-informed symbolic representation of both the good and the bad duality of Hesse's novels, or love and hate in the lyrics of *CTTE*.

Let's examine. By using the phrase a "seasoned witch," Anderson and company could simply be referring to a wise man or woman. In Buddhism, it takes a wise man to rescue another from the hellish realms of suffering. (In December 2012 Anderson told Joe Bosso, of the website Music Radar, that the phrase "seasoned witch" refers to one's "higher self.") In addition, the use of the word "liver" evokes a very powerful image. One can't but help think that the speaker, Anderson, is talking about impurities, toxins, hate.

In 2008, Anderson told me:

> hate is the root of cancer. Things like that, that made
> sense to me at that time, that if you're a hateful, you'll
> get ill. Those types of things [is what I wanted to write
> about]. As time has proved, if you have love in your life,
> you will live a very good life. If you have hate in your
> heart, you will be a cripple. And that's the way it is. That
> was what I was singing about and I was learning about
> it and singing about it the same day. If I read something
> that inspired me, I would write about it the next day.

If nothing else, this double *s* sibilance is reminiscent of the sound of a rushing river, the same river we encounter in *Siddhartha*, a metaphor for the natural mechanism by which we can attain self-realization.

"And You and I"

Some of the same grammatical devices governing "Close to the Edge" reappear in "And You and I." What strikes me, after perusing the second verse of the first section, "Cord of Life," is an actual coherent rhyme scheme (i.e. abcbdefegh).

If we treat each verse as its own separate poem or sonnet, a pattern emerges. Phrases and sentences are broken up in very interesting ways, adding to the mystique of the words and phrasing. Internal rhymes (expression, emotion, and ocean) remind us of "crucifixion" from "Close to the Edge."

Things get even weirder in the third verse. The words of the co-lead vocal section, as they were printed on the original lyric sheet, appear as though they are rungs of a ladder. While the rhyme does not adhere to the scheme used in the previous two verses, a number of odd things are happening. For instance, the word "coins" is reminiscent of "void" from "Close to the Edge" (from "Total Mass Retain"). We also see the infamous double *s* phenomenon rearing its head, again, in the words "crosses" and "fruitless."

Although not identical, the rhyme scheme (abcbdefg) of this first verse of the "Eclipse" section (section two) resembles that of the first two verses of the song, as does the scheme of "The Preacher, the Teacher," the third section of the song.

Meanings?

In the first movement of "And You and I," "Cord of Life," we encounter the concept of a dream, or a dream of self-realization (as far as I can surmise), much like "Close to the Edge." I don't want to get hung up on the word "dream," however. It's likely Anderson is actually talking about real, honest-to-goodness enlightenment, not wishful thinking.

Granted, the record is *Close to the Edge*, but Anderson indicates that the "answer" is in response to a dream and speaks of a goal, a "spiral" aim. Hesse uses the spiral image in *Siddhartha*. As the book tells us, the path of self-awareness isn't a circle but a spiral. Incredibly, on the same page, in my version of the Bantam paperback version of the novel, anyway, on page 18, Hesse actually uses the phrase "and you and I." (For what it's worth, on page 45, we read about the "sparkle of dew"; we also find a "dewdrop" in the lyrics of "Close to the Edge," which may refer to connectedness of all things under the Sun and Moon.)

Labyrinths are related to spirals, which have many meanings—everything from enlightenment to the rebirth of the soul. At Chartres Cathedral, for instance, some say walking the labyrinth leads to the "transformation" of spiritual pilgrims.

For Carl Jung, the image of the *mandala*, or *yantra* (as per *Man and His Symbols*), represented wholeness and the search for self. Jung concluded that mandalas, in the form of spirals, could indicate the Holy Spirit to the faithful.

This does not necessarily mean that "And You and I" is Christian in nature, however. In Zen Buddhism, the figure of the circle represents perfection and enlightenment. In addition, in Hesse's *Demian*, the protagonist, Emil Sinclair, paints a portrait. After being subjected to nature's elements, the painting begins to resemble Max Demian, Sinclair's wise friend/guardian. He treats this painting of half-male/half-female face/daemon as a kind of *mandala*.

"And You and I" paints other images for us, such as cords and coins, crosses and the vision of Mother Earth, in the co-lead or counterpoint lead vocals section.

What Anderson may be saying here is that the symbols of the modern world that we might hold dear—money and, dare we say it, organized religion—may not be the answer or the true path to enlightenment. Our connection to the Earth could prove more vital to our spiritual development. (It could also be indicative of a "landscape of the soul" motif.)

This, along with images of valleys and seas and the concept of calling out over the valley, echoes the Romantic obsession with nature and the ecological interpretation of "Close to the Edge" envisioned by Paul Hegarty and Martin Halliwell in their book *Beyond and Before: Progressive Rock Since the 1960s*. This idea that we are in the cosmic Age of Aquarius also dovetails with the band's growing obsession with Mother Earth, health food, and vegetarianism.

As most fans are aware, in the 1970s Yes had a reputation for being "health nuts," an obsession that sprouted around the time *Fragile* was taking off in the US and the UK. Howe once ran a health food business with Yes drummer Alan White, "and we had it for about one and a half years," Howe told me in 2001. He did call it an "insane business" but said that it "proved that we were committed to that kind of lifestyle." He also noted that Eddy Offord led by example, indirectly persuading the band to refuse meat.

The Neopagan concept of the Triple Goddess—the virgin, the nurturer, and the witch—are in relative abundance in the lyrics, as well, if we care to look. Although I won't go as far as to say that each song represents an individual god, the mere mention of Mother Earth (in "And You and I"), what appears to be a maiden (perhaps both in the title track and "Siberian Khatru"), and the hag (the witch in "Close to the Edge") are unmistakable. Anderson may certainly have caught the scent of Celtic mythology during the writing of the record, adding this to the Christian imagery and Eastern mysticism so prevalent in the aromatic spiritual smorgasbord that is *Close to the Edge*.

We've already seen in chapter 3 that the *om* heard at the opening of "Close to the Edge" could represent some form of countervailing male deific triad baked into the cake of the song. If we try hard enough, we might, quite possibly, detect traces of the patriarchal Holy Trinity in the lyrics somewhere. It's as if, in true progressive-rock style, *Close to the Edge* achieves balance between the masculine and the feminine.

The second section of "And You and I," titled "Eclipse," seems to play off the actual literal definition of astronomical bodies "yoking" together as well as its symbolic meaning. Google the word "eclipse." You'll find a haloed image, like burn holes in film or the iris of an eye, which is unmistakable. It's like looking into the darkness, an abyss. In the case of an eclipse, when we look into the abyss, the "eye" stares back at us. But what does an eclipse really signify? Is it merely some random observable astrological event involving celestial bodies, based on mathematical equations and cosmological coincidence? Is it something more?

Although Roger Waters, in "Eclipse" and "Brain Damage" from 1973's *The Dark Side of the Moon*, was speaking about the more obscure, maddening, and psychologically damaging aspects of life, it's difficult not to think that Anderson got the jump on Pink Floyd here. (It should be noted that as far back as winter 1972, Floyd had been playing variations of songs that would appear on *Dark Side*.)

Interestingly, Yes once used *Also Sprach Zarathustra* as its introduction music—the same piece that captured the imagination of Stanley Kubrick for his film *2001: A Space Odyssey*. The music was employed to represent a confluence of cosmic events with profound implications for mankind. It let viewers know there was something special, evolutionary, and revolutionary to the events that were unfolding.

I'll go out on a limb and say that Anderson didn't choose "Also Sprach Zarathustra" at random, and by the same token he's not talking about random events in "And You and I," either. Words such as "movement," "completeness," and "revealing" imply a kind of cosmic sympathy.

Prior to the release of *Close to the Edge*, Anderson said one could class "And You and I" as "a hymn." This description will inevitably lead some to consider it liturgical in nature. But Anderson took pains to state that he wasn't referring to church or church dogma, but instead ensuring that "And You and I" was really about "feeling very, very secure in the knowledge of knowing there is somebody. God, maybe."

This "otherness" is something to which Anderson alludes a lot. Perhaps he was referring to the process of self-reflection and discovery to find the Christ within. "We're not living a conscious world," he told me in 2008. "We are not conscious to the divine that surrounds us. We are not conscious to God."

Whatever Anderson truly meant, there's plenty of symbolism in "And You and I." Anderson's voice, as he delivers these words, burns through the mists of layered music, puncturing a hole in the sonic atmosphere, if you like, and in so doing sends cold streaks down our spine. The section is symbolic of the heightened state of affairs Yes achieved with the song—a kind of confluence of music, words, and sound.

"And You and I," like "Close to the Edge" and "Siberian Khatru," contains a round, or round robin, effect (that is, overlapping lyrical and vocal sections). Bodies, albeit musical in nature, overlap. In other words, they form an eclipse.

We should point out that during a concert on the *CTTE* tour in Brisbane, Australia, on March 3, 1973, Anderson introduced "And You and I" as being about "possible political situations in the future." Admittedly, this is pretty vague, but Anderson goes on to say that there will be "radical changes" in the coming decades.

What appears to be the entire concert has been uploaded to YouTube by a Yes fan using the handle SaYestoBootlegs2. In addition, in the early 1980s, I heard a radio announcer in New York City refer to "And You and I" as a protest song, putting to rest the unfounded myth that prog rock was and is bereft of political statement. But who was Anderson addressing?

Who Is . . . "You"?

Figuring out who the "you" is "And You and I" is tricky. Who is "The Preacher" and who is "The Teacher"? Much as in "Close to the Edge," Anderson could be referring to himself, recalling the "double projection" present in Hesse's works.

I recall a conversation with Phil "Shiva" Jones of the psychedelic/prog outfit Quintessence about self-realization that seems to shed light on Yes songs such as "Close to the Edge" and, especially, "And You and I."

"My teacher always made it clear: within you is the teacher, the guru," Jones told me in 2008. "You just have to find it and listen to it. We are ultimately our own teachers. It's all about finding that place where you hear the inner teacher speaking to you. That only really comes when you are, in a Native American expression, walking in your truth. When you are no longer BS-ing yourself or anyone else, you *feel* that inner teacher. You hear it."

Siberian Khatru

Compare Yes's lyrics with those of another great wordsmith of the prog-rock world, Pete Sinfield. Although his phrasing can get pretty erotic, weird, and/or sci-fi, Sinfield's words are not nearly so abstract as to be completely meaningless.

Keith Reid of Procol Harum can be equally cryptic, one thinks. I once asked him about Harum's "A Whiter Shade of Pale," a cornerstone of the entire prog-rock movement, and wondered if there was even any meaning behind the song at all. "No, I would not agree with that," he sharply retorted, "because there's definitely a story happening there. There's a journey being taken, and there's a man and a woman involved in the song. There's a beginning, a middle, and an end. There's a lot of imagery, but there's a thread through it."

Unlike "A Whiter Shade of Pale," "Siberian Khatru" doesn't tell a story as such, but is much more impressionistic. The poetic juxtaposing of words, words that might not ordinarily be placed side-by-side in a perfectly grammatically structured sentence, has inspired more esoteric conversations attempting to uncover the song's true meaning than perhaps any other in the prog-rock canon.

Anderson himself didn't seem to want to cause much fuss when he told Tony Stewart of *NME* in 1972, "A lot of my words get abstract because I can't concentrate on one storyline. The 'Siberian Khatru' track is just a lot of interesting sounding words, though it does relate to dreams of clear summer days. The title means winter, but it's meant to be the opposite. It doesn't really mean a great deal."

Yes biographer Dan Hedges muses that *khatru* is a Yemeni word translated roughly as, "as you wish." This could be true, but my college literature professor told me that Shakespeare created words for the English language to present certain amusing turns of phrase or convey certain emotions. From my perspective, Anderson invented the word *khatru* or hijacked it; he brought it aboard the English language and applied to it his own definition.

By inventing or inviting the word *khatru* into his lair, Anderson staged a literary revolt against the pop music lyric-writing establishment. Thus, he introduced a generation or listeners to one phrase they would (dare I say it) incorporate into their everyday vocabulary, at least for a time. (Call it a "Shakespeare revolution," for all you *Big Generator* fans.) Perhaps this is one example of how prog rock imparted esoteric knowledge?

Within the context of *Close to the Edge* a *khatru* could be any number of things, including Yes's nod to the Firebird of Slavic myth. I suppose I'll always associate the phrase with the fawn-like antlered creature roaming the hinterlands of the tri-panel gatefold of *Yessongs*.

Joseph Mileck describes how nature is "a common theme" in Hesse's writing, pointing out that rivers symbolized "life in all its flux," just as birds came to represent the soul and the changing seasons the stages of life. It's the bird symbolism in many of Hesse's major works that closely relates to "Siberian Khatru."

Is *khatru* an example of onomatopoeia? Maybe these questions aren't so crazy. (And, hey, Yes and Anderson started this!) After all, we assign words such as "cuckoo" or "kaw kaw" to suggest the calls of certain type of birds. Might *khatru* be similar?

Anderson made the most of his limited instrumental musical abilities by using his "own" words and actual singing voice—a fantastic human and natural instrument—as a means to make us think and feel.

More than any of the songs appearing on *Close to the Edge*, "Siberian Khatru" doesn't make much sense when we attempt to understand its words as they were literally written. However, if we approach them as abstract thoughts—sounds—in a stream of poetic language, we can acknowledge the deep concepts they convey on a subconscious level.

"Siberian Khatru" is, forgive the term, the "pop" song on the record. Of the three tracks on *CTTE*, it's the only one, despite being nearly ten minutes long, that's not a multi-movement composition. Yes, it resembles "And You and I" in the manner by which it appears, at least initially, to adhere to a strict poetic structure, but the form varies as the song progresses.

The finale is composed of a series of words and images, many of which rhyme. The staccato delivery of the lyrics adds to their starkness and the element of surprise they conjure.

More importantly, the lyrics of "Khatru" seem to give subtle nods to the first two songs on the album. For instance, the appearance of the word "Christian" near the end of the song and the phrase "gold stainless nail" seem beyond coincidence. For that matter, why does Anderson use the image of a man stretching out his arms in "Close to the Edge"? Does this refer to a crucifixion, or a pose the devout strike when praising the Lord? In "And You and I" we also witness a preacher who's been nailed to the "colour door." (Anderson also uses the term "crucify" in an earlier Yes song, "Dear Father.")

An awakening has occurred by the time we reach the ending of "Khatru." One could even say that we've astral traveled from the confines of the river so integral to "Close to the Edge" to the Moon of "Khatru."

CTTE and the Grail Quest?

In the liner notes to the 2003 reissue of *CTTE*, Mike Tiano stresses that few rock artists benefit from the confluence of events that allows their music to transcend time. He even goes as far as to write that, at its creative peak, Yes displayed "fearlessness in the pursuit of perfection."

Although *Close to the Edge* is likely best understood on Eastern terms, or East-meets-West terms, there seems to be some overlap with the Christian tales of the quest for the Holy Grail. Running the risk of sounding Monty Python, or parodying myself, *Close to the Edge* can be interpreted as the Holy Grail of Prog Rock.

The website Alchemy111.com describes the word "grail" as the "vessel [that] carries higher energies into here and now." It's also "used to connect to one's self; to experience the divine here and now; to heal the body through harmony; to find one's Spirit."

In *Close to the Edge*, East meets West in some obvious (and not so obvious) ways, and we know that the concept of self-realization is at the very heart of the record. It's my assertion that the search for the grail is similar to the Buddhist notion of ego loss.

In his book *The Holy Grail*, Giles Morgan writes that the grail stories have roots in ancient Western civilization's history but also "contain elements of Eastern mysticism."

The four sections of "Close to the Edge" might be considered as a loose representation of Buddhism's "Four Noble Truths." The first of the truths involves suffering, motivation to understand suffering, and actually understanding suffering. The second, in a nutshell, urges us to identify why we're suffering and understand it. The third relates to recognizing there's a path to a better well-being and attaining this well-being. The fourth is not only knowing there's a path to well being by living it.

"The Solid Time of Change" seems to foreshadow and actually explicitly tell us that the speaker has achieved a kind of inner peace or balance or nirvana (the want of nothing)—the last of the Four Noble Truths. Yet as one might expect, the final section of "Close to the Edge," "Seasons of Man," also quite rightly picks up on this point.

The second movement, "Total Mass Retain," identifies suffering, and the speaker appears to understand it, making the section a transitional one. It's interesting that Anderson actually even uses words "reasons" and "understood" here.

In "Close to the Edge," these are images of war, although they may not refer directly to combat. It could be that Anderson is identifying the reason for the suffering—war, hatred, combat, and so on.

The "void" Anderson mentions might be the negativity of the world, something he's learning to overcome. (Does this relate to the "depths" of "disgrace?") This could also be the negative aspects of his own inner being, his soul, as Hesse described it. (To be exact, Hesse used the term "abyss" to describe the inner reaches of the soul.) The void could also be interpreted as the so-called "ocean of Samsara," the cycle of life-death-rebirth that must be overcome to achieve nirvana.

Conversely, "Close to the Edge" might follow the path of the sinner who is redeemed, in the Christian sense. Traces of concepts inherent to Christian thought abound. For instance, the "plain" spoken of in the lyrics of "The Solid Time of Change" might be related to the wasteland of the Grail stories and ancient fertility rites.

According to Bonnie Wheeler, associate professor and director of medieval studies at Dedman College, Southern Methodist University, these grail stories were first popularized in Europe at the time of the Crusades, when holy relics were being brought back from the East, giving the West a concrete claim to the mysterious symbolism of ancient concepts such as the grail.

"The Holy Grail . . . is, I think in some ways, very much an attempt to give a concrete visualization of the mystery of the mass," Wheeler told me in 2008. "The grail is the carrier of the blood of Christ. So, you have something, on the one hand, that gives you mysticism and on the other something that is, in the way we have it in the Medieval text, profoundly Christian in its bias."

As German mystic, philosopher, and writer Novalis notes, in ancient times, music and sound were projected unto forests and barren expanses in order to heal the wasteland. The path is clear: music helps us obtain a position of grace and perfection.

Through its vocal harmonies, a sincere search for self, precision, technical ability, the overall production, recapitulation of themes, and more, we surmise that the band is clued in to some esoteric secret to achieve this perfection and restore the wasteland. In peeling back the curtain a bit, and by attempting to understand the band's music, we may find ourselves plugged into this secret, too, and perhaps well on our way to achieving a measure of self-realization.

Listeners I've spoken with have said that they have a difficult time explaining why they feel such an emotional connection to *Close to the Edge* and songs such as the title track and "And You and I."

"It's almost like going up in an air balloon," current keyboardist Geoff Downes told me in 2012, while discussing "And You and I." "The song takes you somewhere else. In speaking with Yes fans, that song is almost the Holy Grail in terms of, I suppose, what epitomized the band."

Other Quests

If *Close to the Edge* can be viewed as a kind of grail quest, it isn't the only example of such in progressive rock. Rush's 1975 sidelong suite "The Fountain of Lamneth" is nothing less than a grail-seeking adventure over Tolkien-esque landscapes, somewhere between pagan and Christian motifs.

Supertramp's 1977 LP *Even in the Quietest Moments . . .* , arguably the band's most balanced record, could be the pinnacle of its artistic success, and perhaps the best fusion of its pop sensibility and prog-rock leanings. Both a spiritual quest and a search for love, the title track incidentally contains bird chirps, the sounds of nature (reminiscent of "Close to the Edge"), and water imagery.

Genesis's "Dancing with the Moonlit Knight" from 1973's *Selling England by the Pound* contains a stanza of lyrics that reference the grail, perhaps to juxtapose concepts of spirituality and commercialism in English society. Some have interpreted "The Cinema Show," which appears on the same record, as having been inspired by T. S. Eliot's modernist poem *The Waste Land*, which was itself partly based on the grail stories and the Arthurian character of the injured Fisher King. And how can we forget "Supper's Ready"? The clue is in the song title. Surely there's a connection to the Christianized grail legends, which stemmed from the mass at the Last Supper?

Questions are at the heart of the grail quest. In Arthurian legend and other works (specifically Wolfram von Eschenbach's *Parzival*), Percival does not ask the ailing Fisher King the appropriate question to restore the wasteland and cure his wound. It's questions such as "Who Am I?" that *Close to the Edge*, and these others, seek to answer.

5
VALLEYS OF ENDLESS SEAS
Roger Dean's Floating World

D ue to the technological advances of audio reproduction and recording, as well as the economics of mass production, a shift in the retail marketplace occurred in the middle decades of the twentieth century.

Ten-inch shellac 78rpm records were relatively fragile and contained a limited amount of audio and, as such, the recording industry was searching for an alternative. What it found was a more durable and flexible *long-playing* audio storage format, which would offer the public four-times more music at a competitive price. (Twelve-inch discs were marketed in the early twentieth century, but at the time stored only a few minutes of audio.)

The LP as a commercially viable recording format had made an appearance in the late 1940s, but discs with a longer playing duration, such as 33 1/3rpm vinyl discs, were produced, with little success, as early as the 1930s. It wasn't until the 1950s and 1960s that the 12-inch 33 1/3rpm long-playing vinyl album began to overshadow the 78rpm. And although the recording industry had once made claims as to the indestructibility of 78s, with the rise of the 12-inch LP, record companies in the 1950s and early 1960s were suddenly promoting vinyl's durability: pick up an old Capitol Records LP and you'll see the word "Nonbreakable" stamped on its label.

Granted, vinyl was not without its drawbacks, but with narrower grooves, or microgrooves, for higher fidelity, it emerged as the standard of the industry. Vinyl was also beneficial for production. A shortage of shellac during World War II forced manufacturers to consider lesser-used recording mediums instead, and vinyl was manufactured from more abundant materials.

More importantly for rock artists of the 1960s and 1970s, the 12-inch LP was more conducive to establishing a continuous lyrical and/or musical narrative than a 10-inch 33 1/3rpm or 78rpm record, or even a series of 78s. In short, the appearance of the 12-inch LP, or album, changed everything. For one thing, the LP simply contained more audio in higher fidelity. Prior to this, a record *album* was just that—it was composed of three or more singles, packaged as a kind of portfolio.

Alex Steinweiss, a one-time art director and album-cover illustrator for Columbia Records, designed the protective sleeve for Columbia's first LPs. (Some credit Columbia Records with introducing the LP format and pioneering the art of album cover design.) Not surprisingly, it was proven that albums with sleeve designs outsold their counterparts in plain brown and gray covers.

Advances in color photography had helped to usher in an era of artist-centric photographic and graphics-heavy album covers with distinctive lettering and/or abstract forms, as seen on many classical and, especially, jazz albums of the 1950s from labels such as Blue Note, Verve, Columbia, Mercury, Philips, and Decca. Designers such as Erik Nitsche, Reid Miles, Paul Huf, William Claxton, and Saul Bass became well-known names, if not by the general public then by industry insiders.

The 12-inch 33 1/3rpm LP was established in large part to accommodate the needs of classical music (such as large symphonic pieces). So, it's no surprise then that classically influenced rock took full advantage of the LP. The LP not only could hold more music, but its packaging fostered the growth of two artistic trends: concept albums, and the golden era of album art of the late 1960s and the 1970s.

Although many music writers and scholars have, for decades, declared Peter Blake and Jann Haworth's iconic design for the cover of the Beatles' *Sgt. Pepper's Lonely Hearts Club Band* album as ground zero for the explosion of interest in album cover art, it was perhaps the psychedelic lettering of 1960s concert handbills and posters seen in New York, London, and San Francisco that were the forerunner to the escapist illustrations that would became synonymous with progressive rock.

Works either created, commissioned, or distributed by Family Dog (courtesy of the likes of artists Victor Moscoso, Rick Griffin, and Stanley Mouse, among others), Athena Posters and Big O posters (founded by Peter Ledeboer), promoting the work of artists such as Roger Dean, H. R. Giger, Martin Sharp, and Mati Klarwein (Miles Davis, Santana), among others, were ubiquitous in the San Francisco and London counterculture.

In the UK, underground publications of the 1960s, such as the *International Times* and *OZ*, were plastered with imagery that was just as influential as its text. The surrealist aspects of these promotional items mirrored the mind-altering effects of the music, for sure but also had developed into every bit the art form as the music they were packaging.

Album cover-artwork for classical recordings, jazz works, and early rock artists, particularly in the 1950s, was fashioned around graphically designed geometric shapes and photographic stills. This changed in the late 1960s and early 1970s to include fantasy themes to match the flights of escapist fancy that music artists were embarking upon.

Expanding the scope and thus the importance of cover-album illustration facilitated a broadening of rock records' commercial appeal. Fantasy elements were in vogue, appealing to the baby boomers, reading sci-fi novels, comics, and other hip counterculture magazines. Sometimes, the more mysterious the joins between the artwork and the music it packaged, the better chance the product had in moving units.

"Prog-rock fans, including myself, are always conscious of art, and the visual presentation and attractive look of the album have always been and still make an important driver for buying it," says illustrator Ed Unitsky. "When it comes to Yes, I recall the music together with Roger Dean's magical worlds, calling us to explore them together with Anderson's magnificent vocal, Squire's bass, Wakeman's keyboard, and Howe's crystalline guitar."

Although Roger Dean had previously illustrated the cover of *Fragile*, his work for *Close to the Edge* would forever and inexorably associate him with Yes's expansive music, prog rock in general, and our perceptions of its escapist qualities. With the exception of a couple stopgap incidents, Dean would carry on a relationship with Yes for most of the next four decades. Steve Howe, of course, continued his relationship with Dean for projects such as his solo work, Anderson Bruford Wakeman Howe, and Asia.

Yes "dated" others—design firm Hipgnosis and Peter Max among them—but always rekindled its romance with Dean. This symbiotic relationship was mirrored by Pink Floyd and Hipgnosis, and also attempted by ELP and artist William Neal.

The Yes and Dean alliance spelled artistic and marketing success. How many Yes fans picked up a Uriah Heep album merely for Dean's signature otherworldly artwork? Perhaps they would have arrived there at some point, anyway, but Dean's visions cinched the deal. In this sense, the band was ahead of the marketing curve, partly thanks to Atlantic Records executive Phil Carson's introduction of Dean to the Yes universe.

Green

Why was the artwork for *CTTE* so special? First, let's look at the cover. It appears to be a virtual 12-inch square, a slice of some untold mythological forest preserve. The denseness of the green, the shading, and the color contain a symphony of subtle complexity. This might be slightly out of context—and certainly the wrong color—but it's difficult not to think of the frothy turbulence of a big glass of tap-served Guinness beer when gazing upon the cover of *CTTE*.

Why green? The tone and shading was inspired by the color and texture of Dean's leather-bound sketchbooks. The original UK pressing of the 12-inch vinyl LP (Atlantic K 50012) possessed a textured sleeve with a silver outline of the Yes logo and the *Close to the Edge* lettering highlighting its importance.

Although this is mere speculation, and it may sound silly, it's possible that another key deciding factor could have been that Chris Squire once stated his favorite color was green.

Even examining the word "green" can be of use to us in this discussion. "Green" can be traced back to Germanic and Celtic languages, which most probably have roots in an Indo-European proto-tongue, as a descriptive word for anything that grows in nature, according to *The Oxford Companion to the English Language*.

In Latin, the word for truth is *veritas* (a term that also figures in Roman mythology). The prefix "ver" may have some affiliation with *verde*, which translates to English as green and also relates to the word *viridis*. The word verdant, of course, means inexperienced, or "green."

Philosophers, literature professors, and etymologists might have a field day with the parallels drawn above, but the definition of green may have been reshaped over many years from a description of someone who is idealistic or uncorrupted to someone who is naïve (or green). Either way, being inexperienced does suggest a kind of purity.

Author Victoria Finlay, in her book *Color: A Natural History of the Palette*, offers another perspective. Finlay discusses a particular shade of green as being a "secret color" in China, although she was referring to the vibrancy of certain rare porcelain. She goes on to say that in Europe, hundreds of years ago, the color green and Western art shared a special bond. Green, she writes, was "associated with Indian mysticism, Persian poems, and Buddhist paintings."

Referencing Kurt Goldstein's article in *Occupational Therapy and Rehabilitation* from 1942, author Faber Birren, in his book *Color Psychology and Color Theory*, echoes Goldstein's concept that green "creates the condition of meditation." Birren goes on to say that green represents a "withdrawal from stimulus . . . and provides an ideal environment for . . . meditation."

More Eastern ties exist. Henry David Thoreau's description of Walden Pond bears a passing resemblance to the color of the cavernous water world of Dean's imagination (more about this in a moment), but more precisely the album cover. Said Thoreau, Walden appears to possess a yellowish hue near the shoreline only to turn "a light green, which gradually deepens to a uniform dark green."

Walden is essentially a series of observations by one individual who retreats into nature, seeks independence, and lives apart from society to find his inner self. Some of the same transcendental qualities Thoreau attributed to the area around Walden Pond, and nature in general, are present in *Siddhartha*, written nearly seventy years later.

The notion that Dean's cover skillfully blends colors in a manner that makes it difficult to tell where one tint begins and another ends fits perfectly with Thoreau's, Hesse's, and even Yes's conception of connectedness.

Cosmic Egg?

CTTE is significant for another major reason: the first appearance of the famous serpentine Yes logo on an album cover. *Fragile* featured a similar, albeit more angular logo. Admittedly, gazing upon the cover of *Fragile*, the *y* of the word "Yes" does appear to be entangled in the title, "Fragile," but I'd like to think that any reasonable and objective observer would note that the two logos are distinct.

On *CTTE*, the *y* loops around and is threaded through the "eye" of the *e* to form the *s*. In wrapping itself around the *e*, the *y–s* hybrid creation is reminiscent of the snake of the Orphic egg of Greek mythology. (The "egg" here being the *e*, appropriately enough.)

The Orphic egg, like the cosmic egg in other ancient cultures, symbolizes the birth of the universe. The Orphic egg of Greek mythology tells us that a god, possessing both feminine and masculine qualities, created other Greek deities. Everything. *Close to the Edge*, then, marks the beginning of nearly everything for Yes—if not personally and musically then certainly visually. The year 1972 and the cover of *CTTE* mark the birth of a new world for the band.

Some in art-world circles have speculated that the lettering on the cover of the Beatles' *Rubber Soul* was an influence on the Dean logo. To be fair, the serpentine typographic designs are, in some ways, an extension of the biomorphic lettering found on many a surreal psychedelic rock album cover and nightclub handbill.

In addition, Dean's work touches upon such art movements as Biomorphism, surrealism, and nineteenth-century *art nouveau*, all of which use curved lines that at least partly resemble and perhaps are meant to represent natural forms. Dean supposedly created the twisting logo on a train ride to Brighton, or so he told *Prog* magazine in 2013.

"All this had a huge effect on the promotion of bands, what we did in our spare time, and of course album covers started to reflect an art form of their own," says artist William Neal, whose artwork can be found on the packaging for Emerson, Lake, and Palmer's *Tarkus* and *Pictures at an Exhibition*. "I don't think it was a deliberate thing at first, it just grew from seeing interesting lettering, and photographic tricks. The lettering conveyed more than just information about the band, it started to have visual voice of its own. The Yes logo by Roger Dean is an example of how far it eventually came."

Gatefold

The final and most crucial component of the Dean artwork for *CTTE* is the inside gatefold. When we open the LP, we're awed by an expansive, mist-shrouded terrain of miles-high emerald streams snaking through a mountaintop of a mysterious, distant land.

Contoured rock cliffs, odd topographical features, what could be a man-made (perhaps Neolithic) land bridge, and waterfalls that float weightlessly lead the eye virtually nowhere. Author and scholar Edward Macan interprets the winding road or land bridge of the gatefold as a spiritual path—what Hesse scholar Theodore Ziolkowski's identifies as "the landscape of the soul."

Still, the fantastical nature of the illustrations seems to transport my mind to some mythical mountaintop paradise, something akin to Shangri-La from *Lost Horizon*, or the ancient Buddhist and Hindu concept of Shambala. Despite Dean's explanation that he was inspired by regions of Venezuela and the Scottish Highlands, the imagery has an exoticism that few places on Earth do, save perhaps for the East.

One thinks of Everest, the mountainous peaks of China's Xianjiang Province, Fuji of Japan, and other such grand natural structures that are as beautiful and towering as they are foreboding, suggesting and symbolizing the eternal, just as Dean's waterfalls seem to be forever refreshing themselves.

Looking East

Art critic/historians have posited that Dean's work may have been informed by Edmund Dulac, Japanese woodcuts, and Alphonse Mucha, among other artists and creative sources. There's some truth in this, but one wonders if Dean also studied the work of environmentally conscious architects and designers such as Frank Lloyd Wright and Richard Buckminster Fuller, whose twenty-story biosphere, constructed of a series of interconnecting triangle shapes and resembling some ginormous magical *yantra*, appeared at the 1967 World's Fair. In addition, Buckminster Fuller based his architectural designs on forms found in nature (the sphere, the egg), signaling underlying themes of birth and rebirth.

Given Yes's affinity for *Sonic Seasonings*, Walter Carlos's 1972 Moog-inflected electronic double album, one wonders if Dean had been shown the cover of that record, as well, which displays an eighteenth-century painting on a six-panel folding screen, titled *Waves at Matsushima*, by Japanese artist Ogata Kōrin. Monumental natural formations appear from seeming nothingness, as if hovering in a surreal floating world. These characteristics are evident in Kōrin's and, we should say, Dean's work. The marbleized technique

Dean employed for his *Yessongs* illustrations hints at the aged color qualities (now) inherent to *Matsushima*.

Some scholars have noted that Kōrin's work is related to Japanese woodblock print art, or *ukiyo-e*, which translates as images depicting the floating world and/or the misery of life, a kind of satirical twist on the Buddhist concept of the pain of human existence. Dean's works do suggest the sadness of Buddhist tenets, but they also capture the playful spirit of *ukiyo-e*, which reflects the beauty of everyday life, the natural elements and the lush colors of expansive Japanese landscapes.

Although we might be instructed to compare the Japanese Rinpa artists of the seventeenth century to those of the Italian Renaissance, who worked hundreds of years prior, there's nonetheless some nod to the Pre-Raphaelites of Britain, who created an art community of sorts in response to Renaissance art. The Rinpa artists and Britain's Pre-Raphaelites seemed to derive inspiration from similar sources, such as classical literature, nature, and an obsession with reviving the ideals and esthetics of the past. In so doing, they created a kind of "natural supernaturalism," to borrow a phrase from the author M. H. Abrams.

As an aside, there are some obvious similarities between Dean's work and the German Romantic painter Caspar David Friedrich's famous *Wanderer Above the Sea of Fog*. Does Dean's gatefold illustration invite us to become "the wanderer" overlooking the shrouds of clouds and distant rocky maw? We feel dwarfed by nature, yet "one with it." Friedrich himself once wrote that the artist paints not "what he sees before him, but what he sees in himself."

Gazing upon the cover of *Sonic Seasonings* and noting the crests of waves, the rocky contoured outcrops towering over them, and the mushroom-topped trees near the apex of the fifth panel of *Matsushima*—not to mention the color tones (largely green, gold, and brown)—it's difficult not to be reminded of the naturally striated rock cliffs seen in the gatefold of *Close to the Edge*, as well as Dean's contemporary illustrations that went unused at the time of the original release. (Fittingly, and I mention this in passing, the tri-fold out panel presentation employed for the *Yessongs* album packaging also seems to suggest the influence of seventeenth- and eighteenth-century Japanese art.)

Of course, the link between Dean's work and the Japanese masters of the Edo period (the years spanning the early 1600s through the 1860s) could simply be the manifestation of Dean's love of art from a certain region of the world.

Since Dean has lived in both Hong Kong and London, and since he made a name for himself in the psychedelic age of the 1960s and early 1970s, it's little wonder that he had the ability to fuse what some perceive as fantasy-based psychedelia of the West with the beautiful traditional, nature-informed styles of the East.

Dean illustrated some very evocative scenes, yes. But never let it be said that he is without wit. He embedded his art with a few clues and peekaboos—or is it *peak*aboos? For instance, the rocks on the cover of Yes's *Tales from Topographic Oceans* and the ribbed and curved cave walls of *Relayer* appear less like natural formations than sculpted Easter Island *Moai* heads. Some have even said they notice a house or even the shape of two people in the rock formation in the gatefold of *CTTE*. (Male and female forms?)

Human genitalia can be detected in the dark grey areas of Uriah Heep's *Demon and Wizards* (penis rocks, vagina tree roots) as well as the wraparound cover of *Relayer*. You might also spot different parts of the male and female anatomy in the *Yessongs* album packaging, if you're so inclined.

Some of this is a kind of Rorschach test, and it can be a case of recognizing your name in photographs of dirt patterns on the surface of the Moon. (Some refer to this phenomenon as pareidolia.) In addition, one of the drawings that Dean created for *CTTE*—one that wasn't used for the packaging at the time of the original release—boasts a monolithic cliff with a winding path, which Dean referred to as "almost monochrome" in his book *Views*, and resembles a jagged, overflowing mug, equipped with handle.

But there's more. Much more. We find humanoid and erotic images amid the mountaintop lake, waterfalls, and craggy outgrowths of the *CTTE* gatefold. A penis tip here, a bloated, floating dead man in the water, there; someone hanging on for dear life, attempting to climb his way back up the waterfalls, off in the distance; we also spy a toothy, snarling gator and a flying dragon. Perhaps the higher mind will recognize the symbolic union of masculine and feminine forms, mirroring the musical marriage of those opposing sonic qualities in the progressive rock of Yes.

All-Encompassing Art

Many in the past have floated the idea that prog rock's ultimate ambition was to present an all-in-one multimedia presentation—a derivation or update of Wagner's dramatic principle of *Gesamtkunstwerk*, which sought to combine the text, performance, and symphonic aspects of a dramatic work. Concentrate hard enough and the act of absorbing the entire artistic progressive-rock package—all the visual and aural stimuli—might induce a form of meditation that could lead to enlightenment, or gnosis.

Images and words are attached in other ways. *Rolling Stone* magazine reviewer Richard Cromelin wrote that "water dominates" the Yes sonic landscape, and that the "liquidity" of the music possesses "a futuristic quality." The metallic elements fuse "with liquid in a heady mix of primordial past and glistening future."

Succinctly, the landscape of the *Close to the Edge* gatefold is matched only by the expansiveness and sometimes quirkiness of the sonic terrain heard on the record. I'm convinced that Rick Wakeman's cavernous Moog- and Mellotron-soaked lines, Howe's evocative 12-string playing, and Bill Bruford's resonant snare sound in "And You and I," for example, give life and meaning—and vice versa—to Dean's gatefold illustration.

In keeping with the Wagner principle, Dean also worked beyond album cover artwork, helping to design Yes's stage productions with his brother, Martyn Dean. Yes's stage shows throughout the 1970s arguably impacted younger generations of designers, thinkers, filmmakers, and progressive-rockers of all stripes, inspiring them to create their own visual extravaganzas, from Dream Theater, with their video rhombuses, to Steven Wilson's use of film-screen cyclorama.

The *Close to the Edge* tour was the very basis of Yes's theatrical presentations thereafter. (See chapter 8.) The stage props for *Tales from Topographic Oceans* included Martyn Dean's fiberglass finned shell canopy, which enveloped newcomer drummer Alan White, creating something akin to an acoustic chamber. White famously noted that the sound of his drums was more resonant because of the pavilion.

One of the amorphous forms of the band's stage set for *Tales*, co-designed by Roger and Martyn Dean, hinted at the shape of a pipe organ. The design called for pipes to be present and change colors. (Talk about a color organ.) This "expressionist organ," as the brothers Dean would call it, was perhaps as close as Wakeman came to playing a pipe organ live onstage with Yes in the mid-1970s.

Although admittedly related to Pink Floyd and Roger Waters' extravagant productions and outrageous stage props, Muse's recent in-the-round "Drones" tour launched floating software-guided, propeller-powered helium objects, which descended upon the audience. A stationary "space station" hovered above center stage and encased the tour's lighting and audio (among other gear).

Surely these enormous oddities owe some, albeit small, debt to the monstrous and circular sci-fi stage creations the brothers Dean incorporated into their production designs of the 1970s. For instance, Muse's designs resembled the lit "barnacle" formations, accompanied by a painted backdrop, featured on Yes's 1975 US dates, as well as Martyn Dean's three-headed alien "crab nebula," with jellyfish-like spines from 1976. The kicker? Mike Tait's mega-successful tour production company built the rotating stage for Muse, no doubt based on Tait's groundbreaking work for Yes's *Tormato* dates . . .

In addition, there seems to be some overlap between Holly-wood CGI effects and Dean's landscapes. The less said about this the better, however. Perhaps more importantly, the crystals for the UK leg of the Yes's *Drama* tour in 1980 reminds the author of another, more recent conceptual design, a Crystal Volcano or pyr-amid, fabricated from Plexiglas by a California production-design firm in service to Krewella, an electronic dance band originating in Illinois.

The Krewella crystals were a complex matrix of single- and double-sided mirrors both containing and displaying interior light sources and effects. Flexible Illuminode LED tape lit the pyramid shaped volcano-like structure from within.

For Yes's *Drama* tour, Dean's internally lit crystals were framed by lightweight aluminum scaffolding that snapped together, easy for load-in and load-out. In addition, Dean's work was a departure from, as much as a complement to, the music. The sharp geometric dimen-sions of the crystals seemed to echo both the clear-cut, streamlined approach the band had taken to the music on *Drama* and the trap-pings of the new-age milieu from which Yes sprung.

Dean's fascination with nature, ley lines, geometric patterns in the landscape, and ancient civilizations continued with the cover of *Tales from Topographic Oceans*. He had just finished working with John Michell, author of *The View Over Atlantis*, which explores the mysterious links between ancient structures such as the Pyramids and Stonehenge.

Traveling with Yes from London to Anchorage to Japan for the *CTTE* tour, Dean gazed out of the airplane window, looking down on the vast landscapes—and those supposed ley lines—crisscrossing three continents. He and Jon Anderson discussed "power" lines, and the substance of this talk found its way into the music and lyrics of Yes by the mid-1970s.

At the same time, Dean's art became more esoteric and "soft." Albums such as *One Live Badger* and Yes's *Relayer* highlighted the greyer end of Dean's color palette. "Roger . . . was commissioned to do it," says Badger's one-time guitarist Brian Parrish. "When we saw the sleeve, if I'm being honest, I thought, 'It is *One Live Badger* and there are two badgers here.' That was my first [reaction] . . . but I still love it. Great cover. The badgers are . . . almost otherworldly, like they come out of the Tolkien world."

Yes. Otherworldly. Beautiful. Subtle. These descriptors are true of both *One Live Badger* and *Relayer*. But in both cases, the image is drained of the tone vibrancy that defined much of Dean's work up until that point. Unfortunately, by the mid-to-late 1970s, this was becoming a trend—for prog-rock artwork in general. Dean-type fantasy-style branding was shunted aside for something, dare we say, a tad bit more realistic and less idiosyncratic.

Artwork for rock and prog-rock records had changed, much like the music, which had become more streamlined, commercialized, and listener-friendly. Yes's relationship with Dean was severed, albeit temporarily, in favor of Hipgnosis's photographic montages (as featured on *Going for the One* and *Tormato*).

Some of the artwork commissioned for the covers of LPs by Yes's contemporaries seemed to follow a psychedelic-meets-photographic formula, sidestepping overt fantasy escapism altogether. Whether it was Genesis's . . . *And Then There Were Three*, Pink Floyd's *Animals*, ELP's *Love Beach*, Tull's *Bursting Out*, or Yes's very own *Tormato*, much of the extravagant otherworldly illustrations and meditative, trance-inducing colors had been filtered out of LPs by major prog bands of the era.

Even the mathematical precision of Shusei Nagaoka's symmetrical visions for Electric Light Orchestra's symphonic art-pop double album *Out of the Blue* spoke less of geographically impossible dreamscapes and more to manned interstellar space travel in nuts-and-bolts rocket-launched vehicles. With a slight leap of faith it could very nearly have been a NASA photo we were witnessing.

Likewise, the debut album of the supergroup U.K.: at the nexus of a diamond-shaped design formed by the disembodied busts of the band's four protagonists is a luminescent, triangle-shaped, UFO-like object, recalling the "insights" from some hallucinogen-induced out-of-body experience. The LP's flip side features a bright aerial photograph of Great Britain taken from space, an attempt perhaps to further precipitate this astral traveling or weightless sensation.

Although the effect may recall the impact of Dean's work, the shift away from Dean-esque landscapes was obvious. A larger movement toward a less color-saturating and elaborate form of artwork typified illustrations of the mid- and late 1970s. Prog rock—and the album artwork that helped to define it—was changed forever . . .

Dean Renaissance

Generations of successful album cover artists, from Ed Unitsky to Rodney Matthews, Per Nordin to Hugh Syme, Manthos Lappas to Thomas Ewerhard, have followed in Dean's footsteps. Each continually, and as a matter of course, apply design tools at their disposal in the digital age.

"Roger's art was actually part of my inspiration," says Per Nordin, who designed prog supergroup Transatlantic's famous dirigible. "On doing *Bridge to Forever* I consciously wanted to combine the dreamy softness of Roger Dean with the stark hyperrealism of Storm Thorgerson."

Unitsky has mastered a number of artistic tools, including digital graphic and 3D-drawing applications. He says:

It's perhaps no surprise that some of my works have

been paralleled with Roger Dean's art. Being far from looking like a blind follower of his style, I can still express my great admiration for his high-class art. And of course I have high regards for the special "Yes-style" spirituality of his artworks, as I've been a long-term fan of this great band, too.

That's why the cover arts for albums I create carry on the best traditions of the prog rock itself, seeking to convey the vibe so much loved by the audience, and invite them to thinking and reflection. The artwork for their releases, too, goes far beyond mere beautiful pictures, being rather a representation of some philosophical ideas that are conveyed in the lyrics and have to resonate with the visual imagery.

6
SEASONS WILL PASS YOU BY
The (Un)solid Time of Change

Jon Anderson was the first to know. Before a word was spoken about it, one cataclysmic event was revealed to him in a vision, as so many other things had been in the *Close to the Edge* era.

Anderson told his wife that he thought Bruford was going to leave the band. He claimed to have foreseen it, but was powerless to stop it. Bruford had made up his mind: he was accepting an invitation from Robert Fripp to join King Crimson.

The following day, with the band set to meet at Advision for a mixing session for *CTTE*, Anderson delivered the news to the gang; emotions, in the wake of Bruford's sudden goodbye, ranged from shock and disbelief to anger and dismissiveness.

Subsequently, Anderson tried to convince Bruford to stay, but it was too late. Bruford wasn't absorbing from the band everything he needed as an artist. Anderson said he and the band could accommodate that, but making exceptions was not what Bruford was aiming for.

"We presumed he wanted to get a different viewpoint for his drumming," Squire told *Melody Maker* in October 1972. But the bassist questioned whether Bruford was fully ready for the jazz-oriented musical styling of Crimson.

Fripp, it was believed by some in the Yes camp, played into Bruford's deep-seated need to be a "jazzer." Yet Bruford was not exactly the kind to jam with other musicians (at least, that was the case when he was a member of Yes). He had sat in with Iron Butterfly once, but his experience with improvisation or flying by the seat of his pants was minimal. Being thrown into deep uncharted musical waters was risky—but exactly what Bruford was seeking. "Fripp was dangling a carrot of a different flavor in front of him," says Mike Tiano, editor of *Notes from the Edge*.

Funnily enough, Fripp referred to the new-look Crimson as being definitive, a "magic band." Fripp's interest in Wicca, the wonders of which he supposedly discovered in New York City while on tour with the *Islands*-era Crimson, may have led to the formation of this new band. Perhaps Fripp knew his *Islands*-era band was doomed. Perhaps he felt lost and needed safe passage into the next phase of his career that only occult spells could grant him. Perhaps some of Yes's magic was being transferred to King Crimson?

As the story goes, Fripp used "Low Magic" for guidance in his musical career—as far as this author understands it, anyway—through means of Pyromancy, or "divination by fire or through forms appearing in fire," according to Dictionary.com. This meant the ritualized burning of candles. Fripp reportedly attributed his adoption of these mysterious methods to his reconnecting with an old friend, bassist/vocalist John Wetton of Family. He also credited Bruford's joining Crimson to the "healing" magic of "a lady in Wimborne," as he told the *New Musical Express* at the time.

If you don't believe in any supernatural hocus-pocus, maybe a more practical reason can be sought for why Bruford joined Fripp. Fripp was actually crashing with Bruford at his home in London for a short time prior to the drummer accepting Fripp's invitation. Crimson had also shared a bill with Yes a few times, most recently in Boston. (A discrepancy has arisen regarding this date. A *Melody Maker* article from April 15, 1972, mentions that both bands performed at the Orpheum Theatre, which had been recently renamed the Aquarius Theatre. However, the liner notes to *Ladies of the Road*, a King Crimson Collectors Club Special Edition release, list the date as March 27, 1972.)

Whether there were any supernatural forces at work or not, Bruford's vanishing act didn't involve any old band. This was the Mighty Crim, one of Yes's earliest and chief rivals.

It was the second time Crimson had lured a Yes member into its corner of the universe. Anderson had appeared on Crimson's 1970 studio effort, *Lizard*, and it's part of prog-rock lore that Fripp had been courted by Yes subsequent to Banks's dismissal. Fripp, or so he told *Melody Maker* in 1972, declined Yes's offer to appear on one of its studio records. (In addition, drummer Ian Wallace had appeared briefly with Yes and later joined Crimson.)

It's curious why Fripp would choose Bruford for this lineup, which was so improv-heavy, but he certainly saw his potential, and likely also knew the kind of precision and economy Bruford employed as a drummer. Fripp may have seen the Crim graduate inside him and brought the Yes drummer along on an apprenticeship in the dark arts of improvisation and minor-chord prog rock.

Although some were skeptical of the move, Bruford has maintained over the years that he was about to leave Yes anyway, and that Fripp was there to catch him before he fell.

Fripp had been through the musical chairs bit himself with Crimson and could sympathize from every angle. Since its earliest days, Crimson had seemingly nurtured a reputation for gathering steam and dissipating its assets. Yet despite its previous two years being topsy-turvy, the band appeared to be more stable than Yes in mid-1972.

Crim co-founders Ian McDonald and Michael Giles had left Crimson for what they thought were greener pastures. I remember McDonald telling me in an interview I conducted with him that he thought that after leaving Crimson he would simply form another band. "It doesn't really work like that," he said, on reflection.

"I still can't figure out why Bill left," Squire told *Melody Maker*, months after the incident. "He could have advanced himself with us just as much as with Bob Fripp." Ironically, six months earlier in 1972, Fripp had told *Circus* something similar about McDonald and Giles regarding their artistic growth within the Crimson band unit.

Well into the twenty-first century, Bruford's dramatic turn still appears to confuse the Yes camp. Jon Brewer, former manager of Yes and Squire, told me in 2013 that he just couldn't comprehend the reasoning behind it. "I don't know why Bill left," he told me. "I don't think *Bill* knows why Bill left."

"I left Yes for the money," Bruford once told me. "I knew I was going to get paid too much." Once a hardworking musician begins to get paid—or perhaps overpaid—his thinking was, "What follows next is repetition."

We'd need to study this in more detail, but Bruford may actually be factually accurate regarding certain musical passages of *Going for the One* and *Tales from Topographic Oceans*, the band's next studio effort after *CTTE*, that either use similar instrumentation or seem to quote from earlier works, including "Close to the Edge."

In *Yesyears*, a band documentary and retrospective released in

1991, Bruford explained that he was having trouble seeing what he could contribute to the band other than "Son of *Close to the Edge*, and I didn't really see any point in that."

"So many things about that are surprising," says Sebadoh drummer Bob D'Amico, a confirmed Bruford fan, who was in a Yes tribute band, the World, in the 1980s on Long Island, New York. "The first thing is that he was only twenty-three years old. Maybe it was an impulsive move, but when you think about it, maybe it was more of a wise man's move. He could have been thinking, 'Let me think about this artistically, not commercially.'"

The process of recording *CTTE* weighed heavily on Bill, and he needed to cut loose of this situation, perhaps for his own musical and mental health. The title *Close to the Edge* certainly could be applied to Bruford's precarious Yes predicament and existential angst. In his own way, Bruford was journeying along a kind of spiritual trajectory of self-realization that would transform the budding artist into a maverick master drummer and adventurous future bandleader.

According to Eddy Offord, it was the long recording sessions that caused Bruford to leave:

> It was a bit too premeditated for him, and he wanted to play more freely. Bill Bruford was very much a purist when it came to music. So, we would lay down a basic track—drums, bass, guitar, maybe, or organ or something, and it sounded really good. Jon was always the one who wanted to push more the classical side. He wanted to add this and that. Or, "Oh, let's try this, let's try that." There was so much going on that you lost the original basis of the band. I remember one day Jon said, "This sounds pretty good. We'll put this in the background and it'll be great." Then Bill said, "Why don't you put the entire record in the background and be done with it," you know? He was sick of his parts being covered up by all of this nonsense going on.

"Bear in mind, though, that once the basic tracks were laid down, Bill's job was mostly done," says Gary Martin. "He contributed musical ideas as the tracks' development went along but

I'm guessing that he got a little bored with the many hours of the minutiae of overdubs and mixes. I had the feeling he was happier playing live, but that's just my impression."

Pivotal Prog Moment

Bruford's blastoff from Yes amounts to a downright paradigm-shifting event in the history of prog rock. It was perhaps as earthshattering to prog as Dylan going electric or George Harrison nourishing a taste for Indian music and philosophy were to the rock culture at large.

Dylan and the Beatles were contemporaries and influenced once another on both a musical and chemical basis, and their relationship went on to change the world. They demonstrated a willingness to disown nearly everything they'd earned as artists, risking prospective commercial profit, the general derision of the public, rendering themselves irrelevant (or worse) and surrendering their status as pop icons for art, for freedom.

Didn't Bill Bruford do the same?

The prospect of comparing Bruford with a Beatle and a poet/folk-rock innovator may not be as blasphemous as one thinks. Don't dismiss this as being outright ridiculous. Bruford had been cut from the same cloth as these icons, as far as I can tell. With a love of jazz in his heart, he wanted to achieve a goal that went beyond just making good music. In addition, and perhaps just as importantly, Bruford's leaving impacted the musical direction and arguably the historical significance of Yes, King Crimson, Genesis, National Health and U.K.—all the bands he touched—and directly or indirectly altered the careers of the individual band members of each of these acts.

Consider this: Bruford helped to push Crimson into a more metallic realm in the 1970s with the recording of the album *Red*, providing fodder for material we'd hear from bands as varied as Dream Theater and Nirvana, while also simultaneously allowing for a more rock-orientated rhythm section to dovetail with Yes's weighty thematic concepts.

Bruford also ensured that public attention was given to lesser-known names of the genre, such as Gong, Genesis (in the States, anyway), keyboardist Dave Stewart (Egg, National Health, Hatfield and the North), bassist Jeff Berlin, and so on. And he facilitated

Phil Collins's move from upstage to downstage by becoming Genesis's touring drummer in 1976, thus helping to offer Collins a path to pop stardom. And, let's not forget, Bruford, along with Wakeman and bassist/vocalist John Wetton, went on to form the prototype for U.K., one of prog's most revered supergroups, itself influential on a range of rock artists, including members of the popular or critically respected bands Megadeth, Van Halen, King's X, and IQ, among others.

Talk had spread for years that Wakeman was forming a band with Wetton, ELP's Carl Palmer, and Manfred Mann Earth Band's (pre-Yes) Trevor Rabin in the early 1980s. Rabin had been kicking around the prog scene for a while, even prior to his involvement with Yes. It's likely this proposed group was the early basis of Asia, before Howe came into the picture. (As of this writing Wakeman was scheduled to tour with Anderson and Rabin.)

The band, in its infancy, even practiced material in the Caped Crusader's rehearsal studios, Complex Seven. That nascent outfit—initially dubbed British Legion, Wakeman once revealed—mutated into something less conservative, prior to the final lineup being solidified. As it happens, a U.K. featuring Wakeman wasn't to be, and Bruford went on record as saying that he had "no intention of playing the kind of music that [Wakeman] wanted to play."

Wakeman soon accepted an offer to return to Yes, ironically enough, and, at the same time, the supergroup dubbed U.K. catapulted former Soft Machine/Tony Williams/Tempest and Bruford guitarist Allan Holdsworth to international fame. Holdsworth's presence and playing helped to inform the revolutionary fretboard acrobatics of '80s guitar god Eddie Van Halen, whose young band gigged with U.K.

To a great degree, U.K. also provided Wetton with a musical template, or a facsimile of such, for yet another supergroup—Asia. Some have pegged Asia as the very embodiment of the failure of the hippie dream sincerely sought by prog rock. It seems the boys couldn't care less.

Thanks to Asia, Wetton graduated from the relative obscurity of prog journeyman to chart-topping hit maker in less than two years. Asia has been his biggest commercial success, a creative outlet he'd been craving as a singer and songwriter since the mid-1970s.

Conflicting stories abound regarding Bruford's migration back to his fusion/instrumental rock band, Bruford. Was he asked to leave U.K.? Did he vacate in solidarity with Holdsworth's dismissal? Either way, U.K. slimmed down to a trio featuring Wetton, lead keyboardist/violinist Eddie Jobson, and Zappa drummer Terry Bozzio, later of Missing Persons.

"I'm close with Bozzio and Wetton, and had a lot of fun with the U.K. reunion, and I was with them in rehearsals in Chicago [in 2012]," says Ed Clift, a Paiste Cymbals consultant who's worked for decades with some of the drumming giants of prog rock, including Carl Palmer and Bruford. "It was interesting to see, up close and personal, how Bozzio got a feel for Bill's drumming and to hear the backstory."

The story goes that Bozzio was unaware of Bruford's hard-won evolution as a drummer, technician, and all-around musician. In short, Bruford had a style and a sound that may have not registered in the mind of Bozzio prior to his joining U.K. in the late 1970s.

"Bruford has had a huge impact on the Bozzios of the world," Clift says. "Most people in the prog genre feel as though Bruford is responsible for so much of what prog means. . . . I always tell people that if Bill had only recorded *Close to the Edge* and did nothing else in his entire career, he would qualify to be a hall-of-fame drummer."

"The common misunderstanding about drummers is that you have to hit [the drums] hard—or that you have to look like you have to hit them hard, or something," Bruford once told me. "My whole thing is to try to be as economical with my movements and as effortless as possible—and elegant. What is the point of having an Englishman playing the drums, if he's not going to be either elegant or economical, or preferably both?"

Once the 1980s rolled around, Bruford further developed his style. The King Crimson of the 1980s sent shockwaves through the music industry. The friction between Bruford and Fripp fueled the new lineup, which included guitarist/vocalist Adrian Belew and bassist Tony Levin, to embrace electronics, new wave, and global ethnic music.

It's impossible to calculate the number of artists who've been impacted by Fripp–Belew–Bruford–Levin lineup that existed at the nerve center of Crimson's pop sensibility and application of musical-instrument technology. We can count a few names, though, such as Primus, Tool, Between the Buried and Me, the Mars Volta, and Mystery Jets.

"I'm very much into Bruford's playing," says Tim Wyskida, drummer for veteran instrumental drone-metal/prog-rock/dub band Blind Idiot God. "King Crimson? Just the way Bruford approached things was incredible. When he got to the era of *Three of a Perfect Pair* [1984], it all flowed. He was doing some minimal shit. The whole leaving space thing had gone further with him."

All of this entices us to entertain thoughts of "What if?"

If Bruford had *not* joined Crimson, either in the 1970s or 1980, or waited to join Crim until after the completion of the *CTTE* tours, it's likely this would have impacted Fripp's musical and spiritual journeys of the 1970s. Without Bill's presence, would Fripp's period of humility, self-reflection, and soul-searching be deferred? Would he have drawn the necessary conclusions to pull up stakes and move to New York City, or reform Crimson circa 1980, in the first place?

It's likely much of this would have occurred at some point, but the larger question remains: would albums such as *Red* or *Discipline* ever have been recorded? (Funnily enough, Fripp broke up Crimson in late 1974, and Bruford had once bemoaned to the London *Times* the arduous process of recording *Red*, the band's final studio record of the 1970s. He didn't appear to have any intention of leaving Crimson, though.)

We can debate whether any of these artistic developments were good things or bad, but it'd be difficult to argue that Bruford was merely a passenger to these events. While I'm aware that it's shortsighted to conclude that he was personally responsible for every twist and turn in the course plotted by prog rock from, say, 1972 through 1982 (or later), his actions, or inactions, nonetheless caused a ripple effect and may have changed the course of the rock and progressive-rock worlds throughout the 1970s—and beyond.

Domino?

Insecurity can be a powerful motivating factor in prompting restless lights to get the fuck out of Dodge. For all his talents and impeccable playing, Bruford may have been the next domino to fall. We may never know, but the manner in which he speaks of Yes is colorful, to say the least. He's likened Anderson to a certain mid-twentieth-century toothbrush-mustachioed dictator for using a unique style of band management to bring out the best qualities in the players around him.

Anderson, he has said, would strum on an acoustic guitar, without really knowing what he was doing, and present feeble ideas to other four members in order for them to piece together a song based on sound musical theory. He did it all "with a look in his eyes which said, 'If you don't like this, quit or make it better,' which is a technique . . . that Hitler would use, somewhere slightly to the right of Hitler," Bruford told Texas radio DJ Redbeard in 2012.

Likening an ex-bandmate to a brutal fascist dictator in retrospect may be the result of all that Bruford had experienced in the music biz since 1972. It also illustrates the pressure the drummer may have felt to conform. It was a demonstrable fact that founding members were dropping like flies: first Peter Banks in '70, then Tony Kaye in '71; Bruford in '72 or '73? Who knows?

Yes entered the next phase of its lifespan: finding a suitable replacement. Of course, Bruford could never truly be replaced. Even the Yes guys knew this, so they knew they needed to find someone who could approach the material in a sensible way to capture the flavor of the original drumming while also bringing something fresh to the table.

As a friend of Eddy Offord, drummer Alan White had been hanging around Advision in recent weeks. With his band Griffin, White would commute from Sussex into London for gigs, but this soon became tiring and expensive. To make life easier, White began staying with Offord at his flat. It was inevitable that White would find himself floating down to the Yes sessions at Advision, as he had when the band was working through "America."

It's been told in several slightly different ways, but the basic skeleton of the story goes that one night in the studio, after Bruford announced he was leaving, he ducked out, stunning the band. Something along those lines. White happened to be hanging around Advision, and Offord told him to sit behind the kit and play. They ran through "Siberian Khatru." As a result of Alan's good showing, Yes was convinced that White, as Anderson would say, was "the guy."

Alan White was born in 1949, about a month after Bruford, in

Pelton, in the north of England, which makes him, as John Wetton once told me, a "Geordie boy." (White was the drummer for the 1987 album *Wetton/Manzanera*.)

As a lad, White would cram his schedule with work, school, and playing gigs, sometimes till early in the morning. His father and grandfather were piano players, and his uncle, who had died when White was young, was a drummer in local dance bands. It was his uncle who persuaded White's parents to buy him a drum kit, practically altering the course of his life.

"As a child growing up there, the north was very depressed in the '60s," says British artist Claire Hamill, once a very close friend of White. "Alan was from a village about fifteen miles north of me, a tiny little village just like mine but more scenic because it was in the countryside. My village was right by the River Tees, and it was incredibly industrial. The people in the north are so warmhearted and easy to talk to and friendly. I think, actually, that was one reason Alan and I got on well, because we were both from the same area."

White had been with Happy Magazine, Alan Price Set (featured on the #4 UK hit "Simon Smith and His Amazing Dancing Bear," among others), George Harrison, Denny Laine and his group Balls, and, most notably, the Plastic Ono Band with John Lennon and Yoko Ono. (Prior to chancing his arm in London, White hooked up with the Blue Chips and, when this band dissolved, the Gamblers, during an extended stay in Germany at the same time, incidentally, the Warriors were gigging there.)

White was a different kind of drummer and a different kind of person altogether from Bruford. He had nurtured a reputation as a rock 'n' roller, having performed or recorded with the aforementioned groups as well as Terry Reid (live work and recording with none other than Eddy Offord), Doris Troy (with members of the Delaney and Bonnie band), and as a member of Chris Stainton's All Stars supporting Joe Cocker on a European tour that wrapped just days before the announcement that White had joined Yes.

The closer you look at Yes's decision to bring in Alan, the more logical it becomes. White and the Yes boys seemed to be orbiting in similar solar systems. For instance, Steve Howe had played with Delaney and Bonnie, as had White, who was on a Johnny Harris album, *All to Bring You Morning*, featuring Anderson and Howe.

"I think at the time [Bill left] we lost a drummer and a writer,"

Howe told me in 2001. "Alan does write, too, but we certainly don't have Bill's identity anymore, which was strong from *Yes* to *Close to the Edge*, to ABWH to *Yesstories*. Bruford's style was unusual. His style was exciting and fresh. Alan forged a style that has its complexities. It is slightly more credible when he wants to play straight 4/4."

"Bill, in the early days, came up with some incredible rhythm parts," Anderson told me. "Chris and Bill in the early days were very adventurous."

Bob Gluck, author, musician, and music professor, saw Yes with King Crimson and Procol Harum in November 1971 at the Academy of Music in Manhattan and once on the *CTTE* tour, but is fuzzy on which date. (It could have been the outdoor concert in Gaelic Park in New York City on August 16, 1972, or the Nassau Coliseum in Uniondale, Long Island, New York, on November 20, 1972, but he's not certain.)

Obviously, Bill was no longer a member of the band. I asked Gluck whether he was aware of this prior to seeing Yes on the *CTTE* tour.

> It was very obvious that Bill was no longer in the band, and that came as a surprise. I . . . was probably one of those people who felt let down by the change. I didn't really understand it, although I came to really appreciate Bill's involvement in King Crimson. I had actually really been a fan of Ian Wallace, having seen the 1971-to-1972 Crimson just north of London, when I was 16, and that caught my attention in a big way. Alan really seemed out of his comfort zone and this was not music that was easy to master.

"I think the band was at their zenith when Bill was in the band, because Bill kept this band grounded, I think," adds Derek Shulman, formerly of Gentle Giant, who toured with Yes in the US during the *Close to the Edge* period. "Alan was a great drummer . . . [but] I think Bill was a great jazz, progressive drummer. . . . Alan was good in his own way."

Gentle Giant was finishing work on *Octopus* for Vertigo Records in August at Advision, about a month after Yes wrapped up *Close to the Edge* there. "We were of the same school—the prog world—and

I guess we got to know them more with that tour, a lot more," Shulman says. "I got to know and understood what they were about. I loved *Close to the Edge*; it was a great piece of music and very well performed for the most part. Jon's voice is certainly unique and Chris's bass playing was much more an instrument than a rhythm section instrument. This was when Bill Bruford was in the band, before Alan White, and that intrigued me because it was quasi-orchestral and that was interesting to me."

In 2005, Steve Howe told me:

> Having a drummer like Bill Bruford was really . . . in a way, we couldn't play "ordinary" with him, and in another way we didn't want to. But the fact that we could have played with a more ordinary drummer, might also have worked, but it wouldn't have worked so well. Having Bill with his integrity and his style and his precision, governed us all. So the individual qualities that we found in ourselves. . . . Unfortunately, Bill didn't stay. I did three records with Bill with Yes at that time and they are really my favorites, because in a way he was holding the band together because it was not only his drumming. He was like a British Frank Zappa. He always had stuff to say and he was always on the edge and never predictable."

As a committed Yes fan, composer and Celtic/ambient artist David Arkenstone told me he felt White "had more balls than Bruford, who was also great, but Alan punched it up a level, I think, adding a bit more of the rock element."

Chris Squire told Chris Welch of *Melody Maker*, for an October 14, 1972 article, that Bruford had "some strange ideas about hitting the snare drum when he should be hitting the bass drum, and the other way round."

In the late 1990s, I asked Bill about his replacement, and he seemed almost intrigued by the question, as if he hadn't been asked it in a while, if very often. As a founding member of Yes, I wondered, how did he feel about a one-time John Lennon drummer replacing him? "You're not asking me why I left Yes," Bill said. "You're asking me what I thought of Alan as a drummer." I concurred, and Bill's answer was: "Solid player. I knew the music wouldn't fall apart with him."

Lindisfarne drummer Ray Laidlaw, who gigged with Yes on the *CTTE* tour, thought of White as "a rock 'n' roll drummer":

> I knew him because he was in a band called the Alan Price Set for a bit, then Happy Magazine, where the keyboard player [Kenny Craddock] was a real good friend of mine and went and stayed with him, about 1968, 1969. They were playing around all the London clubs, The Scotch of St. James, and all those places where Beatles and Stones used to go. I met [White] there. He may have been a year or two older than me. Then . . . he was playing on a bloody John Lennon record.
>
> I'll tell you a funny story about that. When Alan was doing "Imagine" with Lennon, and he got pulled into it on the last moment, Kenny, who was with him in Happy Magazine, was my really close friend, got a call to play keyboards on "Imagine," but he was in the bathroom and falling asleep and didn't hear the phone. One of his great regrets [is that] he didn't have a longer cord on the phone [*laughs*]. Alan likely got the Lennon gig through Terry Doran. Terry was George Harrison's pal, his personal assistant, but he was always out and about in the clubs. He knew everybody. I have a feeling that he had something to do with that.
>
> I met him again a few times after that. He was friends with a few of my pals, who used to live up in Sussex, all musicians from the northeast [of England] who came down to work in various groups. He made a solo album called *Ramshackled*—a bunch of my mates played on it, and I got to hear about it from them. Most of the music was written by Kenny Craddock, Colin Gibson, and all those people.

White has suggested that it was Lennon himself who was aware of his playing, possibly after seeing the drummer perform with his band Griffin, in a London venue. Supposedly, after witnessing White onstage the night before, John rang up the drummer the following day to see if he'd be interested in playing in Toronto the next night with the Plastic Ono Band, featuring Lennon, Yoko Ono, Eric Clapton, and visual artist/Lennon buddy from the Hamburg days Klaus Voormann.

It should be noted, though, that White has also gone on record as essentially corroborating Laidlaw's assertion that it may have been Doran, an old friend of the Fab Four from Liverpool, who put the bug in Lennon's ear about Griffin and White. (As well as "Imagine," White recorded "Instant Karma!," "Gimme Some Truth," and "Jealous Guy" with Lennon at Tittenhurst Park, Lennon's home studio.)

Yes had, of course, performed and recorded Beatles cover songs. And, for cryin' out loud, Yes references "Instant Karma!" and "Give Peace a Chance" in "I've Seen All Good People," from *The Yes Album*. It's no surprise, then, that Anderson indicated that he was already aware of White and that he wanted to collaborate with him "within the framework of Yes."

It's difficult to know *exactly* what this means, but perhaps Bruford, as we'd seen, may have read the writing on the wall, sensing that the band was shifting its musical focus away from jazz—or Yes's interpretation of jazz—and into experimental electronic music and hard rock.

White, it seems, was both a solid drummer and a solid person, as Claire Hamill recalls.

> I was away from home and Alan meant a great deal to me. He was older than me, like a big brother, he looked out for me. Alan and I went on to become really close and we shared a flat together. I was actually with Alan, we were all living together in [White's manager] Tony Dimitriades's house when Alan got the Yes gig. We were just over the moon for him. Yes were just about to reach the absolute pinnacle. I mean, weirdly enough I had toured with King Crimson [on various dates in England and continental Europe in 1973] and I knew Robert Fripp really well, and he'd been one of my ex-boyfriends. It was weird because I went on tour with King Crimson when Bill Bruford had joined the band. And my friend Alan had just taken his place in Yes.
>
> I think Alan thought of the music as being a complete

challenge. It was. Alan wasn't somebody who took anything for granted. He loved his job and he was a dedicated drummer. I know Alan was really thrown in the deep end and was challenged having to learn all of that complex music to take Bill's place. He used to come home and talk about all the time signatures he had to play in. "I have to do a 5/8." Or, "Oh, my God I have to do 7/8." I don't know if you've ever heard my track "Speedbreaker." To me, that is the most amazing drum solo, ever. Alan overdubbed that solo which was so difficult, because in those days no one played with a click track. Alan had to listen to the track and overdub the drums and feel it completely. It was an astonishing feat and in the studio we were just electrified by his performance . . . I was totally in love with him, but also he was my mate.

It seems everyone was feeling the love, at least initially, in the wake of Bruford's announcement. It was once believed that Bruford would tour with Yes until he became an official member of Crimson, on October 1, 1972. Brian Lane posited that Bruford would play drums and White would observe as an understudy of sorts, for a little while. White would then assume the drum throne at some point when Bruford left.

A source told me that when the discussions were underway as to what to do about Bruford, it was Steve Howe who said that if the drummer wanted out, he should leave straight away and not hang around. Howe has supposedly regretted that decision ever since. This may explain why the two recorded together on various projects over the years, especially Howe's solo records, from *Beginnings* to *Turbulence*, and the debut album by Anderson Bruford Wakeman Howe in the late 1980s.

"Nobody wanted Bill to leave," Howe told me in 2001. "Alan had become a friend of the band, anyway, and was already around us. The transition in that sense was easy."

Still, it was a tense, almost panicky, time for Yes. *CTTE* was the band's breakthrough album, and any misstep might ruin everything. As such, the process by which White joined Yes was a bit more protracted and intense than some would have you believe.

Desperate times would have forced certain individuals to resort to torture to salvage what the band, its management, and its agents had built over the last four years. "Chris threatened to throw me out the window if I didn't join the band [*laughs*], number one," White says in *Yesyears*. "And, secondly, as they were leaving, [Squire] said, 'Oh, by the way, we have a gig in front of 10,000 people in three day's time. Can you learn all the material?'"

For a drummer who rehearsed in the back of a plane with John Lennon en route to Toronto, having a few days to master a batch of tunes may have seemed like a luxury. (It may have been as long as a week, however, by White's own words.)

It was White's gig if he wanted it, leaving very little time to waste. (Conversely, and ironically, as it turns out, after Bruford's abrupt exit from Yes, he'd rehearse with the improvising unit Crimson for months prior to performing in Germany and launching into a tour of the UK in November and December.)

A Break in the Action

The Bruford break was messier than some imagined. As the story goes, Bruford was forced to pay to leave Yes, as per Brian Lane's instructions. Hard cash was to be rendered for canceled shows resulting from the switch. In addition, Bruford would have to fork over half the prospective royalties he was due to earn on *Close to the Edge*. The other half, presumably, would go to White, even though the latter had nothing to do with the creation of the album aside from one jam session (if the timeframe is even relevant).

Others in the Yes universe had complained about certain questionable management tactics. Some felt a chilling effect on their personal lives. "I was with [Peter Banks] in Brian Lane's office in 1975, I believe it was," Sidonie Jordan (a.k.a. Sydney Foxx of Empire, the group featuring also her ex-husband, Banks) told me in 2013. "He was getting a royalty check from Yes and he hadn't gotten many through the years, if any at all. . . . Our marriage may have survived had we not struggled so much for money in between record deals."

In researching this book, I eyeballed a number of official Yes documents—everything from riders to contracts involving publishing rights. One, from 1969, for which Banks, Kaye, Bruford, Anderson, and Squire signed on the dotted line, was between Cotillion and Yessongs, the publishing arm of the Yes music-business machine, then just getting off the ground.

I reached out to Bruford via e-mail to check with him the authenticity of the documents, and he believed them to be genuine. I, too, consider them to be such, given that the government office through which I accessed them had transferred them to microfiche and archived them in a searchable database.

The 1969 contract, the term of which was set to expire in May 1973, dictates (among other things) that Cotillion was to pay Yessongs 10 percent of the royalties generated by the printing and publishing of Yes's compositions. The document goes on to say that Cotillion is on the hook for 60 percent of the fees it collects *vis-à-vis* mechanical licenses issued by the company, including performance and broadcasting fees, to Yessongs.

Cotillion also had the legal authority to reprint, in any "folio," Yessongs compositions; it also agreed to pay Yessongs a royalty rate of ten percent of net sales generated from those folios (at wholesale selling prices). The band was given a nonreturnable advance of $15,000 (US) against royalties. Not an insignificant sum of money by 1969 standards, but in retrospect, Yes, as a band on the rise, was likely grossly underpaid.

Those bits about wholesale prices and "net sales" are especially troubling. If nothing else, this document indicates the "pitiful percentages paid to the writers . . . typical of the era," as Bruford put it in an e-mail.

This is, of course, one of many windows into a vast number of dealings Yes and its management had with all sorts of people. Although this may be only one piece of a larger financial puzzle, Yes was so successful that even a terrible contract such as this one must of yielded some financial reward. So what had Bruford truly given up?

The last chapter of Bruford's 1970s Yes saga perhaps shouldn't be defined by dollars and cents, but as a necessary and valuable learning experience. "I think Bill was into being in King Crimson," Hamill says. "I have a photo of him when we were in Italy and he looks exhausted. We did an Italian tour, as well as a British tour, and it was Bill looking really exhausted and Robert and I tucked into a corner of a restaurant . . . I think was really enjoying being with a new outfit."

Some of Bruford's experience with Yes was transferrable to this new situation, and there was new ground to break here. Some of the same qualities present in his drumming for Yes are apparent in his Crimson work, but the context was radically different.

Bruford told Chris Welch in 1973 that he changed his view of drumming and percussion, even calling his previous self "narrow-minded." Bruford was pushed artistically by percussionist Jamie Muir (Assagai, Boris), who surrounded himself with a variety of drums and percussion. Muir had what would qualify as a drum kit but augmented this setup with the likes of plastic bottles, a metal sheet and metal percussive objects, kazoo, whistles, gongs, balloons, metal chains, and parts of traditional instruments used in odd and assorted ways.

Muir was a madman who would crawl on his stomach across the stage floor and bite down on "blood" capsules for vampyric and theatrical effect. Bruford appeared to navigate this madness as well as anyone could—maybe more so. He was the yin to Muir's yang; composed, intellectual, precise, detailed, and steady, while Muir was unpredictable, loud, and violent. (Shades of the kind of showmanship Peter Banks displayed while in Yes?)

The percussionist was not long for the band, however. Disillusioned with the rock lifestyle, its lack of creative productivity, and the recording process, Muir made the decision to leave Crimson, ahead of the March 23 release of this Crimson lineup's debut studio album, *Larks' Tongues in Aspic*, featuring Fripp, Bruford, Muir, bassist/vocalist John Wetton, and violinist/flute player/Mellotron operator David Cross.

In general, Muir seemed to wrestle with concepts of authenticity, convincing himself that his flamboyant stage persona was little more than an act—a line of thinking that, eventually, led to a more introspective and monastic life.

The percussionist's departure was yet another example of the self-destructive nature of the band, or so some in the press thought, and ironically echoed Bruford's escape from Yes prior to *Close to the Edge*. With Muir a mere memory, Bruford, prior to the recording of 1974's *Starless and Bible Black*, began incorporating percussion effects and cymbals similar to the ones Muir used onstage. In fact, after Muir's exodus, Bruford assumed both roles, generating sounds onstage and in the studio that became part of his signature.

In a quirky twist, Bruford assumed the "Muir" role, albeit in a much more electronic capacity, when he shared the stage with White for Mega-Yes's 1991 *Union* tour. For once it wasn't White following but Bruford trying to keep up and carve out a space amid the dense confusion produced by eight players on a single stage.

White may have followed in Bruford's footsteps, historically, but he never aped his predecessor. What would be the point? In fact, White, as of this writing, is the only member of the band to appear in all of Yes's various incarnations since 1972.

By the late 1970s, White had developed his own muscular style, not without a measure of sophistication. Listen to tracks ranging from "Awaken" and "Release, Release" to "Future Times/Rejoice" and "Tempus Fugit." White is forceful but also manages to underscore those classic Yes idiosyncrasies. He'd balanced arty finesse with hard-rock aggressiveness. But that took work—and some time—to achieve.

As if underscoring Ahmet Ertegun's point about British musicians' determination and dedication, Squire said that Yes had redoubled its efforts since Alan White had joined. Yes had a greater amount of potential and seemed to "thrive on set backs. A lot of groups would just give in," Squire told *Melody Maker*.

True. Yes didn't give up but did have to cede ground. The first of the band's scheduled shows on the North American leg of its tour to support *CTTE* were either canceled or rescheduled due to the shakeup in personnel. Yes simply wasn't ready to fly across the Atlantic and play its complicated material for throngs of fans new and old.

Not, yet, anyway.

7

THE JOURNEY TAKES YOU ALL THE WAY

Breakthrough Record, Whirlwind Touring

Close to the Edge surfaced into a strange and dangerous world torn by political scandals, the rise of radical terrorism, and war.

Within a week of Yes's fifth album being released, eight armed Arab terrorists, calling themselves Black September, busted into the Olympic Village in Munich, Germany, where they kidnapped and eventually murdered eleven Israeli Olympic athletes. Five of the terrorists were also killed, alongside one German police officer.

The incident dominated the news cycle, and was just the kind of senseless hatred that Anderson seemed to be discussing in his lyrics. Months earlier, Yes had appeared to be the target of violence when a bomb threat came in to the University of Vermont and disrupted the concert the band was giving there on February 24, 1972. The Patrick Gymnasium needed to be evacuated as a result, according to Mary Jo Dahlbloom, reporter for the *Vermont Cynic*, the university's newspaper.

I checked with the Burlington Police Department, which provided a copy of the entry (entry #7117) from its dispatch log from the night in question. There were actually *two* bomb threats called in by an unknown subject that evening—one at approximately 20:15, and another at 20:58—although police archivist Jen Beane informed me that no official police report regarding this matter could be located.

A Lieutenant Barrett of the University of Vermont's security team also received a threat, at 21:15, and decided to evacuate the building, which is what many in attendance remember. "Having a bomb threat at a concert is very unusual," says J. Geils Band's Danny Klein, who was on the bill with Yes that night. "But, then again, it was early 1970s, fighting against the establishment. . . . You'd burn your draft card . . . I can see it happening."

As bizarre as this incident is, bomb threats were not uncommon in the early 1970s. In 1972, the total number of actual and attempted explosive bombings was 951, according to data the FBI collected for its "Uniform Crime Reports (Bomb) Summary" from 1978.

One of the era's most high-profile domestic anarchist groups, the infamous Weather Underground, wasn't as active as it had been in previous years, but it was still operating. In May 1972, at the Pentagon, a toilet (of all things) was blown up, with the Underground's New York squad reportedly taking credit for the attack. It's doubtful, though, that the Underground was responsible for the UVM mess. The culprit may have been someone with a beef against the establishment as a whole, or the school itself. It's unlikely the band was the target. Why would it be?

Regardless of who was behind the threats, they seem to reinforce the idea that the 1970s was a deadly decade. IRA bombings and a plane explosion in Las Vegas were among the real-life concerns from early spring through early winter 1972. A bomb was detonated in the early morning hours prior to a Rolling Stones concert in Montreal on July 17, 1972, destroying the windows of a nearby apartment building and some of the Stones' audio equipment. Luckily no one was hurt. Add to this the Vietnam War: although the conflict was slowing by October 1972, the US's so-called Christmastime bombing of December 18, 1972 shocked the nation and the world. The bombings had resumed after they were halted for two months due to secret negotiations in Paris. By year's end, however, Nixon had ordered that bombings above the 20th Parallel cease.

Nixon had won reelection in a landslide, but his political victory was curdled by a looming political scandal stemming from a break-in at the Democratic National Committee offices at the Watergate Hotel in June 1972. The burglary trial for this alleged criminal act was set for January 1973. Ironically, Yes was staying at the Beverly Hills Hilton in late March 1973, during one of its sweeps through the West Coast, and it was there that Nixon delivered

a speech in honor of and formally presented the Medal of Freedom to Hollywood director John Ford at AFI's first annual awards
dinner. (Yes was scheduled to play a trio of gigs in New Zealand,
including one at Christchurch Town Hall on March 31, 1973, but
those dates were canceled. Whether they had a brush with history
remains to be seen.)

It was a confused world, macrocosmically and microcosmically.
Things were in disarray in the Yes camp. For one thing, the band
had to either cancel or reschedule the first few dates on its *Close to
the Edge* tour to allow for Alan White to become more familiar with
the band's music. The *Alestle*, the student newspaper of Southern
Illinois University Edwardsville, reported that Yes was forced to
postpone its performance on Wednesday, July 26, until August 21,
when the band would perform in front of 14,500 attendees of the
Mississippi River Festival (MRF), or so the *St. Louis Post Dispatch*
reported. (To show that there were no hard feelings, Yes would
return to the Festival in 1975 and draw 25,300 people, according
to an estimate by the *Alton Telegraph* in July of that year. Yes had
scheduled yet another date at the MRF in August 1976, but the
concert was moved to the Kiel Auditorium in St. Louis to accommodate the band's technical requirements.)

It is commonly believed that Yes actually kicked off the tour
with Alan White in what Count Basie used to call "the driver's
seat," on July 30, in Dallas, at the Memorial Auditorium. Eddy
Offord, the studio wizard, was behind the sound console for the
band's live dates. He proved useful in the concert hall, helping the
band recreate its music live, especially the dense nineteen-minute
track "Close to the Edge."

"I had two tape machines," Offord recalled to me. "[On the
tapes] there were church organs, and there would be vocal parts
and even sound effects and a lot of instrumental parts that they
just couldn't do live. I would be there cuing in these church organ
parts and Rick would actually be kind of miming to some of them,
you know? So, it was really a major kind of production."

Offord had a mixing console courtesy of iconic equipment
company Clair Brothers, which offered the producer and sound
engineer phasing and double-tracking capabilities, among other
functions, in a live setting. A 7,000-watt PA system pumped out
audio in stereo, not mono.

"Yes were the biggest unknown group in the world," says Roy Clair, founder of Clair Brothers. "Even though they could sell out three shows in Madison Square Garden and two shows in Philadelphia, etc., very few people knew Yes."

Yes's relationship with Clair Brothers grew dynamically, and by the latter half of the 1970s, the company's audio system was sufficiently complex to handle the band's complex music, as Clair recalls.

> I set up the console and the house system. I wasn't the mixing engineer. Eddy was at the console. It was a pretty good system for the day. We had high-powered amplifiers, all the best speakers that you could buy, an English console and Eddy Offord. He was probably as famous as the group was, by then. He would bring a duck call along and every now and again, during the show, and blow into it. [*Makes duck call noises.*] Jon would say, "Eddy?!" Yes didn't care. This was Eddy. You know, they all accepted it. He was an artist as well as they were.

Lightheartedness was something Yes needed to have in abundance. The band had been to the US before, but that didn't make the grueling schedule any easier. Wakeman had bemoaned the sheer scale of America, remarking that the US was the size of "fifty Britains." Odd musical pairings only seemed to serve the wackiness of the journey.

In 1972, an up-and-coming country-rock band, called Eagles— whose members would in a few short years become superstars and earn a Grammy nomination for "Best New Artist"—appeared as an opener for Yes in the US and Canada, just as their self-titled debut album, which boasted the Top 10 song "Witchy Woman," sat at #22 on the *Billboard* Top 200 chart. In July of that year, a *Melody Maker* review observed that the band's debut was "full of elegance [and] magical, summery music" and "the finest album of its kind in the country rock idiom."

Clair:

> I think the Eagles were second on the bill, because they couldn't afford a sound engineer. Some nights I was just

going, "Holy shit. This is amazing." Their vocals were just unbelievable. As you can imagine, the people came to hear Yes. How many people have a voice like Jon Anderson? I started out with Frankie Valli and the Four Seasons, back in 1966. They were close to the end of their career. Can you imagine? I went from Frankie Valli to Jon Anderson. Jon's vocal register wasn't as high, but his voice was more melodic. It was more angelic. Frankie was more falsetto.

In August 1972, when Eagles supported Yes in Columbia, Maryland, the *Baltimore Sun* claimed the opening group's performance in front of some 8,000 attendees saw them "living up to their substantial advance reputation." However, when describing Yes's three-part vocals, the review referenced the Hi-Lo's and said the voices were often "drowned out" by Wakeman's keyboards. There was the obligatory jab at Yes's "pretentious" Stravinsky entrance music, and the conclusion that Yes played in a variety of styles but seemed "unable to fashion one of their own."

Not everyone shared this perspective, however. "I worked for a lot of local promoters [in the New England area]," says Les Dinkin, a member of the blues/jazz-rock fusion band Egg Brothers, who opened for Yes at Brown University on February 25, 1972. "I saw Eagles open up for J. Geils and practically get booed off the stage the first time they came out."

On the whole, Yes's North American tour was well received, and curiously Eagles followed up their debut with, of all things, a thematic record, called *Desperado*, which initially infuriated the band's label masters. Concept albums were stuff of British prog rock, no?

After the shows with Eagles, Yes returned to England, where things went as unexpected. Wakeman called the early September Crystal Palace Bowl open-air show, the Garden Party, "a flop." A BBC power transmitter emitted static interference, making it impossible to use the PA. As a result, the band's backing tracks were forfeited for sonic clarity.

Ray Laidlaw of Lindisfarne remembers the show less than fondly. "I think we made the classic mistake of playing the entire new album we made, in sequence," he says. "When people come to see you they come to hear the old stuff and they might want to hear some of the new material, but not all of it. I think there was some great commiserations from [Yes], as in, 'I wish you had spoken with us first.'"

More issues plagued Yes. Back in the US, at the Indiana Convention Center in Indianapolis in September 1972, the police were tamping down on fans for their enthusiasm. The band stopped the show, and both Jon Anderson and Chris Squire tried to calm the crowd—and the police officers providing security. According to *New Musical Express* reviewer Douglas Jones, who filed the report from Milwaukee in October 1972, officers used nightsticks to stop fans in the first few rows from engaging in what they thought was unruly behavior and force them to their seats. (There was a similar issue regarding a concertgoer who attempted to gain access to the Yes show at Brown University in February 1972 without a ticket.)

Early the following year, an article titled "Yes Theft," which appeared in *Melody Maker*'s January 13 edition, detailed a list of equipment that had been stolen from the band's London storage warehouse the previous Boxing Day (December 26). Valued at £3,500, the stolen gear included two of Wakeman's Minimoogs, the main panel of Tait's lighting console, the talkback system for the tour, three amps, and guitar pedal boards. A follow-up piece, which ran in February, explained that Yes had recovered £2,500 worth of gear, although the police were still investigating the missing lighting console panel and Rick's Minimoogs.

It wasn't all misery. Not by far. In September 1972, Yes was awarded a gold record for *CTTE* and, according to *Melody Maker*, advance orders for the record totaled 450,000 copies, with sales climbing past a million dollars.

It wasn't just a great year for Yes but for Atlantic Records in general. Atlantic president Ahmet Ertegun told *Billboard* that the label had "enjoyed its most prosperous year" in '72, in which it celebrated its twenty-fifth anniversary, with strong sales not only from Yes but also ELP, Eric Clapton, Aretha Franklin, Donny Hathaway and Roberta Flack, Rolling Stones, Joni Mitchell, and others.

The good news kept rolling in. In September 1972, *Billboard* called the material Yes performed in concert at the Long Beach Arena in Long Beach, California, "revolutionary" and unlike any rock music that came before it. Yes shared the stage that night with Edgar Winter Group and Eagles, but *Billboard* was none too thrilled about the former, and barely mentioned the latter, having reviewed one of their shows a month earlier. For all the hoopla over Eagles, it was Yes that seemed to excite music fans.

"I saw Yes on the *CTTE* tour, which was indeed the first time," new-age music icon David Arkenstone says. "I think it was at the Long Beach Arena near Los Angeles. Obviously, 'Roundabout' had put them on the musical map, but they took us on a journey way beyond that with *CTTE*. Each song seemed to be a monumental discovery for me. Somehow, the live versions of even familiar songs were actually better than the recording. More punch maybe, and the unique energy that only comes from performing live."

Close to the Edge was a presence on the charts for months after its release. When it debuted on the *Billboard*'s Top 200 Albums chart at #79, for the week ending October 7, 1972, *Fragile* was still on the charts (at #134) and had been there for the last thirty-eight weeks.

New Musical Express had *CTTE* within its Top 5, reaching as high as #3 through the end of September and into early October. In the US, at week two, *CTTE* had climbed to #43, while *Fragile* continued to hang tough at #139.

CTTE had soared to #4 on *Melody Maker*'s Pop 30 by the end of September. Only Rod Stewart, Simon and Garfunkel, and Slade made a better showing. Throughout October the album held strong in the Top 5, amid competition from Roxy Music, David Bowie (*The Rise and Fall of Ziggy Stardust and the Spiders from Mars*), Black Sabbath (*Vol. IV*), Alice Cooper (*School's Out*), Hawkwind (*In Search of Space*), Family (*Bandstand*), Genesis (*Foxtrot*), and Chicago (*V*).

By the end of the month, *Cash Box* reported that *CTTE* was breaking the US market as well, climbing within the Top 15 in America. In early November, it appeared to have gained momentum as it reached the Top 10 in both America and the UK. In its November 4 issue, *Billboard* had *CTTE* at #11, surpassing ELP, whose *Trilogy* was at a respectable #16. In its seventh week of release, *CTTE* was #7. The record had occupied the same position on the chart the preceding week, making its entry on *Billboard* look like the mechanical reels of a slot machine: 7,7,7.

By November 25, *Billboard* reported that *CTTE* was at #4; later that month, it had climbed to #3, and it ended the year in the Top 20.

Yessongs

After the North American dates of the summer and fall of 1972, Yes returned to the UK for the filming of *Yessongs* at the Rainbow Theatre in December. A point of clarification, here: *Yessongs*, the 1975 film shot three years earlier, contains only a portion of the audio featured on the triple-live album of the same title, released in May 1973, most notably "Close to the Edge."

On *Yessongs*, we hear Wakeman lay down Mellotron, blending his keyboard work with the symphony heard on the recording of Stravinsky's *Firebird* ballet. It was something he did on a regular basis during this time period.

Stravinsky's *Firebird* seems to meld into one pot a number of different aspect of Slavic myths and fairytales involving the firebird, including a hero named Ivan (or simply a nameless huntsman), a princess, a selfish magician or monarch, and, of course, the magical bird of prey guiding the hero to victory over evil. The movement used for the opening of Yes's show, "Kaschei's Spells Are Broken," is one of joyous awakening.

Some have thought it pretentious, if not downright vulgar, that Yes chose to use *Firebird* as its walk-on sequence. It is, however, entirely appropriate that this piece of music—one so rich in tonal coloring, steeped in fairytale and imbued with magic—should have been an audience's entrée to Yes's rapturous concerts.

Stravinsky's *Firebird* ballet suite was first used during the band's *Fragile* tour. Prior to this, the band used the first movement of Strauss's *Also Sprach Zarathustra, Op. 30*, reflecting the concept, in Strauss's own words of, "Man [feeling] the power of God."

It's difficult, now, to hear Strauss's music without thinking of Stanley Kubrick's sci-fi classic *2001: A Space Odyssey* and the experimental slit-screen projection techniques applied to the filmmaking process for the "Star Gate" sequence, one adored by many a stoned Age of Aquarius youth keen on mind expansion. This multimedia sound-and-light spectacle is a prelude, a visual journey and soundtrack, to the evolutionary marvel at the center of the movie's plot: Bowman's ultimate transformation into the "Star Child." Filmgoers privy to the psychedelic experience—some of whom were no doubt tripping right there and then in theaters across the country—connected with the movie's cyclical portrayal of life, death, and rebirth—a psychic journey associated with acid trips.

A similar type of rebirth marked *Close to the Edge*. Of further interest: the opening two minutes or so of "Zarathustra"—those everyone is most familiar with—close with a church organ (in what sounds like, to my ears anyway, C). It's difficult to pinpoint how influences manifest themselves in the art, but it appeared that throughout the twelve-month period prior to recording "Close to the Edge," Yes was hearing a church organ on a regular basis.

By commencing its live performances with this piece of music, Yes and Anderson connected to not only the significance of the Kubrick film in the popular imagination, but the actual astrological alignment of the stars. The "magical alignment"—the appearance of the monolithic slab in the movie *2001*—coincides with pivotal moments in humankind's evolutionary development. Cosmically aligned events, of course, linked with the astrologically significant dawning of the Age of Aquarius—the era ushering in world peace and mankind beginning a new chapter of its evolution. In this way, Strauss's Romantic music evoked the hippie idea of the utopian dream.

Yes would generate power from all of this symbolism and soon have its own cinematic moment in the sun . . . but early signs were inauspicious, to say the least.

On March 12, 1972, the Rainbow Theatre shuttered its doors, reportedly due in part to "pop groups who charge unrealistically high fees" and a "lack of sufficient acts with enough pulling power to fill the 3,000-seater," according to the *New Musical Express*.

It was a short run for the Sundancer Theatre Company, the one-time lessees of the Rainbow, which had opened the joint in November 1971. As reported by *NME*, London's Rainbow, formerly the Finsbury Park Astoria, was scheduled to host Alice Cooper, Grateful Dead, and a Jim Morrison-less Doors, among others, when it went dark. That meant there was one less suitable rock venue for visiting American and local British acts to play. The distress caused by the closure was compounded when a few weeks later the Royal Albert Hall announced that it would ban rock or pop acts. This decision was due, it seemed, to rowdy behavior on the part of audiences attending rock concerts.

However, by May '72, the Rainbow was back in business, leased to Biffo Music Ltd., run by Chris Wright and Terry Ellis, famous founding fathers of the Chrysalis booking agency and record company, home of Jethro Tull. Ellis and Wright built an empire based on different aspects of the music and recording business, such as booking, record label, publishing, and even real estate.

On June 30, Deep Purple reopened the place, christening the new Rainbow Theatre with its inaugural concert. Yes had played the Rainbow for two nights on January 14 and 15, 1972, with support from Shawn Phillips. Nearly a year later, Anderson and co were back: conquering heroes, ready for their close ups at the recently reopened Rainbow Theatre for the filming of *Yessongs* on December 15 and 16.

Wakeman, who had been involved in a symphonic performance of the Who's *Tommy*, was not in total agreement with the idea of filming the band's performances at the venue for either a theatrical feature or a television program. While acknowledging the success of the Joe Cocker documentary *Mad Dogs and Englishmen*, he added that if the film, ultimately titled *Yessongs*, was "anything like most rock films, there'll definitely be one vote against it being released," he told *NME*, calling said films "embarrassing."

If Yes did take a vote on whether to move forward with the film, Wakeman was not in the majority. In fact, it may have been Anderson who was pushing for the project from the outset.

"Jon was the guy, way before video, who said we should film [the band's concerts]," Mike Tait told me. "Jon was the one who saw all the shit. Jon saw it all. Jon said, 'Mickey, what I want is a hologram here.' This was decades ago. We were one of the first to have lasers back in the day. I built all that stuff. We shined it over the audience, before there were any laws, we had that equipment everywhere. It was nuts."

Similarly, William Sager, an IT specialist and acquaintance of Anderson, told me that during the mid-2000s, he had worked with Anderson on the prospect of streaming live concerts from his home studio in California. "The fly in the ointment was bandwidth at that time," he says. "It was just a technical limitation. [Anderson] might have been able to stick a truck outside his house but that's not what he wanted. He wanted something set up in his studio, permanently."

We must stress that it was a technical limitation that prevented this from happening, not a creative one. Even though Anderson's plans for streaming live concerts didn't occur, the concept was beyond cutting-edge technology. Other similar music-streaming services have cropped up since, such as Live Nation and Vevo (both of whom have partnered with Yahoo! Music) as well as UphoricTV (dedicated to promoting global festivals), while others went bust before they ever got off the ground.

This story illustrates Anderson's clarity in recognizing trends at the nexus of lifestyle, digital media, and music. And *Yessongs* was just one early example of Anderson's creative vision. Photographed by Ian MacMillan, Anthony Stern, Richard Stanley, and Brian Grainger, the film's mission was to capture the band in action, without narrative. That the camera silently documents the band is its strength. It's not faultless, by any means, but the film is arguably one of the best entries in the burgeoning field of rock concert films, and certainly one of the most enduring prog-rock films. (It is certainly more successful than ELP's movie turn, *Rock and Roll Your Eyes*, a.k.a. *Pictures at an Exhibition*, shot on video by Lindsey Clennell.)

The film opens with an animated version of Roger Dean's illustrations. In addition, during the performance of "Close to the Edge," images of water-based molecular organisms scurrying across the screen and flora twisting to underwater currents recall the natural environment so important to Floyd's *Pompeii*.

Incredibly, filmmakers Peter Neal and David Speechley had arrived without much of an introduction. In fact, no one even knew they were scheduled to film the band at the Rainbow. The crew scrambled to create a workable, photographic scene to shoot for the cameras. In retrospect, the setting does seem overly dark, but this adds to the movie's mystique. On *Yessongs*, Yes's first live album, the quintet is in its element, bathed in multicolored stage lighting, relatively untamed, and breathing new life into grand creations.

Tait, the band's lighting designer/director and all around inventions man, outdid himself for the *CTTE* tour, creating stage elements such as a rotating, flat disco "ball" and custom-made fog machines, while also providing the lighting design for the film event, assisted by Andrew Barker. The flat, mirrored surface was effective but challenging to fabricate, he recalls:

> The problem with the mirror ball is that it's big, and you
> have to have mirrors all the way around it, and it has

to be transported. Those were the days when we would drive a van onto the runway and load the passenger planes ourselves, and off we go . . . I thought, "I'm going to make a flat mirror ball." So I got some wood, Styrofoam, used a soldiering iron to make [the foam] dissolve, so I could stick mirrors on it, one by one. Then when it was rigged, I put all the follow spots on it, you know? It was a great effect. It picked up on that *twinkle twinkle* sound you hear at either end of the song "Close to the Edge." Theater had these types of creations for years, but rock and roll didn't. Then, of course, you need fog, so we needed our own machine. The first ones were like metal trash cans, but we developed them ourselves.

Melody Maker seemed to back up Tait's assertion. A review of the band's performance on Friday, December 15, 1972, praised the use of the "glittering mirror ball" that was lowered near the upstage area "to be lit by powerful spotlights, filling the entire auditorium with circling fragments of light, which were the exact visual counterpart of the sounds we were hearing." Writer Karl Dallas went on to describe the band as high-wire trapeze artists, infusing a sense of drama into their performance without resorting to campy common-denominator destructive art displays, and insisted that Yes was one of the rare groups that could "reproduce on stage the impact of their records" without resorting to a "slavish repetition" of their studio work.

By contrast, *New Musical Express* was taking our boys to task for their "perfect" Friday performance at the Rainbow. It seems that some in the music press, sensing that the band was now primed for the big time, felt betrayed and abandoned by Yes's ability to effectively reproduce their records live onstage. The theatrical nature of the show—the exact element praised by *Melody Maker*—was denounced by *NME*, especially Wakeman's sequined cape and the mirrors erected behind the master keyboardist. To paraphrase: the band was technically adept but lacked the energy of the "old Yes." This was mid-December 1972.

Shown in limited engagements in the US in 1975 and in quadraphonic sound, *Yessongs* was the main event of a double bill featuring Dale Allen Pelton's abstract 1973 sci-fi short *Death of the*

Red Planet, supposedly the first movie to employ ion lasers to create images.

Why would Richard Ellman, of Ellman Film Enterprises, Inc., the distributor of *Yessongs*, choose *Death of the Red Planet* in the first place?

Pelton:

> They needed anything [with] quadrophonic sound, and mine was. It was screened, and Leon Russell and Roger Corman came to the screening. It got some rave reviews in *Hollywood Reporter* and other places and I got calls from all kinds of producers. [Ellman] needed me because *Yessongs* was only seventy-something minutes long. He needed my sixteen minutes. Originally it was twenty. The first time around, it played at least 600 theaters.
>
> *Yessongs* was probably true quadrophonic. For a short time, theaters were set up for true quad. In my case the sound could start in the rear speakers and move slowly over the audience. When there were explosions it would revolve around in all four corners of the room so you would get the sound whirling all around you. That is what makes it really interesting. That's why it was released with *Yessongs*.

According to Barry Schrader, who scored the music for *Red Planet*, a Buchla 200 synthesizer, or "music system," was used to create the otherworldly sounds of the film. "As I recall, just one of CalArts' Buchla 200 systems cost about $20,000 in 1971," he says, "which would be around $100,000 in today's currency. At the same time, I still think that, for 'serious' electronic music, the Buchla 200 was the best system of its day."

It's been said over the years that the band was not totally happy with *Yessongs*, although a second film, *Yessongs II*, was supposedly in the works; Yes biographer Dan Hedges describes it as a work of *cinéma vérité*. But that project went uncompleted.

For its part, *Death of the Red Planet* has made the rounds in the ensuing years. It was screened during the filming of *Fear and Loathing in Las Vegas*, and Pelton, who has since digitized the film, is considering re-releasing it.

Yessongs, meanwhile, was panned by some New York movie critics; the preview section in *Newsday* gave the concert film a one-star rating, calling it "rather dull" and the music from the live album of the same title "uninteresting." The *New York Times* said the film sought "neither to inform nor reveal character nor expand the vocabulary of film," and it wasn't too kind to *Red Planet*, either. Rick Wakeman's nightmare, in other words.

Despite the bad press, or Wakeman's premonition proving to be accurate, fans came out in droves. And they kept coming. Cinemas, at least in Manhattan, Brooklyn, and Queens, and in the suburbs of the city, on Long Island, screened the film well into the early 1980s. Hedges had even reported that *Yessongs* beat Steven Spielberg's timeless horror flick *Jaws* at the box office in Chicago at the end of December 1975—more startling evidence that Yes, and prog rock, spoke directly to the listener and bypassed the most nasty of critical reactions.

National, Regional Recognition

Yes stormed the North American continent with a reported nineteen-person person crew and twenty tons of lighting and audio equipment. The *CTTE* tour was a successful one, so far, in which the group had played to packed houses in arenas, universities (secular and Christian alike), halls, and theaters. In the book *Rick Wakeman: The Caped Crusader*, Dan Wooding reports that Yes earned over seven figures, half of it in America, from touring in 1973.

"Going on the road with Yes was an amazing learning experience," Offord says. "Before, I was just a nerdy kid working in a studio. But live, I experienced good gigs, bad gigs, and some really magical gigs. It was the magic I went after in the studio. They were just starting to get big in America and playing big arenas. The music was complex and to recreate it live was really hard. I am glad I did."

On November 18, Yes played Notre Dame with special guest Lindisfarne. The Notre Dame campus had become a bit more tolerant regarding student behavior. The president of the university at that time, Father Theodore Hesburgh, was a man of faith but also a man of science. (The biological sciences research facility, the Galvin Life Science Center, was built in 1972.)

"I was surprised at how well Yes were received," says Joe Abell, a photographer for the *Dallas Morning News*, who reviewed the show for the *Observer*, the university paper, way back when. "I remember it being a packed house. It was a twin-domed facility and had multiple things going on, so there was a hockey game in the other half of the facility. . . . I remember hearing a lot of talk about it afterwards."

Notre Dame wasn't the only religious university welcoming Yes's *CTTE* tour. Gannon, a Catholic university located in Erie, Pennsylvania, was becoming more socially accepting in the 1970s, as well. One former student I spoke with who was in attendance at the Yes show on November 5, 1972, said there was a lot of "experimentation" going on in the audience—whether the faculty or administration knew it or not.

What's fascinating is that for all the fuss made about progressive rock in the northeast, America's heartland—the Midwest, Rust Belt, and upper south of the United States—rivaled it in fan intensity. The concert archives listed on Forgotten-Yesterdays.com reveal the strings of dates Yes played in the Midwest and the mutual love fans and the band experienced.

Yes even impressed some of its American competitors. Al Jacquez of the Detroit-based psychedelic/prog rock band Savage Grace remembers sharing the bill with Yes, Soft Machine, and Humble Pie, featuring Peter Frampton, in July 1971 for a couple of shows at the Motor City's legendary Eastown Theatre:

> Steve Howe was accomplished as a player. [We thought,] "Those harmonies were cool. We should use more in our material." Everybody can pretend that there's no competition in art and I would like to think there is no vicious competition in art. I mean, some of those shows we were the headliner or second headliner. A band like Yes, technically, opened up for Savage Grace, because we were huge in our area. We were the big fish in the small or medium pond. But you'd see them and say, "Woah. These guys are really well rehearsed." They were tight and they know where they are going. They were organized and in a sense symphonic.
>
> I remember Chris Squire's bass sounded different than any other bass I'd heard, and I think he used bass pedals, so he could add really, really low notes. Bands like Yes,

Humble Pie, they all came to the Midwest on purpose. They wanted to play for those audiences; they knew it was a good place to play and they would get paid etc. I personally think there were times that the whole thing that was happening in the Midwest, which was vibrant and alive, was purposely ignored by both coasts. If you look at things like the Goose Lake [International Music Festival, held in August 1970, in Jackson, Michigan], which was huge, barely got coverage from national music magazines.

There may be some truth in that, but America's heartland nonetheless garnered national attention by churning out bands that synthesized traditional American roots music with European motifs.

Readers and critics alike may have differing tastes, but neither can deny the influence, historical significance, and/or commercial success of the volume of bands raised in the Midwest in and around the progressive scene. They include Styx, REO Speedwagon (specifically guitarist Steve Scorfina), Starcastle, Pavlov's Dog, Savage Grace, Indiana's Ethos (a.k.a. Ethos (Ardour)), faith-based Petra, Kansas; the 1960s band the Serfs, featuring Lane Tietgen and Hammond organ master Mike Finnigan, which mixed folk, blues, soul, and jazz; Glass Harp, featuring Phil Keaggy, from Youngstown, Ohio; the Load, from Columbus, Ohio, led by keyboardist Sterling Smith; and King's X, which has roots in Missouri and Illinois.

"I think [this phenomenon] is due to the college bar circuit and the demands for entertainment," John Schlitt of Petra, and formerly of Head East, once told me. "At that time there were lots of opportunities for live bands to play copy material and for teen dances because live music was preferred. There was room for all of us, from Starcastle to Ted Nugent."

Yes can't take credit for jumpstarting interest in progressive rock in the Midwest, but consider that Styx, Starcastle, Glass Harp, Kansas, and members of King's X and others were, at the least, aware of and in some cases studying Yes's music to varying degrees.

"Your point of view about the Midwest is an interesting one," says the Load's Sterling Smith. "Part of why prog-rock bands could exist in the Midwest is because we had this insulation from the East and West Coasts."

It's likely that a mix of cultural, geographical, regional, economic, and climatological factors contributed to prog rock's flowering in the Midwest.

"How does the mentality of the Midwest, especially Cleveland, micro Midwest, how does the mentality of what goes on in a city that lost its industrial base and has perennial lack of self-esteem issues, affect their listening habits?" wonders Carl Baldassarre, of Cleveland's Syzygy.

"Going back to 1973, 1974, I think everyone was waiting to see what Yes would follow up with *Close to the Edge*," says Randy Jackson of the trio Zebra, which formed in New Orleans, Louisiana, as a foursome named Maelstrom in the 1970s, and covered Yes, Jethro Tull, David Bowie, and Pink Floyd. "Starcastle was doing a kind of Yes imitation."

"Emerson, Lake, and Palmer had a similar sound, around the same time, but Yes took it to a whole other level of beauty, tightness," says Michael Solomon, the promoter of the Yes concert on the November 19, 1972, at Kent State's Memorial Gym in Ohio. "Their music was really refined for that time. They were visionary about the way they combined Jon's voice with [Wakeman's] keyboards and Steve Howe's guitar. It was like an orchestra. You can't deny Keith Emerson's talent, of course, but Yes's music was transportive."

Incidentally, Wakeman met cape-maker Denise Gandrup backstage at the Yes show at Kent State. Gandrup had been backstage earlier and left her own cloak in one of the backrooms. At the end of the performance, when she went to pick it up, she began a conversation with Wakeman. One thing led to another, so to speak, and Gandrup, who was later one of Wakeman's romantic interests, fashioned the famous sparkling dream coat Rick donned for the *Yessongs* concerts at the Rainbow.

Gear

So confident was Yes in its new material, the band dropped beloved songs "I've Seen All Good People" or "Perpetual Change" from the set list to accommodate the longer pieces from *Close to the Edge*. The band's equipment and gear changed, too, depending on the venue. Frank Levi, a Yes roadie during the *Close to the Edge* tour, remembers Wakeman's general set up as: "Two Mellotrons onstage and two Minimoogs, Grand Piano, Hammond organ and, I think, an RMI electric piano." One Mellotron reportedly contained tapes of strings, brass, and flutes, while the other was customized with choir, vibes, sound effects, and harmonized "Yes" vocals. Wakeman also had a pedal board and a Fender Rhodes.

"By the time we got to *Close to the Edge* . . . the bottom of the Mellotron was replaced to raise it up so it would be the right height for him," Levi says. "I think Mike Tait the lighting guy did it. Wakeman was playing through two Hiwatt 100-watt heads, and a Hiwatt 412 square bottom, a Marshall 412 square bottom, and a Univox UEQ 1, equalizer reverb unit. I remember we had to lift the grand piano and put [the legs] on boxes so [Wakeman] could play it standing up. That was a nightmare, every gig."

Articles of the time referred to Wakeman's "computer," which was designed by Tait and boasted panning options and tone controls. It allowed him to plug in all of his instruments, even an acoustic piano played through a Leslie, without any nasty feedback issues.

Wakeman's famous stacked keyboards set up was both visually impressive and musically necessary. It was a bit of an anomaly in the rock world at the time; according to Levi, the crew stabilized the keyboards by "taping them together, or we strapped them together." Wakeman harmonized using the Moog and Mellotron sounds on *Fragile* and *Close to the Edge*, and having the flexibility to play those two instruments simultaneously was essential to reproducing the music live.

Levi claims that Wakeman's keyboards were so hefty that the stage needed to be reinforced. When pressed, however, he didn't remember at which venues, or how this support was achieved. He also claimed that he was one of the few people on the tour who understood how the Mellotron worked, and that he figured out ways "of making it more dynamic through tape realignment and adjusting the height of the keyboard."

Mike Pinder of the Moody Blues was said to have a finger technique for extending the eight-second sound limitation inherent in the Mellotron. I asked Levi if Wakeman had a special Mellotron hand technique, and Levi claimed he did, largely because Wakeman was smart enough to treat the Mellotron as a separate instrument. "Playing a Mellotron like a piano, playing those staccato notes, seemed to work with the flutes [tapes]," says Levi, "but not much else."

It's been said that Hungarian composer/piano master Franz Liszt developed a four- and five-finger technique for the keyboard like no one else before him. Critical focus on Liszt's finger speed, and the rapid succession of notes he played on piano, not only caused naysayers to dismiss him as little more than a fraud; as a result, his compositions and interpretations were oftentimes overlooked. Liszt's technique also allowed for brilliant coloring, original expressiveness, new textures, and an avenue for personal interpretation of well-established and difficult works. "His combination of invented sound are often as astonishing as those in electronic music," writes Charles Rosen, in *The Romantic Generation*.

Wakeman seemed to bring a new playing technique to the Mellotron. "There was something about the way Wakeman voiced the chords he used," says David Bryce, co-moderator of the *Keyboard* magazine Internet forum.

It was as though Wakeman had the ability to skirt the "eight-second rule" and freeze a particular tone in time. In addition, he'd tap the Mellotron to orchestrate his ideas, oftentimes layering sympathetic musical motifs and textures on top of one another.

Not to be outdone, Howe embarked on the *CTTE* tour with his own arsenal of instruments. He bought a Gibson EDS-1275 double-neck guitar in a music shop on London's Shaftesbury Avenue in the summer of 1972. Although it was a bitch to carry around onstage, the EDS-1275 was nonetheless useful to Howe, who found it easier to reproduce "And You and I" and "Starship Trooper" with the twin-necked monster. (It wasn't until years later that he came to the realization that he should be playing "And You and I" with a twelve-string *acoustic*, not an electric.)

Each member seemed to have some form of individual spotlight during the course of the evening's musical proceedings. There was a debate over whether Howe should be playing an extended solo acoustic piece every night. On the *Progeny* boxed set (and the sampler compilation, *Highlights*) he squeezes both acoustic pieces into one performance.

Meanwhile, Anderson would hum a Stravinsky melody in between songs, killing time as the band prepped for the next song; Squire jammed out to his famous solo piece, "The Fish"; and Wakeman rearranged his slightly comical Strawbs keyboard solo, "Temperament of Mind," first introduced during an electrical outage at

Sheffield City Hall in 1970. Styles ranging from ragtime and jazz to classical, TV commercial jingles to silent movie themes, were all stirred into the sonic stew. Some of the same licks spiked his 1972 showcase, "Excerpts From 'Six Wives of Henry VIII'," which also included the "Hallelujah" chorus from Handel's *Messiah*. It seemed that referencing classical bits was popular at the time: even Led Zeppelin's bass player, John Paul Jones, would drop classical references during his keyboard solo at Zep's live performances.

In a review of the Yes show on Thursday, November 16, 1972, at Memorial Hall on the Bowling Green State University campus, Patty Bailey, the entertainment editor of the student newspaper *BG News*, remarked on how the "old-time melodramatic" piano ditties resembled music from *The Hunchback of Notre Dame*.

If elements of "Excerpts" were holdovers from the Strawbs days, it was one of the few retrospective elements seeping into Wakeman's work of the time. After two studio records and half a dozen tours with Yes, he came to the conclusion that not only had his playing altered to suit the Yes environment, but contributing 20 percent of the total sonic effect is often more important than shouldering the brunt of the musical heavy lifting. He once believed that he was the only lead player in Strawbs and, in a way, his solo section of the night ran counter to his role as only one vital component of Yes's sound.

Living with the Law

Once a rock band—or any public figure, for that matter—achieves some level of success or notoriety, it becomes vulnerable to unforeseen attacks. Well, some attacks are more predictable than others, but it doesn't dilute the point: any progressive endeavor invites criticism, or worse. No good deed, as they say . . .

Brian Lane had worked at Hemdale Worldwide and was appointed by Hemdale to manage Yes. At some point later, he broke off into a solo act and grew a management business. As a promoter, Lane had worked with the Floyd, and he was a great networker—a factor that immensely benefitted Yes.

Hemdale was a monster, so to speak. In May 1972, the Hemdale Group, named for its founder, British actor David Hemmings, acquired Worldwide Artist Management, which handled Black Sabbath, Gentle Giant, and the Edgar Broughton Band, among

others, as well as publishing and record production rights, for
$637,000, according to *Billboard* magazine. Worldwide was merged
with Hemdale's music division, which handled Yes and singer/
songwriter Jonathan Swift, who'd shared a few bills with Yes in the
early 1970s.

Business appeared to be going along swimmingly until late
1972, when Yes, Brian Lane (Jelly Music), and the Hemdale Group
were named in a lawsuit seeking to collect punitive damages. Plain-
tiff American Talent International, Inc. (ATI) was suing Yes and
Lane for breach of contract, as ATI founder Jeff Franklin recalls:

> There were two major [booking] agencies in that
> time—Premier Talent and ATI. Between Frank [Barsa-
> lona, founder of Premier Talent] and I, we had a pretty
> good lock hold on the majority of [the rock] bands. We
> brought Yes over to the United States, and I created pack-
> aged tours to break acts, because I didn't have the super-
> stars when we first started. We started with Yes, who were
> a really strong, good band. Brian was the manager, and
> Brian decided—well, his real name is Harvey Freed, what-
> ever you want to call him—decided he always knew more
> than everybody else and was looking for every edge. In
> those days he represented a guy named Jack Oliver, who
> I made a very large record deal for with Buddha Records
> with Neil Bogert, who later in life became my partner
> in Casablanca Records. Brian had a contract with us but
> then decided for some reason he was going to work with
> Premier instead. I sued him over the contract. I sued for
> commission.

Franklin's lawsuit was reportedly filed in the Southern District
of New York City, but when I attempted to verify this through
the County Clerk's computerized database, there was strangely no
record of it. Not finding the lawsuit in the database had led me, for
a brief moment, to entertain thoughts of conspiracy—perhaps the
tentacles of Hemdale were very long. Ultimately, I came to believe
that the matter could be explained by a clerical error or misiden-
tification, or misplacement of the physical file. I did attempt to
contact a one-time Hemdale director, Patrick Meehan.

I spoke with Meehan very briefly on two occasions via phone, but the conversation never got very far. I wanted to set up an interview with him to chat about Hemdale and its history, and also to verify details of the ATI/Premier suit, but a dialogue with the former artist manager proved elusive.

According to documents I obtained, Premier Talent was negotiating on behalf of Yes as early as fall 1971. For a show at SUNY Stony Brook, on Long Island, dated November 28, 1971, Yes received $1,500 in total ($750 prior to the show, with the balance to be paid the night of the show). "The deals all became pretty much the same," Franklin says. "The question is what else did they think they were getting from the deal. . . . I'm not saying kickbacks . . . Frank [Barsalona] would not go down that road—and Frank was the king. . . . We used to steal acts from Frank, too, and he'd *sue us*."

Franklin wasn't specific on what kinds of "incentives," let's say, a band might receive from a contract with a booking agent. It's likely, however, that the sky was the limit, given the type of money a top-shelf name could command in the form of concert ticket revenue in the States.

Why did Yes sign with ATI to begin with? For Franklin, it was simple:

> They were making some noise in England and the record company wanted them over here [in the US]. You would tour bands and pray they broke. . . . We did their first tour. Also, Yes was on Atlantic in those days and we had a great relationship with Atlantic. We did AC/DC and had a lot of urban bands. You took urban bands because you could book those until hell froze over. Yes was a good band, on a good solid record company and it looked like the band had an opportunity to break, which it did.

With such a lucrative and mutually beneficial relationship, it seems surprising that Lane would take Yes across the street and have Premier represent them. Franklin laughed at this suggestion.

> I knew [Lane] pretty well. Did I know what he was doing? No. I woke up one morning and he had sold his management company to Hemdale, and the next thing that

happened was . . . we got a phone call or a letter, I don't remember which one, that said he was terminating us and that he was going to Premier. We talked and talked and we could get nowhere with him and finally we sued him.

Brian was smart enough or someone gave him the knowledge to sell the management company, Hemdale, where he got stock and I don't know whatever happened after that. I think Hemdale got robbed in the end. He probably had a stock deal with them. I never asked; I never cared to. I don't think on any given day the band knew who was managing them. I think these guys [Yes camp] believed they could multiply the amount of money they were going to make and it would not stop. It didn't work that way. It wasn't that Hemdale was wrong in what they were doing, but Hemdale also tried to buy ATI. After that, probably six months or a year later, we lost Yes. And Sabbath. We broke both of them. Oh, by the way, we won both lawsuits.

These business dealings carried some significance, both practically and financially, for a rock band on the rise. Lane received a percentage of Yes's touring revenue, and the band was booked for what seemed like endless tours. (It's been reported that Lane took one sixth of Yes's revenue.)

Even to some fans, Yes was seen as losing a bit off its fastball with the arrival of the controversial *Tales from Topographic Oceans* and the Wakeman-less *Relayer*. Could Yes have created a record of similar scope and magnitude to *Close to the Edge*, had the band been allowed to hop off the merry-go-round and take a deep breath?

In his defense, Lane said he encouraged the boys in Yes to invest their money in real estate or classic cars—tangible assets that would appreciate over time. Wakeman and his then-wife, Ros, took Lane's advice and bought a house soon after he joined Yes. (In later years, Wakeman would become known for his collection of Rolls-Royces.)

The band members were also investing in their joint business venture, pouring money back into Yes at a staggering rate. "The more we earn, the more we spend," Squire told *Melody Maker* in October 1972, now that the band toured with multiple backup instruments, such as more than one Mellotron and Moog, in case of technical glitches or anything else.

"I guarantee you that Brian was probably commissioning $50,000 [during heyday] and, let's say, he was taking 20 percent [of gross commission]," says Franklin. "He pulls ten grand. Now the band members are splitting the balance. Each of them might say, 'Wait a minute. He made 10,000 [dollars]. Why did I only make five?' or something. I can see, if this was indeed the case, where that may have caused a lot of aggravation over the years."

Yes's appearance fee for the time period between late 1971 and end of 1972 seemed to vary within certain parameters. With thanks to Sharon Monigold, a Bethany College archivist, I reviewed a contract entered into by the Student Activities committee at Bethany College and Yes's management company, Hemdale Overseas, Inc., and dated December 16, 1971. The contract was negotiated through the Renner Union Program Board.

Yes was scheduled to play a concert at Bethany, at the Alumni Field House, on February 18, 1972, and contracted to receive $4,000 for the performance, with $2,000 to be paid upfront. The balance would be paid on the night of the concert, prior to performance.

A week later, Yes played Brown University's Alumnae Hall on February 25, 1972, opening for J. Geils Band. Les Dinkin, a student at Brown and also a member of the jazz-rock fusion/blues-rock band Egg Brothers, which went on before Yes, booked acts such as Jackson Browne and Bruce Springsteen, as well as Yes and Mahavishnu Orchestra, for the university. Yes's fee for the evening escaped him, but he recalled that the band had been paid $1,250 for a recent show at Bryant College. (The ticket price for students with IDs for the event was $4.50.)

"Yes were a British act and just breaking in the US," says Dinkin, "[and] $1,250 is a lot more money than it is today. The radio station, WBRU, which was an FM powerhouse in southern New England, was the way I was introduced to the band, and I listened to the music. This was the first time Brown had used an external promoter to produce the concert."

What's fascinating about the Brown show is that Yes was recording it for possible inclusion on a live record. However, I could not find any evidence that audio was ever let out to the public. There may be bootlegs floating around, but nothing has ever been officially released, to my knowledge. And there may be a very good reason why. According to Dinkin, the venue "was a hockey rink, so maybe the acoustics were not warm and wonderful for a concert recording."

Later in the year, on November 11, 1972, Yes performed at Duke University's Cameron Indoor Stadium, recording the performance for an upcoming live album. The material finally surfaced on the boxed set and compilation *Progeny* some forty-three years later. The band was paid a similar rate for this show, says Mark Lehman, who booked the show for Duke through the student union's Major Attractions Committee, which was overseen by the university:

> Yes appeared at Duke twice. The first time they were an opening act for Ten Years After. I think we paid 1,500 dollars for them. At that point . . . they hadn't had any hits in the US, yet. They were building. Duke at the time was very progressive and had developed a good reputation, in part, because the Duke student body was eclectic. It was a very liberal university. The reason we had [Yes] back a second time is because they enjoyed the first time they played Duke and reached out to us and said they wanted to play again. Allegedly they gave us a good deal on the cost.
>
> We had our own hospitality group composed of students. We would pick up the bands at the airport and make sure they were happy. A bunch of people in the band were vegan and we had a vegetarian restaurant in town at the time, run by this hippy girl we were all friendly with. The guys in Yes loved it. Here they were, in the middle of the south, in the middle of nowhere, and here was this cool campus with a bunch of young hip kids and vegetarian food for them.

From many of the contracts I've seen from this time period, $2,000–4,000 per appearance was certainly a normal fetching price for Yes for most of late 1971 and early 1972. (The band kept the money rolling in: the following day's show, at the Academy of Music in New York City, was reportedly sold out within five hours of the tickets going on sale.)

Offord said that Yes was encouraged to spend "a lot of money." And why not? It's similar to the dynamics at play regarding a nine-to-five employer and the people he employs: the more debt a worker racks up, the more inclined he or she will be to exceed at his job.

"Promoters and managers were in bed together to make money from the band," says Mike Tait. "At the end of the tour, 'Here's your thousand dollars.' 'What?' They would give them just enough where they would put a down payment on a house. But they would need to tour next week. This happened all the time."

Was Lane so different from any other rock band's manager operating at the time? Probably not, but it begs the question: who was looking after the well-being of the artists? "If they had someone who said, 'Shut the fuck up, do what I tell you, and we'll do great,' they would have done great," Mike Tait told me. "But no one did that. So, they had a manager, Brian Lane, who would tell each member of the band a different story, because he would tell them what they wanted to hear. But maybe that was a good technique. I'm not sure any other way would have worked."

"I think Brian said, 'I know what I'm doing and let's see how many people I can get to help me,'" says Jeff Franklin. "They all followed Stigwood. In those days the only plan anyone had was [to] tour the shit out of the band, because that was how they broke."

A Badgering Production

At the beginning of 1973, having been off the road for several weeks, Anderson was embroiled in the production of the debut album by Tony Kaye's new band, Badger. The album, *One Live Badger*, was recorded at the Rainbow in London, on the same nights Yes performed its now-famous *Yessongs* shows.

"Badger had been rehearsing and we weren't called Badger until the last minute," says Brian Parrish, the group's founding vocalist and guitarist. "Suddenly we got the call that we were going to be doing some dates with Yes and later on with Black Sabbath, but under the same management umbrella [Hemdale]. They said, 'We can record you with Yes, because we are already there with the Stones mobile.'"

Most bands don't debut in the marketplace with a live album. "I can't remember if it was decided that then your first album will be a live one," Parrish says. "It is not the intention to begin with. If it was, it was only going to cost us two reels of tape to record Badger so the thinking was, 'Let's see what we've got,' the more likely scenario."

The recording took place over two nights:

> In fact there was a third night in Glasgow, and we stormed it. We were better than the other two nights put together, but nobody recorded that. We were booked into Advision studios shortly thereafter, with a view toward seeing what we've got and mixing it. Then, suddenly, it was a question of well, "We have the Black Sabbath tour coming up, we need to mix this and then be on the road." It's interesting, really, because a lot of people thought we were courageous to do a live record, but it was just a series of coincidences that resulted in that.

Most of the recordings for the album were taken from the first night, December 15. Parrish believes the running order of the tracks on the original record was more or less the song sequence for the concerts. One of the biggest "fixes," he says, was a suggestion Anderson made during the overdubbing and mixing sessions at Advision with mixing engineer and co-producer Geoffrey Haslam, relating to a song Parrish initially penned for his previous band, Parrish and Gurvitz:

> We certainly would have finished with "On the Way Home." It had a big kind of . . . quasi-gospel chorus thing at the end. It was the only song that had any extra overdubbing vocally. When Jon got in the studio with us, and Jon is another kettle of fish altogether, he was about precision. His focus is definitely on the vocals and I think he was carrying over his ethos of the Yes recordings. They had no problem multitracking things . . . We were kind of fighting the idea of doing overdubs. It's a live recording and we felt we needed to be true to that. If something needed fixing because it hadn't been recorded properly, that's a different question. But we didn't actually want to do anything that would damage the integrity of [the recordings].

On the end of "On the Way Home," there's a bunch
of vocals on there that Jon got us to track a couple of
times. It was Jon's idea. We didn't do that live. I've never
told anybody that. We had an ending and it was great,
but Jon was saying that [his idea for vocals] will fit in
there, and that's how he heard it. He obviously had significant input in Yes. He wasn't a one-man band, but his
input was huge there. What he was suggesting may have
been a kind of Yes thing.

The Badger sessions were looking more and more like a Yes mixing date. Some editing was involved in creating the final product,
Parrish recalls:

I'm trying to remember which song it was, but I think
it might have been "On the Way Home." It was really
cookin' on the second night, when halfway through the
song the recording went down from the mobile. Not in
the auditorium. Everyone heard the performance and
everything was normal. But when we got in the studio all
we could hear was a little bit of leakage from our vocals
in the drum microphones and the actual vocals were
gone. We tried everything we could. We asked, "Do we
sing it again and try to copy the performance?" Actually,
the vocals were mostly me. That was going to be difficult
to work because of the sound, the ambience, the vocal
track was completely different.

Thanks to Haslam, whose credits include Atlantic acts J. Geils
Band, Bette Midler, MC5, Aretha Franklin, Ornette Coleman, Eddie
Harris, The Velvet Underground, Jan Akkerman, and, of course, Yes,
there was a third way for *One Live Badger*. "He said, 'Can we see if
it is possible to splice the end of the recording from the first night
onto the . . . second night?'" Parrish says. "We spliced that together
and I think there may be a slight lift in tempo, but that worked. The
performance we had to sacrifice had definitely been better. But we
didn't have the vocals, so we were between a rock and a hard place."
It is odd that Anderson seemed to take an interest in Badger
but never showed the same kind of appreciation for Banks's band,

Flash—or at least not publicly, anyway. "There may have been a guilty conscience involved," Parrish says. "I've never been in Jon's head—perish the thought—but he might have felt a little bit guilty. I don't know. I can only talk from a point of view of working with Tony Kaye, who I respected enormously. He's a very intelligent guy."

Australia Freedom

In March 1973, the boys were at it again. A concert tour of Japan began on the 8th. Roger Dean tagged along and began formulating ideas for the band's next studio album cover artwork—what would be illustrations for *Tales from Topographic Oceans*. Squire summed up the handful to Japanese dates as something close to "Beatlemania."

These shows were the precursor to the band's dates in Australia, many of which are remembered with great affection by attendees, decades on. Yes played five dates in Australia, in Brisbane, Adelaide, Melbourne, and the final stop, Sydney, for two concerts at the Hordern Pavilion.

The band appeared at precisely the right moment in Australia to garner maximum reception from the crowds. "In Australia, if you say you've been to the Yes shows in Australia in the 1970s, it is like, 'Ah, '73,'" says Brian Draper, who wrote a book about Yes's momentous tour of Oz. "It is a reference point as being memorable rock concerts, even those who would not go on to be great Yes fans. Some were stunned at the virtuosity of what they'd seen and questioned their own abilities."

"Prog-rock bands from all around the globe influenced Australian prog bands in a big way," says Mario Millo, guitarist for the Australian progressive rock band Sebastian Hardie. "'Your Move' by Yes was a major hit for the band here in Oz. It was played by all the mainstream radio stations and was the band's ticket to success in Australia."

Although Australia, a constitutional monarchy, was becoming more ethnically diverse at the time of Yes's *Close to the Edge* tour, there was some consternation within the band ranks about making the trek Down Under. Artists from the Who and Joe Cocker to the Rolling Stones were being hassled, if that's even the correct term, about what they might be "importing" into the country, as Draper recalls.

Yes were paranoid about . . . the way Australian authorities treated Joe Cocker, who was arrested in Adelaide for possession of marijuana, and this was just before the change in government. There was a lot of paranoia about that. Rock tours of Australia hadn't been that common for quite a while prior to 1973. There had been a hiatus of overseas musicians, rock musicians, coming to Australia. At the end of 1972, the conservative government that had been in office for many years lost power and a more liberal state of government, from the American perspective, was voted in. The labor party, the leftwing liberal style of politics, made some massive changes quickly and focused very much on younger people. Yes came a few months after they came to power.

The combined impact of Yes's rapturous extended songs, otherworldly stage design, and saturating lighting looks was elevated to the realm of mystical religious experience in a newly liberal country. *Circus Raves* magazine picked up on this phenomenon in 1975, with reviewer Steve Rubenstein from Las Vegas describing Yes's shows as "more spiritual awakenings than musical events."

I've talked with Greg Lake (RIP), Gustavo Moretto (Alas), a number of Italian prog musicians, Józef Skrzek (Poland's SBB), Nicolae Covaci (Romania's Phoenix), and Nick Barrett of Pendragon, who agreed that people living in communist countries have cherished their progressive rock as a symbol of freedom. Australia is not communist, of course, but Yes's shows there coincided with a broader cultural and social awakening.

"Jon Anderson . . . remembered the Sydney concerts and he said they were peak performances," says Draper. "I think they sensed it in themselves. You could tell that there was something more going on there then just playing a concert."

The Wagnerian heights Yes reached, the almost *synesthesian* aspects of the band's shows, were taken to another level in Australia. These performances have been interpreted as a "total artistic package," according to Draper.

It was kind of like walking into an ambush. It was complicated music and nobody had seen such integrated lighting shows in Australia, in my opinion. You're seeing the colors of the lights change with the shift into different passages of the songs. It was a total experience.

Rick was the center point of the group. I remember my own particular sense that this was the first time I had been to a concert that the keyboard player was a soloist and he had interacted with the band as well. People who attended those shows—it's another reference point for them—remember the Firebird introduction, and how Rick, with his back to the audience and that sequined cape, melded Mellotron with the sound of Stravinsky.

Veteran rock 'n' roll photographer Philip Morris was also in attendance, and recalls:

As the photographer for the Australian music bible, Go-Set from 1969, it was my job to cover all the major concerts, especially from the big overseas touring bands. We had just witnessed Led Zeppelin and the Stones, and Yes were on their way. Their album *Close to the Edge* was getting rave reviews and Yes were the next big band to hit our shores.

On the evening of the concert I chose a position front of stage at the Hordern Pavilion with a 5,000-capacity crowd in attendance not knowing what was about to unfold. The lighting was the best I had seen; it was amazing for photography. The large "mirror ball" flashed beams of light onto Rick Wakeman's glittering full-length cape. I had a cross screen filter on my lens, a bit overused in the '70s, but it was effective this time. Smoke like thick fog started rolling across the stage and down into the audience. It wasn't until the house lights went on—a half an hour after the end of the show—that the stunned crowd were able to physically move toward the doors. Yes had left a lasting impression on Australian Rock fans.

"All of the reviews had said that they outdid the Stones," says Draper. "It's my understanding that after they left Australia they sold their lighting equipment to lighting people. In itself it started a trend, here, regarding the lighting industry. Rick returned to Australia with his own tour and brought *Journey to the Centre of the Earth* out here. He'd later return and maintained a kind of presence in Australia."

Renée Geyer, a legendary blues/soul voice in her native Australia, fronted the R&B band Mother Earth, the support act for Yes's two shows in Sydney. Geyer had joined Mother Earth after departing a jazz-rock outfit called Sun, which recorded its debut album with veteran jazz industry man Horst Liepolt.

"I do remember that *the* talk about everything was the crazy magician/weird guy on the keyboards with a cape," says Geyer. "It was like some magician with smoke coming out of his ears, you know, on the keyboards."

Despite their aloofness, the members of Mother Earth quickly claimed Yes as fans:

> I remember hearing that they were impressed with our band. Maybe Jon Anderson was impressed with my voice. I'm not sure. It was all quite foreign to us. Jon Anderson probably started in rhythm and blues and he would have known that stuff, years ahead of any of us. His voice was an amazing instrument. Incredible. I remember everyone was impressed with that. I remember the fact that he was short and had a huge voice and how high his voice could go. I was the opposite. I was a tall girl, who had a big deeper voice. I think I even commented that, that would make an interesting duet, you know?

Geyer admits that, at the time, she and the band had no real working knowledge of Yes's history or the careers of the individuals in the band, many of whom had played on top-shelf sessions or in blue-eyed soul cover bands and the like. "We didn't know about Rick Wakeman's sessions with David Bowie and Elton John," Geyer says. "When I started mixing with other people, I realized that Rick Wakeman is huge. We were so green and innocent, and also snobbish. We were into the blues and the real nuts and bolts, which is completely away from the kind of theatrical rock the English brought. Still, we watched them."

Geyer takes a trip down memory (mammary?) lane, recalling one of her most unforgettable experiences of the Sydney shows. "I was walking around and it was one of the first times I remember that I had to wear a bra," Geyer. "I used to walk around, bounce around, and I think one of [Yes's] road crew was obsessed with my chest. One of the crewmembers was talking to one of the band members about my chest and said, 'Check out those tits!' I will never forget. That's my biggest memory of Yes. How do you like that?"

"After the Australian dates, the band were supposed to play three shows in New Zealand, but those shows got canceled," says Draper. "That left a gap in their program in the Australian leg and the start of another American leg of the their tour."

Wakeman indicated that the break derailed the band, not only physically but also mentally. "It was sort of an interruption of a band at its peak, and they never reached that peak again," says Draper.

Yes's first show in North America after the Australian tour, in April 1973, was delayed by almost two hours. Fans at the San Diego Sports Arena went stir crazy as the crew wrestled with issues with the PA system.

By this point, delays were normal occurrences. Even during Yes's Australian splendor, there were technical glitches with Rick's keyboards. "There were some issues that came up in and around Melbourne," says Draper. "There were some interactions with journalists as well. . . . In that era, I think Australian journalists had a reputation for being in-your-face, whether they were music or political journalists."

This despite the members of Yes ingratiating themselves to Australian audiences. Howe even picked a snippet of Aussie Rolf Harris's folky, country-ish song "Tie Me Kangaroo Down, Sport," a Top 10 hit in Britain, during his acoustic showcase of "Clap" and "Mood for a Day."

"There were some in-your-face type of interviews with journalists that particularly upset Steve, I understand," Draper says. "By the time they got to Sydney, things were more relaxed."

Prior to that, at the University of Waterloo in Ontario, Canada, on October 30, 1972, sound equipment troubles were reported by the *Chevron*, student newspaper, and confirmed by local reporter

Victor Stanton, of the *Kitchener-Waterloo Record*. An hour separated Tranquility's set with Yes's. Likewise, at Yes's show at Brown University, sound system problems caused an hour-plus delay between sets.

With the bulk of the *CTTE* tour completed, new plans were being formulated for the band's upcoming studio record, the double LP *Tales from Topographic Oceans*, a thematic work that would emerge as the band's most controversial studio effort. Yes had been in Tokyo in February 1973 when Anderson and Howe began conducting writing sessions via candlelight, formulating the general arc of the new songs. In Savannah, Georgia, Anderson and Howe hammered out vocal, instrumental, and lyrical sketches during a six-hour writing session that lasted until seven in the morning.

The germ of the concept for *Tales* was planted by King Crimson percussionist Jamie Muir, who was in attendance at the now famous wedding reception of the former Yes (and at the time current Crimson) drummer Bill Bruford. Muir introduced Anderson to the book *The Autobiography of a Yogi* by Paramahansa Yogananda, and the die was cast. Given the lukewarm reaction over the years to *Tales*, one has to wonder (with tongue planted firmly in cheek): was this Muir's way of attempting to "take down" a more commercially successful progressive rock band?

Each of the four pieces that would emerge on *Tales*, one song per side, is inspired by a footnote appearing in the book, representing the four classes of scripture mentioned in the footnotes. (Interestingly, *The Autobiography of a Yogi* also influenced members of the Beatles, having been given to the Fab Four by writer Barry Miles, according to one source. Other sources credit Ravi Shankar with introducing George Harrison to the book. Yogananda, of course, appeared on the cover of *Sgt. Pepper's*.)

As history tells us, *Tales* was the tipping point: it was a nightmare to manage in the studio, sent one band member packing, confused longtime fans, and pissed off and all-out bored critics who suffered through live performances of it. It was the type of thing Bruford always wanted to avoid.

Keyboard magazine online forum founder and co-moderator David Bryce and I discussed the comparisons between Yes and Led Zeppelin in the 1970s: how *Houses of the Holy* and the album unofficially dubbed *Led Zeppelin IV* were balanced records that fed the band members' artistic egos but also managed to please a large volume of fans; and then how, as much as *Physical Graffiti* and *Presence* are classics in their own right, the band lost a bit of its edge in the mid- and late 1970s.

Tales from Topographic Oceans and *Relayer* are classics, too, in their own ways, but (more than *CTTE*) were born of artistic self-consciousness. "Yes moved beyond what made them great and were more concerned with the Yes they thought they were supposed to be," Bryce says. "Kurt Vonnegut, who I used to love to read, at one point in time was just writing. But later on you can see there's a clear turn where he just obligatorily being 'Kurt Vonnegut.'"

"With most bands that you might call special—they are a combination of strong individuals, the Beatles being the most obvious example of that," Wishbone Ash co-founder Martin Turner offers. (Wishbone Ash's *Argus*, issued months prior to the release of *CTTE*, was one of the most popular rock albums in Britain in 1972.) "You're talking about four strong characters. But when that goes out of whack and it breaks and you change one or two people it becomes a different thing entirely."

Amid this, in May 1973, the triple-live album *Yessongs* was released, and included tracks that featured both Alan White and Bill Bruford. *Yessongs* was really the culmination of ideas Yes had hatched two years earlier, when the band was formulating plans to record *Fragile*. Reports indicate that Yes wanted its fourth studio release to be a double album, the second disc featuring live material, including a version of "America."

According to *Melody Maker*, the sold-out shows and tracks for the soon-to-be million-selling *Yessongs* were recorded on the band's previous North American tour in the late summer/early fall 1972. Initially, the hope was to have *Yessongs* ready for release by January 1973. After the band's tour of the UK and North America, it had planned on mixing the proposed live album; a revised date fell in April. This date, too, was postponed.

Yessongs was eventually released in May, to generally good reviews. *Melody Maker* said that no other band in the world could maintain diversity and excellence across its six sides. But not everyone saw it this way. While praising Rick Wakeman's 1973 solo album, *The Six Wives of Henry VIII*, in a compound review, the *Baltimore Sun* blamed the record company as much as the band for the overall quality of the presentation of the music on *Yessongs*, calling the triple-live offering "a cop-out release." The music certainly had its moments, the *Sun* reviewer wrote, but neither Yes nor Atlantic should have been satisfied with the lack of "new" material on the live behemoth.

Anderson once said that *Yessongs* was the end of an era. In a way, it was. The band left behind the "concise" and economically epic tracks of *Close to the Edge* to embark upon ever-lofty musical goals, the aggregate results of which are still being debated even as I write this.

Squire later said the band had been spending so much time overseas, specifically in the US, that the idea had been floated that they would record in America. A change of scenery seemed to be the order of the day, although, ultimately, the band didn't so much "change" scenery as add it to the studio setting.

The band was split on where to record its next studio effort—some members wanted to record out in the country, others wanted to stay in town. It was said that Anderson wanted to literally track in the woods, but a deal was struck whereby Morgan Studios would be transformed into a pastoral recording paradise, complete with electric cows, haystacks, and wooden fences to create a faux-countrified atmosphere in the concrete canyons of London.

Offord:

> That was Brian Lane's fault, in a way. The band and I
> had discussed putting an environment together that was
> conducive to creating and maybe being in a farmhouse
> somewhere, getting away from London. A lot of bands
> were doing it at that time. Go somewhere and create in
> a nice environment. As a comical gesture he brought all
> of these cutout cows and plants in a kind of tongue-in-
> cheek way, to make it seem like the country. I remember
> after a few weeks, all the cows had graffiti all over of
> them and the plants had died and that was the end of
> that.

While *Tales* is not nearly as riddled with padding as some—even members of the band—would have you believe, one can't escape the notion that the expansiveness and coherency of *Close to the Edge* was never again to be achieved. *Tales* and its follow-ups, *Relay-*

er (1974) and *Going for the One* (1977), contain some breathtaking material that goes way out, even to the point of being dissonant or what some might class as atonal.

This disharmony was evident in the music, the times, and the band. During the period 1973–1974, the world and political winds begin to weirdly warble: Nixon resigns before certain impeachment in 1974; the IRA targets the British government with more bombings; the world experiences global inflation; Americans feel the pain at the pump in the fall of 1973 due to an energy crisis; and, in July 1973, the Trilateral Commission is formed, inciting some conspiracy theorists to demonize the body, as they do the Freemasons, for attempting to keep a stranglehold on the world population, its global economy, and major faiths.

"The beauty of Lennon and McCartney was you had two totally opposite people with different musical tastes coming together and creating something special," says Offord. "You had John's real, not punky, almost real-street kind of stuff and then McCartney came in with the melodic material with nice chord changes. You put those two together and you had magic. In a way, Chris and Jon were the same way. Later on as the careers developed, the rift between Chris and Jon, same as John and Paul, kind of, it got to a point where it was not quite so healthy anymore."

"What no one can take away from the band is that those initial years, and those initial ideas, were absolutely amazing," Tait says. "Hence their success. Their later success was in spite of all their problems. People trying to hold it together. Getting new people in . . . It was bloody hard going."

Yes's rivals were also gaining ground. Just before the Yes caravan came off the road for five months in the spring of 1973, as if on cue, Emerson, Lake, and Palmer announced that they were going to carry the world's largest mobile musical production in rock history for their Get Me a Ladder tour, which was scheduled to take them through some of the same global territories Yes had just visited. Fifty tech hands and a thirty-foot-high proscenium arch, securing dozens of lighting fixtures and theatrical curtains, was to be constructed each night at every venue.

This was but a preview of ELP's worldwide jaunt to support *Brain Salad Surgery*, which was released in November 1973, for which the group pulled all the stops. The trio commanded four semis to haul and a forty-two-member crew to set up thirty-six tons of equipment, including an oval projection screen, a two-ton-plus stainless steel kit (with wildlife engravings on its drum shells). The kit revolved on its own iron stage and included a 130-pound church bell (that Palmer would ring with his teeth). A thirty-channel quadrophonic sound system (designed by the late Bill Hough of IES) delivered crystal-clear sound, and a Persian rug costing a reported $6,000 was laid at Lake's feet.

Following 1973's *Yessongs*, ELP released the triple-live set *Welcome Back, My Friends, to the Show That Never Ends—Ladies and Gentlemen, Emerson, Lake, and Palmer*, two years or so after the popular *Pictures at an Exhibition*.

"There *was* a certain amount of competition, but there was nothing which was out of order," Carl Palmer told me in 2007. "The competition was purely on a gentlemanly basis, you know. That was the general atmosphere in the UK at the time. It is a very small place England and London, which was the hub, is even smaller. So, that particular time, you could meet and greet a lot of people."

"Jethro Tull was doing well at the time, but obviously ELP was closer to our field of play," Steve Howe told me in 2005. "I didn't have competition with them much because there wasn't a guitarist in there. But Chris and Greg, maybe. Maybe Carl and Alan, maybe a little bit. Obviously, there was respect for what they did. Rick and Keith Emerson. . . . In a way, you had to think of them in the same breath. They weren't doing the same thing, but they were in the same era that had a wealth of rich music."

"Here's my favorite quote I can offer in any of this," says New York radio personality/DJ Ken Dashow, whom I spoke with prior to Emerson's death.

> Keith is a lovely guy, and when I talk to him about the era and about these kinds of questions, I'd ask Keith about the rivalry between Yes and ELP. "Was there a Rick–Keith rivalry?" "Was there a Yes–ELP rivalry?" "Where does Genesis fit in?" Honest answer, "Not rivalry as in we are trying to make more money than them, or trying to sell more records than them." He said, "Believe me, when a Yes album came out, I was the first guy on

line. I wasn't even going to wait for them to send it to me. It made me proud to know that Rick said I was the first in line waiting for an ELP record." The point was, "Could they take it further?" He said, "I'd like to think that hopefully *Pictures at an Exhibition* helped them to get to *Close to the Edge*. And, without a doubt, *Close to the Edge* helps to take us to "Karn Evil 9."

"I think . . . everyone was just trying to outdo everyone else to see who could be more adventurous, more cutting edge and . . . who could go the furthest," Offord says. It seems others were asking some of the same sorts of questions. On the same page as *NME*'s review of Yes's show at the Rainbow, the magazine featured a write-up of King Crimson's concert at the same venue two days earlier, on December 13.

It's obvious that some in the music press were aligning themselves with what may have been perceived as a hipper form of mainstream prog rock, in King Crimson. Crimson appeared to be gaining in strength and on the brink of a major musical and commercial breakthrough during 1972–1974.

Yes had become superstars; no one is denying that. But efforts such as *Starless and Bible Black*, *Red*, and *USA*—three examples of Crimson releases of the time period—are arguably just as concise, consistent, passionate, and earthshattering as Yes's studio and live efforts around the same time (*Yessongs*, *Tales*, and *Relayer*).

As 1973 came to a close, Yes finished the lengthy recording sessions for *Tales* and hit the road in November. The group would soon embark on what would be its most controversial and divisive tour ever.

Meanwhile, in New York City, the performance venue CBGB became the virtual wellspring for the punk and new-wave revolution. Esoteric rock need not apply. The years 1974–1976 saw progressive rock reach its commercial zenith. By 1977, the division between progressive-rockers and their target audiences widen. In fact, the summer of 1977 in New York was a study in contrasts. New York, one of the last refuges of prog-rock music on the East Coast, was experiencing "a second English Invasion," or so wrote Wayne Robins in *Newsday*.

You could catch Pink Floyd in Midtown in early July at Madison

Square Garden and then trek downtown to CBGB on Bowery for Sylvain Sylvain and the Criminals. Likewise, you could witness ELP for three dates in July "playing opposite" the Cramps; and Yes, in August, opposite DMZ.

These were two historically significant and distinct worlds—one losing the power of its currency and another gaining strength—operating independently of one another in the same geographic location. It's the stuff of Erik Larson or Caleb Carr. Prog-rock caravans swept through large venues in numerous North American cities, avoiding the seedier aspects of a metropolitan life. For many, it was this side of life that would become the most interesting aspect of 1970s pop culture.

Prog's commercial and cultural dominance had ended. Discontinuity in recording patterns and the emergence of more aggressive music genres distracted and diverted fan attention. Several years later, we'd witness a kind of prog resurgence during the so-called second and third waves of the 1980s and 1990s, a movement in which the Trevor Rabin–era Yes participated.

"Progressive music hasn't stopped," Anderson once told me. "It will always go on. In some ways you're writing a book about something that hasn't stopped yet. In fact, some of the early James Brown, was really avant-garde as far as his use of a band. I don't know if you know Sun Ra? But it's totally, 'Let's all get in the room and we'll start playing.' You play for two hours and you feel like you've finished this cosmic event."

Looking through the lens of the late 1970s and early 1980s, 1972 seems so distant. Back then, the universe was balanced—and boundless—due to these "cosmic events."

Of course, progressive music had evolved into ever more obscure and confrontational subgenres—spinoffs from the mother musical tongues such as the Canterbury Scene, Zeuhl, and Rock in Opposition. Yet few would deny that Yes reached a creative peak circa 1972, teetering on the edge between commercial success and earnest exploratory songwriting, internal harmony and disunity, self-indulgence and universal appeal.

No one can repeat what's past, and most are not foolish enough to attempt to do so. What had transpired all those years ago—the classically structured rock music, the inhuman technical prowess, the studio experimentation, the spiritual awakening, the confounding and life-changing career decisions—are there for all to study . . . and for aspirants to imagine.

"I think that experience changed me a lot . . . because I was a little kid locked up in a studio recording records," Offord says. "Then suddenly I was in Australia and America and learned a lot about music, too. You play the same set every night and most nights it's good, some nights not so good and a few nights it is magical. And to be there to experience those magical nights showed me a lot about the magic of music, you know?"

8

THEY REGARD THE SUMMIT

The Impact of Yes and *CTTE*

Yes's influence on modern music is almost incalculable. One simple way to illustrate how deeply ingrained this music has been in the popular psyche is to list the number of progressive-rock or hard-rock or mainstream or so-called alternative bands who cite Yes as an influence.

The diversity is staggering: from Riverside to Spock's Beard, Dixie Dregs to King's X, Porcupine Tree to members of Weezer and the Flaming Lips, Dream Theater to Foo Fighters, P-Funk to Klaatu, Rush to the Flower Kings, Marillion to Glass Hammer, Transatlantic to the Tangent.

Mixing engineer Rich Mouser (Spock's Beard, District 97, Transatlantic) told me:

> "Close to the Edge" intrigued me. It was an acquired taste, but once I was able to digest and start to understand it more and listen to it more, it had legs. From a spiritual side, it used to get me through some highly introspective and semi-dark times in my eighteen-to-twenty-year-old time period, when you're trying to figure it all out and what are you doing with your life kind of stuff. I used to listen to that album and it had some way of centering me. You know, "I get up, I get down." The lyrics just struck a chord in me that had a way of calming me down and making me realize: you know, it's all going to be okay.
>
> I bought a pedal steel and I ended up with an electric sitar and got so deep into it that I tried to copy all the guitar parts on *Close to the Edge*. On the Transatlantic album *Kaleidoscope*, there's a cover of "And You and I," and

when it came time to mix, I told Neal [Morse, vocalist, guitarist, keyboardist] that it would be great to have some steel guitar playing on the song, like the original. Neal said, "Hey, man, why don't you throw something down." I pulled out my pedal steel and Echoplex and laid down a slide part. Mike Portnoy said, "I just sent it off to Jon Anderson." I was thinking, "I got to play 'And You and I,' and Jon Anderson will hear it."

The legacy of *Close to the Edge* can't be overstated. Yes would follow the long-form composition model through records such as *Tales from Topographic Oceans*, *Relayer*, and *Going for the One*. Take "The Gates of Delirium": the incessant cymbal work hints at natural element, such as rain. This centerpiece of *Relayer* seems to organically sprout music from a fertile and sonically rich environment.

One could argue that the experimental aspects of *Relayer*, like those in "The Gates of Delirium" and "Sound Chaser," mirror the intense jazz-rock workouts heard at the beginning and end of "Close to the Edge." *Relayer*'s final track, "To Be Over," concludes with its hymn-like chant and the use of eclectic instrumentation (sitar guitar, Mellotron) closely resembling the finer moments of Yes's grand 1972 studio album.

The impact of Yes's recordings spans far and wide. This is not meant to be a complete list, by any means, but it does show you the diversity of individuals who have been influenced by Yes's music: Robert Downey Jr., Major League Baseball's Tony La Russa, Hollywood writer and director Joss Whedon (*Buffy*, *Agents of S.H.I.E.L.D.*), house-music godfather Marshall Jefferson, the late actor Sherman Hemsley of *The Jeffersons*, the late NPR broadcaster Tom Terrell, and more.

La Russa told me:

My wife is a huge rock 'n' roll fan. I'm more the classic rocker, still am. But when I first heard Yes, I said, "Wow. The sound is different." One time, I was with the White Sox and Yes performed in Chicago, the old Chicago Stadium, the arena there. I remember I was the manager of the team, so they got me seats in the front row of the balcony directly across from the stage. I was totally enthralled. I remember Jon singing up to the microphone on his tiptoes and hitting those high notes and ever since then that was it. Yes was the one. Even though the songs were long, I was buying the albums and getting into them and . . . they remain my favorite band. One of the neat postscripts to this love affair with Yes is having a personal relationship with Jon and [his wife] Janey. I don't know if you know that Elaine and I had started an animal foundation twenty-five years ago, called ARP [American Rescue Foundation; www.arflife.org]. We do a concert and Jon has taken part in it twice.

My favorite Yes song is "And You and I." Jon Anderson performed that song . . . there was a twelve-year-old guitarist helping him out. I have video on that. My first favorite is "Close to the Edge." Why? Because of the way I was taught to manage, especially strategic decisions during the game, was to play it *close to the edge*. "Close to the edge, down by the river . . . " I was always on the edge of the cliff—no guts no glory kind of management. That was the way I was taught, the philosophy I was taught. I love that. *Close to the Edge*. That's how you survive in what I do.

All of this is to say nothing of the undeniable impact Yes has had on British rival and contemporaries such as ELP, Crimson, Genesis, and, for obvious reasons, Flash. Hollywood soundtrack and TV music composers from Mark Mancina (who co-wrote material that would find its way onto Yes's 1991 record *Union*) no doubt learned from Yes and the way they composed music.

Yes, and British prog in general, had an impact on acts across America, from Kansas and Styx to Zebra (Louisiana and New York), Starcastle, and obscure prog band Polyphony.

"I look at *Close to the Edge*, and the song itself, and point to that as the peak of the combination of all the elements that were going on at the time," says Randy Jackson of Zebra, once signed to Yes's former label, Atlantic. "I don't think it has been repeated by anyone. They gave you everything in that song. It was about the art and they were in control of it at that time. They were using everything they had in a musical fashion—and not just to show off. You can hear that, even today."

"I had the dubious honor of seeing Starcastle," says Mike Tiano. "They opened for Gentle Giant in Massey Hall in Toronto, and my friend and I went to see them. They were entertaining. What they were trying to do was not copy Yes but do a Yes-type project. But you can't do that without . . . sounding like you're pretending to be them."

"We were from Dover, Delaware, but we'd drive to New York City for all the record stores," says percussionist "Chatty" Cooper of the American progressive rock band Polyphony, which released its debut album, *Without Introduction*, in 1972. "They'd have a space at the back of these stores for European imports. We'd learn some of these things and it wasn't easy music to play, either. But pretty soon the guys in the band wanted to write music similar to Yes or Genesis. Even Todd Rundgren. Soon we decided to move out of Dover and down to Virginia Beach where the music scene was a bit more happening."

"The first time I heard Yes, my friend and I were driving, and had to pull off the road when we heard 'Roundabout,' and for me, especially, Rick Wakeman's solo," says David Arkenstone. "The clarity and musicianship of Yes were staggering."

One of the enduring mysteries of Yes's extensive catalog is how the band was able to write a song that's nearly nineteen minutes long yet make it accessible, enjoyable, and gripping. Stephen Marsh, who along with mixing engineer extraordinaire Steve Hoffman worked on a remastered version of *Close to the Edge* for the Audio Fidelity label, made a similar observation as he was working on the record.

"The one thing that struck me was the grandeur," he says. "The thing about *Close to the Edge* that I most connect with is that it is very anthemic. It's also natural for progressive rock to veer into, not to use it as a super pejorative, but to veer into math rock and there's definitely intricate elements of Close to the Edge, but it is also accessible, melodic and flowing. Whereas you put the record on and you say, 'How much time went by?'"

CTTE isn't a concept record in the sense that it doesn't tell a linear story with a plot line. But a case could be made that it's thematic work. Records such as *CTTE* and *Tales from Topographic Oceans* have impacted later artists in their own desire to build drama and stress musical storytelling to bring the listener on a sonic adventure.

"I think I can attribute my desire at making 'concept' records directly to Yes, and some of the symphonic repertoire," says Arkenstone. "My album *In the Wake of the Wind* was a direct reflection of some of Yes's expanded musical concepts."

"Regarding *Close to the Edge*, the LP was available in Czechoslovakia in 1974 when the Czechoslovak label Supraphon bought the license from Atlantic Records," says composer Peter Machajdik. "This album was, for me, the biggest discovery of my life. I could not believe that something like that would even exist. The music had for me and for many of my friends an incredible power. But, I think that, at that time my generation in Czechoslovakia and other Eastern countries was not ripe enough, mature and/or ready to perceive any form of symbolic power in this kind of music."

"I was just listening to *Close to the Edge* this morning," singer Geoff Tate, a solo artist formerly of Queensrÿche once told me. "I took my kids to school and I came back to the house and it is a beautiful sunny fall day and the sunlight was coming through and the birds were singing and I thought, 'I want to hear *Close to the Edge*.' I blasted it, and stood outside and looked at the surroundings and just blasted it."

"The main lesson I take away from *Close to the Edge* is one of humility," says Australian progressive-rock musician Ben Craven. "If you're going to attempt a side-long composition, if you're going to ask someone to take twenty minutes out of their day to listen to your song, you'd better make sure it's a good one, because [*CTTE*] is the benchmark. Arguably, even Yes themselves have never been able to top it."

Yes's music has even crossed into the electronica arena, having been remixed for 310's limited-edition 12-inch vinyl EP *Prague Rock*, issued by the Leaf label in 1999. The piece in question, "Sharp / Distance," contains an audio recording of Bill Bruford talking about Chris Squire's bass playing being in the "high frequencies" and how he adjusted his own sound in order to cut through amplification (by applying rim shots to the snare). We also hear a Rick Wakeman keyboard solo from *Yessongs*; the opening twinkling noises and nature sounds of "Close to the Edge"; and bits of "And You and I," such as Howe's twelve-string tune up and steel guitar, and part of Bruford's signature beat.

Howe's son Virgil, a keyboardist, drummer, and DJ, released a record of Yes remixes in 2003 (*Remixes*), featuring Skrillex-esque cut-and-paste manipulations of "Siberian Khatru," "Arriving UFO," "Tempus Fugit," "Heart of the Sunrise," "Awaken," and "Five Percent for Nothing," among others, mastered at Abbey Road studios.

> At the time I was only using MPC 2000XLs going into a live mixing desk [Soundcraft Spirit Folio] and that leading to a Minidisc. There was no actual computer, or interface, there wasn't any software program in use. There wasn't any Logic or GarageBand. I was only using a sequencer on the MPC itself to build up all of those things. I wouldn't do it like that, again, but at the time that was what I did.
>
> I did "Heart of the Sunrise" and I put a beat over it and played it for Dad, and he literally said, "Why don't you do some more?" I did one from every album that I liked. It was literally like that. There wasn't much concept beyond that. It wasn't much beyond, "Just do it, Virgil. Do what you want and then I'll present it to the band." It got the go-ahead from everyone. The only money I really put into it was for the mastering. We got the best mastering we could. We went into Abbey Road with an M-disc. Crazy. It was all off the vinyl. I didn't have any stems or individual files or anything. I used all the finished product and chopped it up into eight or four bars.

What's so incredibly striking about *Remixes* and *310 Prague Rock* is how the band's classic material is still recognizable and enjoyable in the context of twenty-first century recording and mixing equipment. Tate:

> Our record industry has been in a decline since the early 1990s. [Major labels] were interested in sales and counting beans. The arena for this progressive music, challenging music, is not supported by the industry and that way the public didn't get it. But back in the 1960s and 1970s it was a freer time for musical expression. A radical time in a lot of areas, social areas, the country was going through big changes and the music reflected that. The people that

made the music were interested in social change and there wasn't a stranglehold on the artist to have to conform to any sort of sales chart. It wasn't that competitive then. You saw that in the music.

Yes and the Rock and Roll Hall of Fame

I have mixed feelings about Yes being inducted into the Rock and Roll Hall of Fame. I think the institution is a good one, when educating the public at large about little-known or underappreciated (however we may define that term) artists. It performs a great service, actually. However, I'm less enthused about the induction process, which pinpoints who "gets in" and who doesn't.

If rock 'n' roll was born of youthful rebellion, as purist critics always like to remind us, why do we create an institution around such music? The very same kind of institution any red-blooded American (or any other nationality) rocker would rail against? And why are we being selective about a music that was, from the start, built on a kind of democratization?

Rock and rock 'n' roll was meant to be inclusive—in theory, anyway. A rebellious generation turned its back on the past, finding thrills, spills, and shakes in cross-cultural expression. For that matter, and this is merely my opinion, the progressive-rockers— Yes, ELP, Tull, Gentle Giant, King Crimson—were, by very definition, breaking down barriers and opening new avenues of artistic growth and thought. Pretty rebellious—but I don't want to get ahead of myself.

With the recent deaths of both Chris Squire, Greg Lake, and Keith Emerson, I can't help but think that an opportunity was lost. These gentlemen will never see such an honor bestowed upon them—not in this life, anyway. I don't know the mental anguish Emerson went through his final days, before he died of a self-inflicted gunshot wound to the head, although I've heard things, as we all do. (If it's as I surmise and as I've heard, a day of reckoning will come for a certain billion-dollar-a-year industry. This should happen sooner, hopefully, rather than later. But this is for another day.)

More to the point: If other acts I would not consider to be either rock or rock 'n' roll have been nominated and then given the go-ahead for induction, then Yes certainly should receive a retroactive gold-plated invitation to the Hall's exclusive club—with sincere apologies. Especially considering that Atlantic's own Ahmet Ertegun, such a champion of Yes, was instrumental in the Hall breaking ground in the first place.

Part of the dilemma is how to categorize Yes's music. This issue was addressed by Dr. Lauren Onkey, former vice president of the education and public program department at the Rock and Roll Hall of Fame, who went as far as to say that the music world considered a band such as Yes to be pretentious, because it drew on "classical elements," seemingly implying that these artists believed that "rock, itself, wasn't interesting or important enough to contain its complex ideas."

I'm not in total agreement with this remark, but Onkey has a point. But here's the rub: despite their commercial success, Yes and some of the more popular British progressive-rock bands mentioned above were working within the system to fight preconceived notions about what rock is—and what it could be. What better place to recognize a band that had blurred the definition of what rock is than an institution whose curatorial mission is to document this music in all its many forms?

Perhaps it's not the Yes organization that needs to shift its perception of rock. A *Rolling Stone* magazine review of *Close to the Edge*, published in November 1972, nicely sums up the dilemma: "If there's a problem involved in placing or defining Yes's music, it's a direct result of our establishing rigid criteria and admitting only that which qualifies, rather than expanding our own border of perception in accordance with what artists choose to present."

Ironically, as I'd hinted at earlier, some of the material released by Hall of Fame artists is not what many listeners would even consider to be rock or rock 'n' roll music. The Beatles would be a great example of this. Who would deny these rock deities entry?

Still, what do we make of the harp-heavy "She's Leaving Home"? A Dylan-inspired folk song that includes sitar, titled "Norwegian Wood"? The orchestral version of the ballad "The Long and Winding Road"? Many of the later George Harrison Beatles tunes, from "The Inner Light" to "Within You Without You"? Furthermore, it seems that with every release, the Beatles were in many cases extravagantly redefining the parameters of the style with brilliant and frighteningly eerie audio-visions, using whatever tools were available to them at the time, from their own musical talents and psychological projections to recording equipment at EMI's Abbey Road and Trident Studios. Dare I say it, the very same artistic ideals that were held dear by Yes for large swathes of its career.

Of course, in the mid-to-late 1960s, the Hall was still decades away from its brick-and-mortar existence, and some will call parts of my argument cherry picking. Perhaps, but did Yes not retain elements of rock and the influences of rock 'n' roll in its music? Further to the point, check the organ solo in Yes's "Roundabout"—a Top 20 hit in the US, by the way—and find the influences of blues and soul—part of the very essence of rock and roll 'n' music. For that matter, when Yes reimagined "Roundabout" for the stage in the early twenty-first century, the group performed it as an acoustic blues shuffle. This is to say nothing of Steve Howe's American roots-washed guitar stylings on tracks as varied as "Going for the One," "And You and I," "Siberian Khatru," and "Clap." (Howe gives a little taste, a sneak peak, of his countrified picking in "Perpetual Change," from the live album *Yessongs*, prior to the official start of the song.)

Material on *Fragile, Close to the Edge, Tales from Topographic Oceans, Relayer,* and *Going for the One* contains nods to jazz-rock fusion, classical, country, electronic music, rock 'n' roll, the avant-garde, and God knows what, contributing to the belief that Yes was often operating outside the realm of what was, and apparently *is*, considered rock.

Progressive rock often confounds critics who attempt to describe and define the genre, in large part due to a combination of opposites, such as its postmodernist mash-up of ancient and modern motifs cutting-edge keyboard technology, and interpretations of classical works—works that have been in the public consciousness for well over one hundred years.

"There's a whole argument that says rock should only ever have three chords," Bill Bruford told me in 2001. "Then there's the guys who say, 'We like that, but let's add this other stuff. Let's add Berlioz, Bartok; this country music, this Indian music.'"

Rock has often begged, stolen, or borrowed from many different sources; prog rock, and Yes's music, is no different. Maybe it is all in how the dish is being served that ultimately appeals to the listener's taste.

Still, prog rock touches upon something much deeper: by combining the aggressive and the pastoral, the music reflects both the "masculine" and "feminine" aspects of music. (Carl Jung differentiated between the two parts of the psyche, being the male, *animus*, and female, *anima*.) Despite its complexity, "Close to the Edge," like much of Yes's recorded output, cuts to our very core as human beings. In this sense, Yes, and prog in general, is (wait for it) *soul music*.

But back to Onkey's point. As we know, Yes is *not* a normal rock band, and on this basis alone the group's work is not grounds for admittance into the Hall, at least with regard to the institution's own perceived guidelines. Progressive-rock fans should not run from this but embrace it and move on. Yes's music apparently still operates outside "the system."

In other words, if Jon Anderson or Ian McDonald, Carl Palmer or Kerry Minnear, Peter Hammill or Phil Ehart, Robert Fripp or Fred Frith never find themselves standing at a podium of a black-tie event, in front of a packed house in some swanky New York City or L.A. hotel ballroom, fear not. It'll simply underscore how misunderstood, how innovative—and dangerous—their music still is. That's nothing to get *hung about*. That's a badge of honor.

EPILOGUE
River Running Right On Over My Head: An Immersive View of '72

In his book *The Redeemer Reborn*, author Paul Schofield explores links between Wagner's *Parsifal* and *The Ring* cycle, principles of Buddhism, philosophy of nineteenth-century German metaphysician Arthur Schopenhauer, and the search for the Holy Grail as a means of explaining that each individual springs from a "karmic stream."

In Eastern religions, karma and reincarnation provide a mechanism through which we can finally achieve perfection, or nirvana. The river of "Close to the Edge" and *Siddhartha* could be a physical representation of this karmic stream. It's only upon achieving nirvana, escaping the circle of birth-death-rebirth, that "all the karma in that particular stream is converted and cleansed," Schofield writes.

In other words, we are doomed to this cycle of rebirth if the stream, or river, is not cleansed. Near the conclusion of *Siddhartha*, the main character returns to the river after he realizes that his son must cut his own path through life, a situation similar to his relationship with his own father. It's these "cycles of the past" (some Hindus and Buddhists might say this is related to the concept of *samsara*), this repetition of events, with which Siddhartha wants to break.

Hesse wasn't making a point about "sins of the father" but rather about how Siddhartha finally realizes that he can't control or change this cycle and instead decides to devote his time to matters of the soul, spending the rest of his life as a ferryman. The river offers serenity without conflict, unity in a confused world. The *om*, or the clamorous sounds of everything known to the Earth, good and evil, is conducive to contemplation of the human condition, and coaxes Siddhartha—the budding Buddha—to accept life as it is.

Rivers, seas, and large bodies of water could symbolically represent change, reincarnation, and rebirth—all concepts found in *Siddhartha*, which culminates in the title character's epiphany, his near-death experience, if you will, at the water's edge.

Carl Jung interpreted dream imagery of rivers as representing the direction of our lives. Bodies of water could be viewed as representing the collective unconscious—our true inner selves, our souls.

A River Runs Through It

The London music scene can be interpreted as a river as well. Musicians paddled freely in the currents of creative consciousness streaming all around them. Of course, the insurgency of prog rock can be attributed to a number of factors, as we've seen.

Having rejected their parents' traditionally held beliefs, a younger generation staged a cultural coup, exploring everything from non-Western spirituality to mind-expanding illicit substances. It was this inclusivity and even multiculturalism that set the younger generation apart from earlier ones. It certainly helped to lay the groundwork for the social revolution of the 1960s, the explorations and hedonism of the 1970s, and a postmodernist musical style that permitted artists to experiment with and add ingredients to psychedelic rock, giving rise to a codified and, dare we say it, "new" musical form.

Sharing not only common artistic goals but also the same pieces of real estate ensured that a certain kind of hothouse weirdness was growing in what could be termed the artist incubator of London. The early British progressive-rock musicians frequented and played the same clubs—clubs that were in proximity to one another, where like-minded musicians brushed elbows on the regular basis.

"Keith [Emerson] and Chris [Squire] used to go out boozing and jamming together," says Clouds' Billy Ritchie. "The Pied Bull in Islington was a favorite haunt. It used to have jam sessions for all concerned. Musos love all that, even though all it produced is an unholy row."

"For a short period of time I shared a flat with two other people and a guy named Eric Clapton in London," says veteran radio DJ, nightclub operator and promoter Russ Gibb, who was instrumental in feeding the "Paul is dead" phenomenon in the late 1960s on WKNR in Detroit. "Within the radius of five blocks or so you had the entire music industry, it seemed. You could go to the main rock club, the Marquee; the studio, EMI studio; and these things were a few blocks away. Then you could also go to all the music magazines. It was all within walking distance, the whole music industry in London. It was very coordinated, whereas in America it was spread out to the West Coast and down south in Nashville and over to New York."

"Everybody knew everybody," Bill Bruford told me in 2003. "It's not a big world. There were a couple of clubs in London that everybody went to. The Speakeasy was one, and Yes's manager Roy Flynn managed that. A lot of musicians went through there. You'd sit at the bar next to Keith Emerson or Jimi Hendrix or Noel Redding or some guy from the Canterbury Scene and everybody knew everybody."

"About one or two o'clock in the morning, bands would meet at a service station, in Hatfield, north [of] London, off the M1, a major English motorway," says Stewart Goldring of Gnidrolog. "If you were going anywhere in England to play, you were quite often using the M1. About half the gigs, wherever they were, between one and three in the morning, a selection of bands would be meeting up there for dinner."

You mix all of these ingredients in a high-pressure environment, and *voilà*! You have an instantaneous breeding ground for a germinating artistic movement called progressive rock.

As American author Norman Maclean writes in his autobiographical short story "A River Runs Through It," which contemplates the metaphysical join between love, God, and (of all things) fly-fishing, "Eventually, all things merge into one, and a river runs through it."

It's in the river that these characters, who are mysteries to one another, find themselves. Likewise, through the cultural environment and through a flow of new ideas, these progressive-rock musicians found their voices and changed the course of popular art, spreading out like musical tributaries through England—and the world. It's what lyricist Pete Brown was talking about, at least partly, I believe, in Jack Bruce's "Theme for an Imaginary Western."

It should come as no surprise then that some musicians in the scene—the "stream" of consciousness of, as Paul Stump calls it, "the Progressive Imagination"—helped to solidify a newfangled music genre. This was happening throughout 1972.

When I looked at works from 1972 competing with *Close to the Edge*, a number of curious and intriguing connections emerged. The symbolism most of the major British progressive-rock bands seemed to share was uncanny—and it couldn't be ignored.

Water imagery resonates with so many listeners and British prog-rock artists, perhaps due to England's proud nautical heritage and its geographic designation as an island nation. The Brits may have subconsciously chosen to pursue water symbolism as representations of the self, the soul, and life.

The Moody Blues' 1972 studio album *Seventh Sojourn*, released via the band's own Threshold label a month after *Close to the Edge* appeared, closed a chapter on an incredible stream of classic albums.

By the early 1970s, the group had earned the reputation of spiritual guides (something, by the way, it had never really sought). Bassist and vocalist John Lodge's "I'm Just a Singer (in a Rock and Roll Band)" highlights this fact: Lodge seems to be plagued by some of the same mysteries and uncertainties of his times as his listeners.

If "Close to the Edge" represented an individual searching the wilderness of the soul, then most of the songs appearing on *Seventh Sojourn* are a collective cry in the wilderness (see keyboardist Mike Pinder's politically charged and topical "Lost in a Lost World").

The album echoes the faint calls of a confused generation desperate to find meaning in the current political and social climate. (Nothing too heavy, eh?) Contrarily, Justin Hayward's "New Horizons" speaks of finding inner peace in an outer world of turmoil.

Although no actual "river" appears in the lyrics of the songs on *Seventh Sojourn*, there's an awful lot of water imagery here (not to mention references to love and prayer). "I suppose people in life always look for watershed moments and I suppose the watershed for the Moody Blues was that we became part of the progressive-rock avalanche," Lodge told me in 2008. "At the time we thought we were writing and recording very own personal music with no regard for anyone else. We are always looking for new avenues to explore, I think."

The Search, The Self, and Social Commentary

Gentle Giant's 1972 studio album *Octopus*, recorded at Advision Studios at nearly the same time as Yes was finishing *Close to the Edge*, marks the conception of the band's high progressive period, also encompassing such releases as *In a Glass House*, *The Power and the Glory*, and *Free Hand*.

Three Shulman brothers—Ray, Phil, Derek—formed Gentle Giant, which evolved from the soul band, Simon Dupree and the Big Sound. The band was fairly diverse, otherwise. Guitarist Gary Green was from Chicago, with blues leanings; Welsh drummer John Weathers, who replaced a jazzier Malcolm Mortimore, was so mischievous in his youth he had to be sent to live with family in Liverpool; keyboardist/percussionist Kerry Minnear attended the Royal Academy of Music and soaked up Romantic classical, baroque, and early church music.

While Gentle Giant has always been closely identified with austere musical forms such as European liturgical, Renaissance, medieval, and classical, much of the band's approach revolved around rhythm in all forms, from intricate counterpoint/polyphonic melodies to polyrhythmic and polymetrical passages.

Perhaps one of the reasons Gentle Giant's music sounds so dense is because multi-instrumentalist Ray Shulman wrote angular harmonies that didn't appear to be composed for any particular instrument in the band.

Minnear once told me that Ray's music was initially difficult to learn precisely for this reason. Ray would begin writing music, starting with one line, only to build a matrix of counterpoint parts and pockets of hockets that impossibly meshed. (The 1997 two-disc boxed set *Under Construction*, featuring unreleased tracks, demos, and other vaulted material, fully displays Gentle Giant's embryonic musical ideas.)

Drummer Weathers burrowed his way through these complex and quirky Gentle Giant tracks, somehow finding a groove that worked for the recording of *Octopus*, as exemplified by songs "Boys in the Band" and "Knots," the latter influenced by R. D. Laing, author of *The Divided Self,* who challenging traditional notions of normalcy, sanity, and insanity.

Weathers does a great job laying down the solid rhythm but also occasionally comments on the knotty intricacies intertwining all around him. A song titled, interestingly enough, "River," refers to the subject as "a friend." The song features experimentation with "electronic devices," the liner notes read, and Weathers once told me that he blew into a plastic tube threaded through the air hole of his snare drum to achieve ascending notes.

The concepts discussed in "Knots" and "River" are more clinical, psychological, and even personal than spiritual, but it's all in service to finding and understanding oneself and how the individual interacts with the world at large.

Ian Anderson's search for self was filtered through Jethro Tull's spoof—a one-song concept album called *Thick as a Brick*. The concept revolves around a fictional character, nine-year-old literary prodigy Gerald "Little Milton" Bostock, the winner of a local poetry competition, who was later disqualified due to the "unwholesome" nature of his work.

Bostock's entire sordid tale was reported in a mock parochial newspaper, the *St. Cleve Chronicle*, a physical copy of which served as *TAAB*'s original LP packaging. The words of this so-called shocking poem conveniently provided the lyrics for the song "Thick as a Brick." (It was, of course, Anderson who actually wrote the words, although Bostock receives co-writing credit.)

"Thick as a Brick" is "reprinted" in these funny papers with phrases such as "across the sea," "swelling mountain water," "whirlpool," "down by the river," and "your real self sings the song." These words, and their relative proximity to one another, are unmistakable, and could represent tide pools of social change in an overregulated and morally corrupt world.

Emerson, Lake, and Palmer, prog rock's first so-called supergroup, culled the talents of the Nice's underground keyboard hero Keith Emerson, angelic-voiced bass player Greg Lake from King Crimson, and Buddy Rich–influenced drummer Carl Palmer, previously with the Crazy World of Arthur Brown, Atomic Rooster, and Chris Farlowe. ELP's *Trilogy* rings in sympathy with older Yes material in its preoccupation with the American Old and Wild West. Tunes such as "The Sheriff" and "Hoedown" are self-evident in this obsession; the latter is based largely on the Aaron Copland composition of the same title, from his *Rodeo* ballet, which owes its greatest debt to Kentucky fiddler William H. Stepp's "Bonaparte's Retreat," an interpretation of a traditional song.

Like nearly every other electric keyboardist of the 1960s and 1970s, Emerson noted the influence of Walter Carlos's synthesizer-based reinterpretation of classics, such as the groundbreaking *Switched On Bach* and others, which sought to demonstrate and test the possibilities of the Moog synthesizer. These efforts may or may not have been an initial inspiration for ELP's "Abaddon's Bolero," the closing tune on *Trilogy*, which bears only a passing reference to Ravel's lulling "Bolero."

The virtuoso Emerson wielded great power by commanding Moog technology, layering a dizzying array of buzzing, trumpeting, and circling synth lines, which were propelled by Palmer's unnerving martial pulse and Greg Lake's bottom-end bump. The aggregate of these myriad elements nearly suffocates the listener with its intensity. Quite fittingly, "Abaddon's Bolero" sounds as though it's the insolent devil spawn of some demonic fife-and-drum brigade, spinning further out of control with each subversive, modulated turn.

The opening suite, "The Endless Enigma," is composed of two mid-tempo, Moog-laced ballads (more or less) sandwiching a piano "Fugue" written by Emerson, who by this point had a history of writing similar pieces, dating back to the Nice. The heartbeat-like pulse opening of "Enigma," common to the era (see also *A Passion Play*, *The Dark Side of the Moon*), is the salvo to a journey that transports us from blindness to awakening from a life of artificiality. "Enigma" could be interpreted as an open letter to a lover, or former lover, as much as a search for self. Like "Close to the Edge," it's unclear who the speaker is and who he's addressing.

Interestingly enough, the album's Top 40 hit, the largely acoustic "From the Beginning," a Lake composition and easily the most popular song on the record, seems to mimic the sounds of nature (birds, babbling brooks) with its bleeps, chirps, and sonic whirling. To boot, the acoustic guitar opening is very similar to "Roundabout."

"It was a good chance that they are in the same key," says Offord. "I would have to play the thing again. But didn't Greg play some harmonics and stuff? Everyone knows if you play harmonics, stick to the key of E if you can, you know?"

Hipgnosis's cover artwork for *Trilogy* depicts the three-headed hydra (ELP) gazing off into the distance at mountains, and what appears to be a river or some body of water on the back sleeve of the wraparound image . . .

Rivers and Revelation

Although a bit disjointed—and I say this not as a sleight to Genesis or its writing ability—"Supper's Ready," from 1972's *Foxtrot*, soars with revelatory fervor at its climax with anthemic calls for the coming of a New Jerusalem.

There are many interpretations of the phrase "New Jerusalem," but, interestingly enough, in the New Testament's "Book of Revelation," John of Patmos had envisioned this heralded city as a metropolis with the curious natural formation of a river cutting its way through its center. (The Lamb of God stands at the middle of this most Holy City.) In biblical terms, the river, or water in general, is eternal life through Christ.

Genesis was still a fairly young band, and its synthesis of individual song parts doesn't appear to have been as smooth as the joins in "Close to the Edge." Perhaps there's a reason for this: the absurdist "Supper's Ready" is composed of different pieces, and was written at various different locations.

Genesis spent much time on the road, fixing recording dates whenever possible to finish the record, rehearsing and writing parts of "Supper's Ready" at Una Billings' dance school in the summer of 1972. Guitarist Steve Hackett once said that the tap-dancing feet on the ceiling above the band's rehearsal space alleviated stress. This is purely a guess, but it's entirely possible that the rat-a-tat-tat rhythms above their heads may have influenced the songwriters in Genesis to pursue such staccato and odd rhythms in their music at the time.

Perhaps no other staccato rhythm in prog rock has caught the imagination of fan and musician alike as the one featured in the opening song of *Foxtrot*, "Watcher of the Skies." In an interview for the 2007 *Foxtrot* CD reissue, drummer Phil Collins does not reference the dance school students but rather admits to seeing Yes at the Marquee Club in the early 1970s, right around the time "Watcher of the Skies" was being written and completed. Collins cited Yes's "trickier arrangements" as one inspiration for the track.

Although not as "prog" as some of the above-mentioned records (it might rightly be termed progressive R&B), Badger's debut, *One Live Badger*, co-produced by Jon Anderson and featuring former Yes keyboardist Tony Kaye, boasts bits of blues, funk, and gospel-esque rock laced with a touch of jazz-rock fusion. And, of course, *One Live Badger* was recorded at the Rainbow Theatre in London on December 15 and 16, 1972, the dates associated with the *Yessongs* concert film.

Badger's personnel was as diverse as its music. Bassist and lead vocalist Dave Foster was a member of the Warriors, Anderson's old band. Kaye had known Foster from his involvement with Yes, of course, and had also completed a session with Foster for the single "310 to Yuma" by Legs Larry Smith. In addition, it was reported at the time that Kaye helped to re-record Foster's solo material, originally tracked with members of Head, Hands, and Feet in 1970. Some may remember that HHF featured vocalist Tony Colton, who produced Yes's *Time and a Word*. (Adding to these incestuous activities, Kaye had also participated in Alexis Korner sessions with members of King Crimson.)

When the re-recorded Foster solo tracks couldn't attract label interest, Foster and Kaye turned to the advice of Anderson, who suggested they write all-new material. The resulting band, initially called Angel Dust, featured drummer Roy Dyke of Ashton, Gardner, and Dyke (and the earlier Liverpool band the Remo Four, featuring Ashton); guitarist and vocalist Brian Parrish; Foster; and Kaye; and was soon renamed Badger.

Parrish told me that he was responsible for the name change in and a greater portion of the writing credit than was indicated in the liner notes of the original album. He wrote "On the Way Home" for the Parrish and Gurvitz debut in 1971, but the song went unreleased until *One Live Badger*. The record also contains the songs "River" and "The Preacher," both titles that would be right at home on *Close to the Edge*.

Parrish:

> There has always been a spiritual aspect to what I do. I would say I was searching and I didn't have any answers . . . "On the Way Home" was an example of that. I was singing about Jesus before I knew who Jesus was. I knew the name but I hadn't met Jesus . . . I was thinking . . . that all roads would lead to what you might call the godhead, a spiritual path. That might be music; that might be mathematics.
>
> In those days we were all reading *The Tibetan Book of the Dead*, the *Upanishads*, and people were going off to India. I didn't want a guru, but . . . we felt that this searching was all part of the same thing, if that makes sense to you.

Foster's "Fountain" and "Wind of Change" were slightly different, says Parrish.

> David said he wrote "Fountain" on the Tube, on the London underground. He was looking at people's faces and there was a kind of mistrust, a fear. "My fear is always greater than my judgment," is one of the lines. It's about the difficulty in coming to trust.
>
> I suppose the origins of "Wind of Change" date back to 1967, when he got hit on the head by a policeman outside the American embassy. There may have been some demonstrations of the involvement in Vietnam or whatever. But it seemed that in his head his whole life was returning to or staying in 1967. It was like a Groundhog Day thing. "Wind of Change" is singing about flying high above all this shit.

"Wheel of Fortune" rang in sympathy with some of the other ideas Parrish had explored at the time. "I had begun to practice Buddhism," he says, "and, on the one hand, the song is saying that if the world has let you down, don't sit there complaining and don't be negative; just hang in there. These days I wouldn't be as passive as that. I wouldn't say, 'Wait until the wheel of fortune turns around.' I would say, even in pure Buddhism, it is a process, a chain reaction, a process of cause and effect, so you do something."

In "River," we encounter a female that easily could be interpreted as the divine. George Harrison had said that his iconic tune "Something" was really about Krishna, not a flesh-and-blood female, for which he had romantic feelings.

"'River' is about a girl who can't be reached," says Parrish. "The river is a symbolic obstacle: the guy in the song doesn't know how to cross it to get to her. Having said this, whatever spiritual message was there [in Badger's music], it was flawed at best, which isn't to say it wasn't sincere. I've spoken to people who've said that the Badger album saved their life."

Finally, Germany-based UK natives Nektar, as of this writing led once again by Englishman Roye Albrighton, released *A Tab in the Ocean* in 1972, an album premised upon a Utopian dream of universal consciousness through lysergic acid diethylamide.

Albrighton explained to me once that drugs provided the inspiration for some of the band's most beloved songs, including the epic "A Tab in the Ocean," which opens and closes with the foamy rush of noises of the sea, and "King of Twilight." Another, "Desolation Valley/Waves," concludes with multi-part harmonies, recalling the magical *om*. Clearly, these were not anthems for substance-using dropouts, but introspective and speculative tracks asking, "What if?"

Despite its Teutonic bent, Nektar was part and parcel of the same stream of consciousness, the same river of dreams, from which British prog sprang, as Albrighton explains:

> The idea of using a piece of music and having themes repeat throughout the piece and keep reprising it but in slightly different forms, is what they do in film music. In the 1960s that was what these theatrical composers were doing and I think some of that rubbed off on musicians. You can hear this in Emerson, Lake, and Palmer, and even down to Rick Wakeman's stuff. I think the accessibility of musicals made some ears prick up. I know ours did. It was also a combination of classical and rock. I thought, "You can't do that?" But apparently you could. "Why can't we?" That is how it progresses. The likes of *Time and a Word* wasn't quite there, but *Close to the Edge* hit it. That was when it started. I know that was the era that we started. We thought, "If everybody else had a go of it, why not us?"

Later "Main Stream" Artists

The concept of self-realization popped up in some unlikely places in 1972, like folk-rock. This may, or may not, make you chuckle: John Denver's pleasant and largely acoustic hit from 1972, "Rocky Mountain High," is nonetheless spiced with some pretty heavy mystical imagery, environmental awareness, and Eastern philosophy. In the song, a twenty-seven-year-old man experiences rebirth in the quiet of the wilderness while overlooking rivers and lakes. (Okay, Denver doesn't actually use the word "river," but he does reference streams.)

This image is eerily similar to the final episode—the silent valley of Anderson's dream—we encounter in "Close to the Edge."

Neither the dogma of organized faith nor the guidance and influence of a holy man can help transform the speaker by opening "doors" for him. He seeks "grace" by communicating directly to the divine, climbing "cathedral" mountains.

The song also operates largely along the same lines as "Close to the Edge" in that all of the individuals mentioned in the song may actually be different sides of the same personality. The "friend" Denver lost could be, in part, himself; he's shed his older unenlightened self, coming home to a place he's never been before. A more enigmatic statement hinting at reincarnation had rarely been uttered in "pop" music at the time, or since.

Pop records aside, prog-rockers were trading in the mystical currency of "the self" beyond the borders of 1972. A case in point: Camel wrote and recorded a song called "Riverman," based on the *Siddhartha* saga. Whether due to the popularity of *Close to the Edge* or the esoteric slipperiness of the subject matter, the notion of basing an entire record on Hesse's popular tome was scrapped. The band's two songwriting protagonists, guitarist/vocalist Andy Latimer and keyboardist/vocalist Pete Bardens eventually collaborated on a largely instrumental album based on Paul Gallico's short fiction tale "The Snow Goose," itself based on Japanese myth. Despite the false start, this episode does show the power *Siddhartha* commanded over the psyche of British progressive-rock musicians at the time.

Genesis' "Firth of Fifth," from 1973's *Selling England by the Pound*, was supposedly inspired by the River Forth in Scotland. From Tony Banks's rippling, classically influenced piano opening to the piece's breathtaking dynamics, Genesis was, in its own way, mirroring Yes's "Close to the Edge" with a narrative flow highlighting the turmoil and change brought to the fore through life's ebbs and flows.

In 1974, Genesis released *The Lamb Lies Down on Broadway*, which is as much a coming-of-age of story as a slide show streaming Jungian archetypes streaming through one young man's subconscious. In "In the Rapids," the protagonist, the Puerto Rican street tough Rael, is surrounded by cold dark waters and thundering noise as he spirals down to the riverbed. It's in the river that Rael comes to a realization of who he is.

Italian progressive-rock band Premiata Forneria Marconi's (PFM) dynamic "Appena un po'," from 1972's *Per un amico*, resurfaced as the English-language song "River of Life" on the 1973 crossover album *Photos of Ghosts*, issued on ELP's Manticore label. PFM's music can be, at times, counterpoint-heavy, even menacing, yet gentle melodies honor both the pastoral and classical aspects of its collective European heritage.

Greg Lake's buddy from King Crimson, Pete Sinfield, penned the lyrics for *Ghosts* and later for ELP, most notably on *Brain Salad Surgery* from 1973. Sinfield seems to use the image of river as a metaphor for life; how we experience moments of purity, pain, and rejuvenation. Buddhist concepts, really, intentional or not.

The Alph River courses through Canadian power-prog trio Rush's supernatural epic "Xanadu," a tone poem from its 1977 studio effort, *A Farewell to Kings*. "Xanadu" was based on the opium-fueled Romantic poem "Kubla Khan," alternately titled "A Vision in a Dream," by author Samuel Taylor Coleridge. (The Alph, it seems, symbolizes a source of power or the eternal.)

Lyricist and drummer Neil Peart alludes to Shangri-La or Shambhala in "Xanadu," which some interpret as an Earthly mountaintop paradise or a heavenly state of mind—an inner peace. Whether heaven is a physical place, and whether the concept of paradise or nirvana carries the same connotation in "Close to the Edge" as it does in "Xanadu," may be a matter of interpretation.

Again, much like in the opening moment of "Close to the Edge," we hear sounds of nature in the song's instrumental intro. The buzzing of synth and volume-controlled electric guitar, the whistling winds (created by keys), and the popping of pitched temple blocks, all evoke the mysticism of the East.

Guitarist Alex Lifeson's arpeggiated guitar line cuts through a misty cloud of audio as Peart and bassist Geddy Lee introduce penetrating patterns in 7/8. As in "Perpetual Change," we get the sense of dual or dueling bands, and because of this effect, the music is very much like the Coleridge poem that inspired it: it retains a dreamy, supernatural quality.

The overlap of sea-based imagery in the lyrics, the archetypal iconography of the river, and the expansive oceanic effect of British prog rock can be explored in more depth and vigor at some later date. For now, all of these elements appeared to link many of the major prog bands in and around 1972.

What *was* in the water back then?

CTTE TOUR DATES

Through my own research, the help of archivists at various universities, daily newspaper archives, and with a hat tip to sites such as Forgotten-Yesterdays.com, here's a list of the shows Yes played in support of *Close to the Edge*.

7/30/1972 Dallas Auditorium
Memorial Auditorium

7/31/1972 Houston, Texas
Sam Houston Coliseum

8/1/1972 Oklahoma City, Oklahoma
Fairgrounds Arena

8/3/1972 Denver, Colorado
Denver Coliseum

8/4/1972 Long Beach, California
Long Beach Arena

8/5/1972 Berkeley, California
Berkeley Community Theatre

8/6/1972 Portland, Oregon
Memorial Coliseum

8/7/1972 Vancouver, British Columbia
PNE Coliseum

8/8/1972 Seattle, Washington
Paramount Theatre

8/10/1972 Dayton, Ohio
Hara Arena

8/11/1972 Akron, Ohio
The Rubber Bowl

8/12/1972 Asbury Park, New Jersey
Convention Hall

8/13/1972 Columbia, Maryland
Merriweather Post Pavilion

8/15/1972 Philadelphia, Pennsylvania
Spectrum Arena

8/16/1972 New York City, New York
Gaelic Park

8/18/1972 Louisville, Kentucky
Commonwealth Convention Center

8/20/1972 Memphis, Tennessee
Mid-South Coliseum

8/21/1972 Edwardsville, Illinois
Mississippi River Festival

9/2/1972 London, England
Crystal Palace Bowl

9/4/1972 Glasgow, Scotland
Kelvin Hall

9/5/1972 Glasgow, Scotland
Kelvin Hall

9/9/1972 Bristol, England
Colston Hall

9/10/1972 Manchester, England
Kings Hall

9/12/1972 Newcastle, England
Newcastle City Hall

9/15/1972 Hollywood, Florida
Hollywood Sportatorium

9/16/1972 Tampa, Florida
Curtis Hixon Hall

9/17/1972 Jacksonville, Florida
Jacksonville Veterans Memorial Coliseum

9/19/1972 Cincinnati, Ohio
Cincinnati Gardens

9/20/1972 Indianapolis, Indiana
Indiana Convention Center

9/21/1972 Detroit, Michigan
Cobo Arena

9/22/1972 Chicago, Illinois
Arie Crown Theatre

9/23/1972 Minneapolis, Minnesota
The Armory

9/24/1972 Milwaukee, Wisconsin
Mecca Arena

9/25/1972 Hartford, Connecticut
Dillion Stadium

9/26/1972 Boston, Massachusetts
Music Theatre

9/27/1972 Richmond, Virginia
Richmond Coliseum

9/29/1972 New Orleans, Louisiana
Morris FX Jeff Municipal Auditorium

9/30/1972 Atlanta, Georgia
Atlanta Municipal Auditorium

10/1/1972 Tuscaloosa, Alabama
Memorial Coliseum

10/2/1972 Columbia, South Carolina
Carolina Coliseum

10/3/1972 Charlotte, North Carolina
Charlotte Coliseum

10/28/1972 Millersville, Pennsylvania
Sports Arena

10/29/1972 Syracuse, New York
Onondaga County War Memorial

10/30/1972 Kitchener, Ontario
The University of Waterloo

10/31/1972 Toronto, Ontario, Canada
Maple Leaf Gardens

11/1/1972 Ottawa, Ontario, Canada
Ottawa Civic Centre

11/2/1972 Montreal, Quebec, Canada
St. Denis Theatre

11/3/1972 Flint, Michigan
IMA Auditorium

11/4/1972 Columbus, Ohio
St. John's Arena

11/5/1972 Erie, Pennsylvania
Gannon University

11/6/1972 Struthers, Ohio
Struthers Field House

11/7/1972 Pittsburgh, Pennsylvania
Pittsburgh Civic Arena

11/8/1972 Huntington, West Virginia
Veterans Memorial Field House

11/9/1972 Norfolk, Virginia
Norfolk Scope

11/10/1972 Roanoke, Virginia
Roanoke Civic Center

11/11/1972 Durham, North Carolina
Duke University

11/12/1972 Greensboro, North Carolina
Greensboro Coliseum

11/14/1972 Athens, Georgia
University of Georgia

11/15/1972 Knoxville, Tennessee
Knoxville Civic Auditorium

11/16/1972 Bowling Green, Ohio
Bowling Green State University

11/17/1972 Terre Haute, Indiana
Tilson Auditorium

11/18/1972 South Bend, Indiana
University of Notre Dame

11/19/1972 Kent, Ohio
Kent State University

11/20/1972 Uniondale, New York
Nassau Veterans Memorial Coliseum

12/15/1972 London, England
Rainbow Theatre

12/16/1972 London, England
Rainbow Theatre

12/17/1972 Manchester, England
The Hardrock

3/8/1973 Tokyo, Japan
Tokyo Kōsei Nenkin Kaikan

3/9/1973 Tokyo, Japan
Shibuya Koukaidou (Public Hall)

3/10/1973 Tokyo, Japan
Kanda Kyoritsu Kouduo

3/11/1973 Nagoya, Japan
Nagoya-shi Koukaido

3/12/1973 Osaka, Japan
Kouseinennkin Kaikan

3/14/1973 Kyoto, Japan
Kyoto Kaikan

3/19/1973 Brisbane, Australia
Festival Hall

3/21/1973 Adelaide, Australia
Apollo Stadium

3/23/1973 Melbourne, Australia
Melbourne Festival Hall

3/26/1972 Sydney, Australia
Hordern Pavilion

3/27/1973 Sydney, Australia
Hordern Pavilion

4/4/1973 San Diego, California
San Diego Sports Arena

4/5/1973 Los Angeles, California
Los Angeles Forum

4/6/1973 Las Vegas, Nevada
Ice Palace

4/7/1973 San Francisco, California
Winterland Ballroom

4/8/1973 Albuquerque, New Mexico
Johnson Gym

4/9/1973 Phoenix, Arizona
Civic Hall

4/11/1973 Wichita, Kansas
Century II Civic Center

4/12/1973 Oklahoma City, Oklahoma
Fairgrounds Arena

4/13/1973 San Antonio, Texas
San Antonio Municipal Auditorium

4/14/1973 Houston, Texas
University of Houston

4/15/1973 Dallas, Texas
Memorial Auditorium

4/16/1973 St. Louis, Missouri
Kiel Auditorium

4/17/1973 St. Louis, Missouri
Kiel Auditorium

4/18/1973 Nashville, Tennessee
Municipal Auditorium

4/19/1973 Atlanta, Georgia
Georgia Tech Coliseum

4/20/1973 Savannah, Georgia
Savannah Civic Center

4/21/1973 Tampa, Florida
Curtis Hixon Hall

4/22/1973 West Palm Beach, Florida
West Palm Beach Auditorium

SIBERIA GOES THROUGH THE MOTIONS
A Selected Discography

The following is a partial overview, a selected discography, of Yes albums containing material that relates to the original *Close to the Edge* (*CTTE*) album. I've also included a general Yes discography here as well.

CTTE and Related Releases
Close to the Edge (LP SD-19133)
Close to the Edge (cassette CS-19133)
Fragile / Close to the Edge 80002-4 (cassette)
Close to the Edge (Atlantic CD, SD19133-2, 1987)
Close to the Edge (Elektra/Rhino, R27390, 2003)
Close to the Edge (Panegyric, GYRSP50012, 2013)
Close to the Edge (SACD, AFZ 147, 2013)
Close to the Edge (Japan, HDCD mini LP, Atlantic / East West Japan AMCY-2732)
Close to the Edge (Blu-Ray)
Close to the Edge (8-track)
"A Revealing 14-minute interview with the Yes" [sic] 7-inch, 33rpm flexidisc (Amsco Music Publishing Group manufactured by Eva-tone Soundsheets)
Yessongs (1973)
Classic Yes (1981)
Yesyears (1991)
Yesstory (1992)
Highlights: The Very Best of Yes (1993)
Symphonic Music of Yes (1993) (Bruford, Howe with the London Philharmonic Orchestra)
Keys to Ascension (1996)
Key to Ascension 2 (1997)
House of Yes: Live from the House of Blues (2000)
Magnification (2001 Borders limited edition)
In a Word (2002)
Remixes (2003)
The Ultimate Yes—35th Anniversary Collection (2003)
Magnification (2004 reissue with bonus tracks)
The Word Is Live (2005)

Essentially (2006)
Yesstories (2006)
Live at Montreux 2003 (2007)
In the Present—Live in Lyon (2011)
Union Live (2011)
Wonderous Stories: The Best of Yes (2011)
The Studio Albums—1969–1987 (2013)
Songs from Tsongas (2014)
Like It Is: Yes at the Bristol Hippodrome (2014)
Like It Is: Live at the Mesa Arts Center (2015)
Progeny: Seven Shows from Seventy-Two (2015)
Progeny: Highlights from Seventy-Two (2015)

Anderson Bruford Wakeman Howe
An Evening of Yes Music Plus (VHS, 1993)
An Evening of Yes Music Plus (DVD, 2006)
An Evening of Yes Music plus (CD) (1993, 2006)
Live at the NEC October 24, 1989 (2012)

Selected Singles
"America" / "Total Mass Retain" (US, 45-2899)
"America" / "Total Mass Retain" (Brazil, ATCS-10.036, 2899)
"America" / "Total Mass Retain" (Spain, HS- 871)
"America" / "Total Mass Retain" (Germany, ATL 10226, 2899)
"America" / "Total Mass Retain" (Japan, Warner-Pioneer Corporation P-1161A)
"America" / "Total Mass Retain" (Australia, 45-2899)
"America" / "Total Mass Retain" (Netherlands, ATL 10 226)
"America" / "Total Mass Retain" (Turkey, 72506)
"And You and I" (Part I) / "And You and I" (Part II) (US, 45-2920)
"And You and I" (Part I) / "And You and I" (Part II) (Brazil, Atco ATCS 10.045, 2920)
"And You and I" / "Roundabout" 1974 extended play (Yugoslavia, Atlantic Records K 10407)

DVD, Video
Yessongs (VHS/DVD, 1984)
Yesyears: A Retrospective (VHS, 1991)
Keys to Ascension (DVD, 1996)
Live in Philadelphia, 1979 (1998)
Symphonic Live (2002)
YesSpeak (2003)
Songs from Tsongas (2004)
Live at Queens Park Rangers Stadium (2001)
Live at Montreux (2007)
Classic Artists: Yes; Their Definitive, Fully Authorized Story (DVD, 2008)
Live in Chile, 1994 (DVD, 2009)
Union (DVD, 2011)

Selected Yes Albums: Compilations, Studio, and Live Releases

Yes (1969)
Time and a Word (1970)
The Yes Album (1971)
Fragile (1971)
Close to the Edge (1972)
Yessongs (1973)
Tales from Topographic Oceans (1973/4)
Relayer (1974)
Yesterdays (1975)
Going for the One (1977)
Tormato (1978)
Drama (1980)
Yesshows (1980)
Classic Yes (1981)
90125 (1983)
9012Live (1985)
Big Generator (1987)
Union (1991)
Highlights: The Very Best of Yes (1993)
Affirmative: The Yes Solo Family Album (1993)
Talk (1994)
Something's Coming: The BBC Recordings 1969–1970 (1997)
Open Your Eyes (1997)
The Ladder (1999)
Magnification (2001)
Keystudio (2001)
Wonderous Stories: The Best of Yes (2011)
Fly from Here (2011)
Like It Is: Yes at the Bristol Hippodrome (2014)
Heaven and Earth (2014)
Like It Is: at the Mesa Arts Center (2015)

Selected Solo Releases

JON ANDERSON

Olias of Sunhillow (1976)
Song of Seven (1980)
Animation (1982)
3 Ships (1985)
In the City of Angels (1988)
Deseo (1994)
Toltec (1996)
Earthmotherearth (1997)
Survival and Other Stories (2010)

With Vangelis:
Short Stories (1979)
The Friends of Mr. Cairo (1981)
With AndersonPonty Band (feat. Jean-Luc Ponty):
Better Late than Never (2015)
With Rick Wakeman:
The Living Tree (2010)

STEVE HOWE

Beginnings (1975)
The Steve Howe Album (1979)
The Bodast Tapes (1981)
Turbulence (1991)
Grand Scheme of Things (1993)
Mothballs (1994)
Not Necessarily Acoustic (1995)
Homebrew (1996)
Pulling Strings (1998)
Quantum Guitar (1998)
Portraits of Bob Dylan (1999)
Homebrew 2 (2000)
Natural Timbre (2001)
Skyline (2002)
Spectrum (2005)
Homebrew 3 (2005)
Motif Volume 1 (2008)
Homebrew 4 (2010)
Time (2011)
Homebrew 5 (2013)
Anthology: A Solo Career Retrospective (2015)

With Paul Sutin:
Voyagers (1995)

As Steve Howe's Remedy:
Elements (2003)
Live (DVD) (2005)
As Steve Howe Trio:
Haunted Melody (2008)
Travelling (2010)

BILL BRUFORD

As Bruford:
Feels Good to Me (1978)
One of a Kind (1979)
The Bruford Tapes (1979)
Gradually Going Tornado (1980)
Master Strokes (1986)
Rock Goes to College (2006)

With King Crimson:
Larks' Tongues in Aspic (1973)
Starless and Bible Black (1974)
Red (1974)
USA (1975)
A Young Person's Guide to King Crimson (1976)
Discipline (1981)
Beat (1982)
Three of a Perfect Pair (1984)
The Great Deceiver (1992)
THRAK (1995)
The Night Watch: Live at the Amsterdam Concertgebouw, November 23, 1973 (1997)
Absent Lovers: Live in Montreal 1984 (1998)
The Beat Club, Bremen (1999)
Live in Central Park (2000)
Live in Mainz (March 30, 1974) (2001)
Live at the Zoom Club (October 13, 1972) (2002)
Champaign-Urbana Sessions (January 17–30, 1983) (2002)
Live in Guildford November 13, 1972 (2003)
Live in Philadelphia, PA (July 30, 1982) (2004)
October 23, 1973, Apollo, Glasgow, Scotland (2006)
June 27, 1974, Kennedy Center, Washington, D.C. (2006)

With Genesis:
Seconds Out (1977)
Three Sides Live (1994, remastered reissue)
A Trick of the Tail (2007, "Definitive Edition" remaster with DVD concert)

With U.K.:
U.K. (1978)
Alive in America Classic Concerts Volume 4 (1999)
Live in America (2007)

With Patrick Moraz:
Music for Piano and Drums (1983)
Flags (1985)
In Tokyo (2009)

With Michiel Bortslap:
Every Step a Dance, Every Word a Song (2004)
In Concert in Holland (DVD) (2004)
In Two Minds (2007)

With Absolute Elsewhere:
In Search of Ancient Gods (1976)

With Pete Lockett's Network of Sparks:
One (1999)

With Pianocircus:
Skin and Wire (2009)

With Tony Levin:
Bruford Levin Upper Extremities (1998)
Blue Nights (2000)

With David Torn:
Cloud About Mercury (1987)

With Pavlov's Dog:
At the Sound of the Bell (1975)

With National Health:
Missing Pieces (1996)

With Al DiMeola:
Scenario (1983)

With Ralph Towner and Eddie Gomez:
If Summer Had Its Ghosts (1997)

For Paiste Cymbals:
insert included in *Modern Drummer* magazine May 1984

With Earthworks:
Earthworks (1987)
Dig? (1989)
All Heaven Broke Loose (1991)
Stamping Ground (1994)
A Part, and Yet Apart (1999)
The Sound of Surprise (2001)
Footloose and Fancy Free (2002)
Random Acts of Happiness (2004, featuring Tim Garland)
Earthworks Underground Orchestra (2006, credited as Bill Bruford and Tim Garland)

With World Drummers Ensemble:
A Coat of Many Colors (2006)

CHRIS SQUIRE
Fish Out of Water (1975)
Chris Squire's Swiss Choir (2007)

With Alan White:
"Run with the Fox" (1981)

With Squackett (Steve Hackett):
A Life Within a Day (2012)

With Billy Sherwood:
Conspiracy (2000)
The Unknown (2003)
Conspiracy Live (2013)

ALAN WHITE
Ramshackled (1976)

As White:
White (2005)

With Claire Hamill:
October (1973)

With the Plastic Ono Band:
Live Peace in Toronto 1969 (1969)

With John Lennon:
Imagine (1971)

With Levin Torn White:
Levin Torn White (2011)

With Eddie Harris:
E.H. in the UK (1974, also featuring Chris Squire)

With Wetton/Manzanera:
Wetton/Manzanera (1987)

With Johnny Harris:
All to Bring You Morning (featuring Jon Anderson) (1973)

RICK WAKEMAN
*Piano Vibrations** (1971)
The Six Wives of Henry VIII (1973)
Journey to the Centre of the Earth (1974)
The Myths and Legends of King Arthur and the Knights of the Round Table (1975)
No Earthly Connection (1976)
Criminal Record (1977)
Rhapsodies (1979)
1984 (1981)

Rock N' Roll Prophet (1982)
Cost of Living (1983)
Beyond the Planets (1984, with Jeff Wayne)
Silent Nights (1985)
Country Airs (1986)
The Gospels (1987)
Time Machine (1988)
A Suite of the Gods (1988, with Ramon Remedios)
Zodiaque (1988, with Tony Fernandez)
Nights Airs (1989)
Sea Airs (1989)
Black Knights at the Court of Ferdinand IV (1989, with Mario Fasciano)
Aspirant Sunset (1990)
Aspirant Sunrise (1990)
Aspirant Sunshadows (1991)
Visions (a.k.a. *Visions of Paradise*) (1995)
The Piano Album (1995)
The New Gospels (1995)
Seven Wonders of the World (1995)
King Biscuit Flower Hour Presents Rick Wakeman in Concert (1996)
Return to the Centre of the Earth (1999)
White Rock II (1999)
The Masters (1999)
Chronicles of Man (2000)
Preludes to a Century (2000)
Simply Acoustic (2001)
Two Sides of Yes (2001)
Classical Variations (2001)
Songs of Middle Earth (Inspired by The Lord of the Rings*)* (2001)
Two Sides of Yes: Volume II (2002)
Live in Nottingham (2002)
The Legend: Live in Concert 2000 (DVD, 2002)
Live (2005, credited as Wakeman and Cousins)
Amazing Grace (2007)
Live at the BBC (2007)
The Six Wives of Henry VIII Live at Hampton Court Palace (2009)
In the Nick of Time—Live in 2003 (2012)
Journey to the Centre of the Earth (2014)
Live at the Empire Pool—King Arthur on Ice (2014)
Starship Trooper (2016)
Life on Mars (2016)

Soundtracks

Lisztomania (1975)
White Rock (1976)
The Burning (1981)
Crimes of Passion (1984)

With Strawbs:
Dragonfly (1970)
Just a Collection of Antiques and Curios—Live at Queen Elizabeth Hall (1970)
From the Witchwood (1971)

* Produced by John Schroeder; Wakeman doesn't consider this to be his first solo album

BIBLIOGRAPHY

Books, Literature

Agel, Jerome (ed.). *The Making of Kubrick's* 2001. New York, NY: Signet, 1970.

Barnett-Jones, David. *Sibelius*. London: Omnibus Press, 1989.

Best of Yes for Bass. Milwaukee, Wisconsin: Hal Leonard Corporation, 2013.

Birren, Faber. *Color Psychology and Color Therapy*. Secaucus, New Jersey: The Citadel Press, 1961.

Blavatsky, H. P. *Isis Unveiled: A Master-Key to the Mysteries of Ancient and Modern Science and Theology. Volume II: Theology*. Sixth Edition. New York: J.W. Buton, 1891.

Bruford, Bill. *The Autobiography: Yes, King Crimson, Earthworks and More*. London, England: Jawbone Press, 2009.

Bruford, Bill. *When in Doubt, Roll!: Transcriptions of Bruford's Greatest Performances, with Bill's Personal Commentary and Suggested Exercises*. Transcriptions by Michael Bettine. Cedar Grove, New Jersey: Modern Drummer Publications, Inc., 1988.

Burrough, Bryan. *Days of Rage: America's Radical Underground, The FBI, and the Forgotten Age of Revolutionary Violence*. New York: Penguin Press, 2015.

Case, George. *Led Zeppelin FAQ*. Backbeat Books, an imprint of Hal Leonard Corporation: Milwaukee, Wisconsin, 2011.

Cavanagh, John. *The Piper at the Gates of Dawn*. New York: The Continuum International Publishing Group, Inc., 2004.

Cousins, Dave. *Exorcising Ghosts*. Kent, England: Witchwood Media Limited, 2014.

Covach, John and G.M. Boone (Eds). *Understanding Rock: Essays in Musical Analysis*. New York: Oxford University Press, 1997.

Classical Music. John Burrows (ed) with Charles Wiffen. New York: Metro Books/Sterling Publishing Co. Inc., 2010.

Davie, Cedric Thorpe. *Musical Structure and Design*. New York: Dover Publications, 1966.

Davies, Hunter (Editor). *The Beatles Lyrics: The Stories Behind the Music, Including the Handwritten Drafts of More Than 100 Classic Beatles Songs*. New York: Little, Brown and Company, 2014.

De Givry, Grillot. *Witchcraft, Magic, and Alchemy*, translated by J. Courtenay Locke. New York: Dover Publications, 1971.

Dean, Roger. *Views*. Petaluma, California: Pomegranate Artbooks, 1975.

Drum Techniques of Rush. Transcriptions by Bill Wheeler. Secaucus, New Jersey: Warner Bros. Publications, Inc./Core Music Publishing, 1985.

Fellezs, Kevin. *Birds of Fire: Jazz, Rock, Funk, and the Creation of Fusion*. Durham, North Carolina: Duke University Press, 2011.

Finlay, Victoria. *Color: A Natural History of the Palette*. New York: Random House, 2004.

Fong-Torres, Ben. *Eagles: Taking It to the Limit*. Running Press, Philadelphia, PA, 2011.

Forrester, George, Martyn Hanson, Frank Askew. *Emerson, Lake & Palmer: The Show That Never Ends . . . Encore*. London: Foruli Classics, 2013.

Gallo, Armando. *Genesis: I Know What I Like*. London: Omnibus Press. 1987.

Genesis Anthology. New York: Warner Bros. Publications, Inc. Unknown Date.

Godwin, Joscelyn. *Harmonies of Heaven and Earth: Mysticism in Music, from Antiquity to the Avant-Garde*. Rochester, Vermont: Inner Traditions International, 1995.

Goulding, Phil G. *Classical Music: The 50 Greatest Composers and Their 1,000 Greatest Works*. New York: Fawcett Books, 1992.

Greene, Joshua M. *Here Comes the Sun: The Spiritual and Musical Journey of George Harrison*. Hoboken, New Jersey: John Wiley and Sons, Inc., 2006.

Hedges, Dan. *Yes: The Authorized Biography*. London, England: Sidgwick and Jackson, 1981.

Hegarty, Paul and Martin Halliwell. *Beyond and Before: Progressive Rock Since the 1960s*. New York: The Continuum International Publishing Group, 2011.

Hesse, Hermann. Demian. New York: Bantam Books, 1981.

Hesse, Hermann. *Journey to the East*. New York: The. Farrar, Straus and Giroux: New York, 2003.

Hesse, Hermann. *Narcissus and Goldmund*. New York: Bantam Books, 1984.

Hesse, Hermann. *Siddhartha*. New York: Bantam Books, 1971.

Holm-Hudson, Kevin. *Genesis and The Lamb Lies Down on Broadway*. Surrey, England: Ashgate Publishing Limited, 2008.

Hurwitz, David. *Sibelius: The Orchestral Works, an Owner's Manual*. Pompton Plains, New Jersey: Amadeus Press, 2007.

Jung, Carl G. (ed). *Man and His Symbols*. New York: Dell, 17th printing, 1978.

Jung, Carl G., Aniela Jaffé (ed). *Memories, Dreams, Reflections* (Revised Edition), translated by Richard and Clara Winston. New York: Vintage Books/Random House, 1989.

Lachman, Gary. *Turn Off Your Mind: The Mystical Sixties and the Dark Side of the Age of Aquarius*. San Francisco, California: Disinformation Books, 2001.

Laing, R. D. *The Divided Self*. Middlesex, England: Penguin Books, 1971.

Leary, Timothy; Metzner, Ralph; Alpert, Richard. *The Psychedelic Experience: A Manual Based on the Tibetan Book of the Dead*. New York: Citadel Press Books, 1992.

LoBrutto, Vincent. *Stanley Kubrick: A Biography*. New York, NY: De Capo Press, 1999.

Macan, Edward. *Rocking the Classics: English Progressive Rock and the Counterculture*. New York: Oxford University Press, 1997.

Mardsen Thomas, Anne (compiler). *The Organs of St. Giles Church Cripplegate*. Independent release, 2012.

Martin, Bill. *Music of Yes: Structure and Vision in Progressive Rock*. Peru, Illinois. Open Court Publishing Company/Carus Publishing Company, 1997.

Matthews, W. H. *Mazes and Labyrinths: Their History and Development*. New York: Dover Publications, Inc., 1970.

Mileck, Joseph. *Hermann Hesse: Life and Art*. Berkeley, California: University of California Press, 1978.

Mish, Frederick C. (ed.) *Merriam Webster's Collegiate Dictionary Tenth Edition*. Springfield, Massachusetts, 1993.

Moore, Allan F. *The Beatles: Sgt. Pepper's Lonely Hearts Club Band*. Cambridge, UK: Cambridge University Press, 1997.

Moore, Allan. *Rock: The Primary Text: Developing a Musicology of Rock*. New York, New York: Routledge, 2001.

Morgan, Giles. *The Holy Grail*. Edison, New Jersey: Chartwell Books, 2005.

Morse, Tim. *Yesstories: Yes in Their Own Words*. New York: St. Martin's Griffin, 1996.

Nhat Hanh, Thich. *The Heart of Buddha's Teachings*. New York, New York: Broadway Books, 1999.

Nef, Karl. *An Outline of the History of Music*, Third Printing, translated by Carl F. Pfatteicher. New York: Columbia University Press, 1939.

Ortenberg, Veronica. *In Search of the Holy Grail*. London, England: Hambledon Continuum, 2007.

Perrine, Laurence. *Sound and Sense: An Introduction to Poetry* (Second Edition). New York: Harcourt, Brace and World, Inc., 1963.

Rodriguez, Robert. *Revolver: How the Beatles Reimagined Rock 'n' Roll*. Milwaukee, Wisconsin: Backbeat Books/Hal Leonard, 2012.

Rosen, Charles. *The Romantic Generation*. Cambridge, Mass.: Harvard University Press, 1995.

Rubin, Dave. *Yes: Guitar Signature Licks: A Step-by-Step Breakdown of the Guitar Styles and Techniques of Steve Howe and Trevor Rabin*. Milwaukee: Hal Leonard Corporation, 2015.

Sandbrook, Dominic. *State of Emergency: The Way We Were: Britain 1970–1974*. London: Penguin Books, 2010.

Schafer, R. Murray. *The Soundscape: Our Sonic Environment and the Tuning of the World*. Rochester, Vermont: Destiny Books, 1994.

Schofield, Paul. *The Redeemer Reborn*. New York: Amadeus Press, a Hal Leonard imprint, 2007.

Serrano, Miguel. *Jung and Hesse: A Record of Two Friendships*.

Stump, Paul. *The Music's All That Matters*. Chelmsford, Essex, England: Harbour, 2010.

Thoreau, Henry David. *Walden and "Civil Disobedience."* New York: Signet Classics, 2012.

Walsh, Stephen. *Stravinsky: A Creative Spring: Russia and France, 1862–1934*. New York: Alfred A. Knopf, 1999.

Warwick, Neil, Jon Kutner and Tony Brown. *The Complete Book of the British Charts*. Third Edition. London: Omnibus Press, 2004.

Watkinson, David. *Yes: Perpetual Change*. London, England: Plexus Publishing Limited, 2002.

Welch, Chris. *Close to the Edge: The Story of Yes*. Omnibus Press, 2008 (Third Edition).

Wheeler, Tom. *American Guitars: An Illustrated History*. New York: Harper and Row, 1982.

Whitburn, Joel. *The Billboard Book of Top 40 Hits*. New York: Billboard Books; an imprint of Watson-Guptill Publications, 1989.

Wooding, Dan. *Rick Wakeman: The Caped Crusader*. London: Robert Hale Limited, 1978.

Yogananda, Paramahansa. *Autobiography of a Yogi*. Los Angeles: Self-Realization Fellowship, 2002.

Ziolkowski, Theodore. *The Novels of Hermann Hesse: A Study in Theme and Structure.* Princeton, New Jersey: Princeton University Press, 1974.

Liner Notes

Coltrane, John. John Coltrane: *A Love Supreme,* 1964. (MCA Records/GRP)

Gottlieb, Doug, and Glenn. Yes: *The Word Is Live* "That '70s Show: Madison Square Garden, 1978." (Rhino/Elektra/Atco, 2005, R2 78234)

Lewisohn, Mark. The Beatles: *Past Masters, Volume Two,* 1988 (Apple/Parlophone/EMI)

Vivaldi: The Four Seasons. (Infinity Digital/Sony Music Entertainment Inc., 1993, QK 57243) No author credited.

Magazines and Periodicals

Achard, Ken. "Steve Howe talks to Ken Achard." *Guitar: The Magazine for All Guitarists,* February 1973.

Achard, Ken. "Steve Howe talks to Ken Achard." *Guitar: The Magazine for All Guitarists,* March 1973.

Album Reviews: Pop. "Emerson, Lake, and Palmer—*Pictures at an Exhibition.*" *Billboard,* January 22, 1972, page 64.

Album Reviews: Pop. "Yes—*Close to the Edge.*" *Billboard,* October 7, 1972.

Album Reviews: Pop. "Yes—*Fragile.*" Billboard, January 22, 1972, page 64.

Alexander, Phil. "The Seeker." *Mojo '60s,* issue #3, 2015, page 115.

Andrews, Graeme. "UK Indies, US Labels Bid for Dominance in Britain." *Billboard,* June 29, 1968.

"Any Questions? Diary of a Yes Man." (Questions posed to and answered by Jon Anderson.) *Melody Maker,* September 16, 1972.

"Around the Studios: Floyd, Blunstone at Abbey Road." *New Musical Express,* July 1, 1972.

"Atlantic Has Banner Year." *Billboard,* January 6, 1973, page 3.

"Beck, Genesis, Gallagher, and Strawbs Tours." *Melody Maker,* January 13, 1973.

"Billboard Pick: Pop: Yes: Fragile." Billboard, January 22, 1972.

Bivona, Joe. "Now Howe on Solo LP." *Circus Raves,* October 1975, page 56.

Black, Alan (Q&A with Rick Wakeman transcribed). "Rick Wakeman and the Making of The Six Wives of Henry VIII." *Melody Maker,* February 10, 1973, page 25.

Bosworth, Penny. "Caught in the Act: Yes Is No Disgrace." *Melody Maker,* September 16, 1972, page 12.

Brooks, Michael. "'Yes': Steve Howe." *Guitar Player,* April 1973, pages 24–26, 41

Buskin, Richard. "Use It or Abuse It." *Studio Sound,* March 1997, page 60.

Charone, Barbara. "One of These Nightmares: Say a Prayer for the Pretenders." *Crawdaddy,* April 1977.

Coral Electric Sitar ad. *Billboard,* April 13, 1968.

C. R. "Eagles' First Flight." *Melody Maker,* July 29, 1972.

Crescenti, Peter. "Guitar Synthesizer: $7,000 Is Cheap." *Circus,* September 1975.

Crescenti, Peter. "The Sunhollow Saga: Jon Anderson Delivers Fourth Yes Solo Album." *Circus,* October 26, 1976.

Crowe, Cameron. "Journey to the Center of the Stage." *Rolling Stone*, January 30, 1975.

Crowe, Cameron. "Yes: The Band That Stays Healthy Plays Healthy." *Rolling Stone*, June 7, 1973.

Cromelin, Richard. "Yes: Close to the Edge." *Rolling Stone*, November 9, 1972.

Cromelin, Richard. "Yes: Fragile." *Rolling Stone*, March 16, 1972.

Crowe, Cameron. "Yes Soars Back to Earth with 'Tales from the Topographic Ocean.'" *Circus*, March 1974.

Dellar, Fred, "Around the Studios." *New Musical Express*, July 15, 1972, page 30.

Dellar, Fred. "Around the Studios." *New Musical Express*, July 22, 1972, page 39.

Dellar, Fred. "Around the Studios." *New Musical Express*, August 12, 1972.

Dallas, Karl. "Caught in the Act: The Yes Circus." *Melody Maker*, December 23, 1972.

"Don't Release 'Pretties', says Alice / Yes album price mix-up / A and M 'insult.'" *New Musical Express*, September 16, 1972.

Dwyer, John. "Diary." *Studio Sound*, September 1972, page 34.

Dwyer, John. "Diary." *Studio Sound*, March 1973, page 27.

Dwyer, John. "Diary." *Studio Sound*, April 1973, page 38.

Dwyer, John. "Wessex-Chrysalis." *Studio Sound and Broadcast Engineering*, September 1974, pages 59–62.

"ELP Go Global." *Melody Maker*, March 17, 1973, page 6.

"ELP Label." *Melody Maker*, February 10, 1973.

Farber, Jim. "The Emerson, Lake, and Palmer Tapes, Part 3: Keith Emerson." *Circus*, September 8, 1977.

Farber, Jim. "Yes Is Going for the Big One: Wakeman Rejoins Former Partners for Mammoth US Tour." *Circus*, September 8, 1977.

"FM Action." *Billboard*, July 29, 1972.

"FM Action." *Billboard*, October 7 1972, page 20.

"FM Action." *Billboard*, October 14, 1972, page 14.

"Full Yes." *Melody Maker*, December 16, 1972.

General News: Gold Awards. *Billboard*, April 24, 1972, page 6.

Grossman, Loyd. "Records: *Emerson, Lake, and Palmer* Cotillion, SD 9040" (review). *Rolling Stone*, April 15, 1971.

Hall, Claude. "Progressive Rock Gives Life to Dead-Weight FM Radio Stations." *Billboard*, April 20, 1968.

Hall, Claude. "Says Hip Public Cues Hip Rock." *Billboard*, June 8, 1968.

Heber, Shelly. "Talent in Action: Yes, Edgar Winter, Eagles." *Billboard*, September 2, 1972, pages 10, 12.

Hedges, Dan. "Steve Howe: Renaissance Man of the Guitar." *Guitar Player*, May 1978, pages 38–39, 43, 46, 48, 50, 52, 54, 58, 60.

"Hemdale Buys NEMS, Sabbath's Disk Pact." *Billboard*, Sept. 2, 1972, page 54.

Holman, Pamela. "Yesman Steve Howe: A Self-Assessment." *New Musical Express*, February 5, 1972.

Houghton, Mick. "Sabbath's Sabotage: Rock Magicians on Tour—End Sabbatical with Devilish LP." *Circus Raves*, October 1975, pages 20–24.

"International: The Battle of Britain, 1974." *Newsweek*, February 11, 1974.

"Jethro Smash Stones." *New Musical Express*, February 12, 1972.

Jones, Douglas. "Yes concert stopped by police raid." *New Musical Express*, October 14, 1972, page 47.

"Kama Sutra Helms Draft Waxing Plans for Hippops." *Billboard*, June 17, 1967.

Kelleher, Ed. "Record Reviews: Emerson, Lake, and Palmer: *Pictures at an Exhibition*." *Circus*, April, 1972.

"King Crimson's British Dates." *Melody Maker*, January 6, 1973.

"KPIX-TV Show on S.F. Scene." *Billboard*, May 27, 1967.

"KSHE-FM Outlet with Difference." *Billboard*, December 16, 1967.

"Lux Awards." *Melody Maker*, January 27, 1973.

MacDonald, Ian. "Matching Mole: Cosmic Music and a Weird Fripp Trip." *New Musical Express*, September 30, 1972.

MacDonald, Ian. "Meaningless Magnificence from Yes?" *New Musical Express*, September 2, 1972.

Mangle, Harry. "Martin Rushent Tells All." *Studio Sound*, January 1982, pages 62–64.

Menn, Don and Chip Stern. "John McLaughlin: After Mahavishnu and Shakti, a Return to Electric Guitar." *Guitar Player*, August 1978.

Micallef, Ken. "Roy Haynes, Terri Lyne Carrington, and Jack DeJohnette." *Modern Drummer*, June 2012, pages 38–51.

"NME Charts: British Albums." *New Musical Express*, September 30, 1972–October 28, 1972.

Norman, Tony. "Jon Anderson of Yes Talks to Tony Norman: Confessions of a Musical Idiot." *New Musical Express*, June 3, 1972

Norman, Tony. "Wakeman Swallows Ego, Yes Surge Ahead." *New Musical Express*, November 18, 1972, page 10.

O'Connor, Jim. "ELP Split for Solo Exploits." *Circus*, November 1974.

"Ouch." *Melody Maker*, February 10, 1973.

Paige, Earl. "Programmers Rip Too-Long Singles." *Billboard*, November 4, 1972.

Palmer, Philip. "From the Music Capitals of the World: London." *Billboard*, May 13, 1972, page 56.

Partridge, Bob. "UK Industry Hurt by Albert Hall Rock Ban." *Billboard*, May 6, 1972, page 12.

Podolinsky, Gil. "Clair Bros. Audio, Lititz, PA." *Modern Recording*, December/January 1977, pages 36–41.

"Polydor Classical Sales in 30 Percent Spurt Over '71." *Billboard*, February 10, 1973.

"Pop 30." *Melody Maker* charts dated September 3–December 30, 1972.

"Progressive Rock All the Way in WNEW-FM's Format Future." *Billboard*. December 9, 1967.

"Progressive Rock Dilemma." *Billboard*, April 13, 1968.

Proops, Tony. "Anderson's Fairy Tales: The Rocker Who Wouldn't Roll with the Times." *Circus*, August 10, 1976.

"Radio-TV Programming: Programming Aids: Progressive Rock Radio." *Billboard*, June 29, 1968.

"Rainbow Is Re-Opening." *New Musical Express*, May 27, 1972.

Rensin, David. "The Eagles: Desperado." *Phonograph Record*, June 1973.

"Rick Wakeman's Mini Moog." *New Musical Express*, February 19, 1972.

Ridder, Fred. "Creating Utopia with Todd Rundgren." *Modern Recording*, May 1977, pages 38–42.

Roberts, Chris. "Heaven Can Wait." *PROG magazine*, November 2012, page 37.

Rose, Frank. "Rick Wakeman—The King of the Klassics Jousts with 'King Arthur.'" *Circus*, July 1975.

"Rosko Mercer to Do DJ Show with WNEW-FM." *Billboard*, October 28, 1967.

Rubenstein, Steve. "Yes Takes a Gamble." *Circus Raves*, October 1975, pages 55–56.

Schact, Janis. "Emerson, Lake, and Palmer: The Dagger Does More Than You Think." *Circus*, March 1972.

Scoppa, Bud, with Billy Cioffi. "Squire and Rabin Say, "Yes, I Do." *Guitar World*, September 1987.

"S.F. 'Hippop' Music Format of the Future?" *Billboard*, June 24, 1967.

Smith-Park, Paul. "Emerson Hopes to Break Banco." *Circus*, January 1973.

Sobel, Robert. "RCA Classical Sales Up 3.5 Percent." *Billboard*, August 5, 1972.

Stable, Simon. "Peter Sinfield—It Was Fripp or Me: One of Us Had to Quit." *New Musical Express*, January 8, 1972, page 17.

Stable, Simon. "Robert Fripp—It Was Sinfield Or Me: One of Us Had to Quit." *New Musical Express*, January 15, 1972.

"Stargazing: The Big Names of Music on the Shape of Things to Come." *Melody Maker*, December 30, 1972.

Stewart, Tony. "Flash: Concert Review." *New Musical Express*, March 4, 1972.

Stewart, Tony. "Yes on Edge." *New Musical Express*, July 15, 1972.

"Studio Directory: Advision (entry)." *Studio Sound*, April 1971, page 171.

Sutherland, Sam. "Talent in Action: Eagles, Jackson Browne, J. D. Souther—The Felt Forum." *Billboard*, October 14, 1972.

Sutherland, Sam. "What's Happening." *Billboard*, October 14, 1972.

Swenson, John. "Longplayers": "Yes: Tormato" record review. *Circus*, November 7, 1978.

"Talent: Signings." *Billboard*, December 23, 1972, page 10.

Tan, Anne and Howard Bloom. "Yes: Weaving the Fragile Web." *Circus*, March 1972, pages 20–23.

Taylor, Spike. "Rick Wakeman Embarrassed by Success." *New Musical Express*, April 22, 1972, page 8.

"The End of the Rainbow." *New Musical Express*, March 18, 1972.

"The Rock Report: Yes." *Melody Maker*, April 23, 1973, page 33.

Tiegel, Eliot. "KYA Boost 'San Francisco' Sound and Doubles on Music." *Billboard*, June 10, 1967.

"Top Tape Cartridges." *Billboard*, January 22, 1972, page 34.

Top 200 Albums charts. *Billboard*, issues January 15, 1972; May 13, 1972; May 20, 1972; July 29, 1972; August 5, 1972; September 2, 1972; September 9, 1972; September 16, 1972; September 30, 1972; October 7, 1972; October 14, 1972; November 4, 1972; November 18, 1972; November 25, 1972; December 2, 1972; December 9, 1972; December 16, 1972; January 6, 1973

Turner, Steve. "The Great Yes Technique Debate." *Rolling Stone*, March 30, 1972.

"Two Kings." *Melody Maker*, February 10, 1973.

Tyler, Tony. "Genesis Poised on the Brink." *New Musical Express*, November 18, 1972.

Tyler, Tony. "Instruments: Mellotrons in Use." *New Musical Express*, February 12, 1972.

Tyler, Tony. "The King Is Dead. Long Live the King." *New Musical Express*, November 11, 1972, pages 8–9.

"Under the Influence: This Week, Carl Palmer." *New Musical Express*, November 11, 1972, page 8.

Watts, Michael. "The Man with the Midas Touch: An Interview with Ahmet Ertegun, Boss of Atlantic Records." *Melody Maker*, December 16, 1972.

"WDAS-FM's Lit Seeks Progressive Rock Net." *Billboard*, June 1, 1968.

Webb, Julie. "Music to Lay Chicks By: Uriah Heep's David Byron Talking." *New Musical Express*, April 15, 1972.

Webb, Julie. "Self-Indulgent Yes." *New Musical Express*, December 23, 1972.

Welch, Chris. "Angel Dust—the Latest Ex-Yes Band." *Melody Maker*, October 28, 1972, page 13.

Welch, Chris. "Squire Route." *Melody Maker*, April 28, 1973, page 9.

Welch, Chris. "Still Bill." *Melody Maker*, February 3, 1973, page 9.

Welch, Chris. "The Anderson Tapes." *Melody Maker*, April 22, 1972.

Welch, Chris. "The What, Where and Why of Howe." *Melody Maker*, January 8, 1972.

Welch, Chris. "Yes—Stricken by Studio Stupor!" *Melody Maker*, July 8, 1972.

Welch, Chris. "Yesquire." *Melody Maker*, October 14, 1972, page 22.

West, David. "The Pioneers of Prog Dumming." *Rhythm*, July 2015.

"Wetton Quits Family." *New Musical Express*, July 22, 1972, page 4.

"What's Happening." *Billboard*, October 14, 1972.

Wicks, Keith. "Around the Studios: Number 3: Advision." *Studio Sound and Tape Recorder*, May 1970, pages 204–205, 207.

Wicks, Keith. "Studio Diary." *Studio Sound*, May 1971, page 219.

Williams, Richard. "Can Do." *Melody Maker*, January 27, 1973.

Williams, Richard. "Jamie: Why I Quit Crimso." *Melody Maker*, March 17, 1973, page 8.

"World-Wide Yes." *Melody Maker*, January 20, 1973.

"Yes in new style Whistle Test." Melody Maker, March 24, 1973, page 6.

"Yes Man to Join Crimson." *Melody Maker*, July 22, 1972.

"Yes Mania Hits US." *New Musical Express*, February 12, 1972.

"Yes Theft." *Melody Maker*, January 13, 1973.

Young, Charles M. "Emerson, Lake, and Palmer Go for Broke." *Rolling Stone*, July 14, 1977.

Newspapers

"Apollo Splashed Down for Good." *Newsday*, December 20, 1972, page 7.

"Arabs Kill 2 Israelis in Raid at Olympics." *Newsday*, September 5, 1972, page 1.

Bailey, Patty. "Good Concert? Yes." *The BG News*, November 21, 1972, page 5.

Baker, Robb. "The Sound: Music and Radio: For Young Listeners." *Chicago Tribune*, April 28, 1968.

Baker, Robb. "The Sound: Music and Radio: for Young Listeners." *Chicago Tribune,* July 5, 1968.

Binder, David. "A 23-Hour Drama." *New York Times,* September 6, 1972, page 1.

Blair, W. Granger. "Britain to Outlaw Pirate Radio Stations." *New York Times,* July 29, 1966.

Brown Daily Herald ad for upcoming Yes show with J. Geils Band (Friday, February 25, 1972), February 23, 1972, page 8.

Bungey, John. "To Beat, or Not to Beat—That Really is the Question." *Times* (UK), November 23, 2007, page 15[S].

Christgau, Robert. "No, No, No, No, No, No." *Newsday,* February 15, 1974.

Christgau, Robert. "Records: Curious? Read on." *Newsday,* October 27, 1972.

Christgau, Robert. "Records: Waxing prosaic." *Newsday,* August 4, 1972.

Dahlbloom, Mary Jo. "Winter Week Considered Successful By Directors." *Vermont Cynic,* March 2, 1972, front page.

Dilts, James D. "The Eagles and Yes Appear in Columbia." *Baltimore Sun,* August 14, 1972, page B4.

DeWan, George. "After Giant Leap, Slow Steps in Space." *Newsday,* July 14, 1974, page 6.

Feron, James. "British Pirate Radio Stations Thrive." *New York Times,* January 3, 1965.

Ferretti, Fred. "FM Radio Grows Up to Have Its Own Convention." *New York Times,* April 2, 1970.

Gent, George. "Jimi Hendrix, Rock Star, Is Dead in London at 27." *New York Times,* September 19, 1970.

Goldstein, Richard. "Freedom Can Be Costly." *New York Times,* February 4, 1968.

Gould, Jack. "Radio: British Commercial Broadcasters Are at Sea." *New York Times,* March 25, 1966.

Gray, Stephen. "Wakeman: On the Verge." *Baltimore Sun,* September 16, 1973.

Griffiths, Kathie. "Baildon musician who left Bradford for Belgium dies at 67." *Telegraph and Argus,* November 3, 2010.

Hamilton, Thomas. "Yes Group Performs at River Festival." *St. Louis Post Dispatch,* Aug 22, 1972.

Heckman, Don. "Melodrama Marks Rock by Emerson, Lake, and Palmer." *New York Times,* November 27, 1971.

Jahn, Mike. "British Band Makes Debut at Fillmore." *New York Times,* May 2, 1971.

"Last Pirate Radio Continues to Defy New British Law." *The New York Times,* August 17, 1967.

Lingeman, Richard. "Offerings at the Psychedelicatessen." *New York Times,* July 10, 1966, page 182.

Mason, Bob. "Over the Edge." *Chevron,* November 3, 1972.

Mayer, Ira. "From Kongos to ELP." *New York Times.* Feb. 20, 1972.

Palmer, Robert. "Emerson, Lake, and Palmer Go Classical." *New York Times,* July 8, 1977.

Robins, Wayne. "English Rock Invades Anew." *Newsday.* June 21, 1977.

"Rocket Pioneer Von Braun leaves NASA for Fairchild." *Newsday,* May 27, 1972.

Rockwell, John. "Cliched and Casual, Wakeman Rocks in Garden Concert." *New York Times*, October 16, 1974, page 35.

Roberts, John Storm. "Progressive Rock's Classic Synthesizers." *Newsday*. July 3, 1977.

Shelton, Robert. "Rick Wakeman: Crystal Palace." *Times* (UK), July 29, 1974, page 7.

Shelton, Robert. "Yes: Rainbow Theatre." *Times* (UK), November 21, 1973, page 11.

Sinclair, David. "Battle of the Yes men." *Times* (UK), February 4, 1989, page 38.

Smith, Stephan. "Backstage: More Blood Than Song." *Brown Daily Herald*, February 28, 1972, page 3.

St. John, Jeffrey. "In Defense of the Space Program: An Achievement of Epic Proportions." *Newsday*, April 11, 1972, page 40.

Stanton, Victor. "An Endless Wait for Fine Music." *Kitchener-Waterloo Record*, October 31 1972.

Stewart, Bob. "Music: J. Geils." *Brown Daily Herald*, February 28, 1972, page 3.

"The Year of 1972." *Newsday*, December 31, 1972, page 20.

Thompson, Doug. "25,300 say Yes at River Festival." *Alton Telegraph*, July 10, 1975.

Wale, Michael. "Pop find of the year." *Times* (UK), July 13, 1970, page 5.

Walsh, Stephen. "Philomusica: Burlington House." *Times* (UK), July 10, 1972, page 7.

"'Yes' Appearing Tomorrow in Semester's First Event." *Bethany Tower*, February 17, 1972, page 3.

"Yes Rescheduled." *Alestley*, July 27, 1972.

DVDs and Videos

Bruford and the Beat. Axis Video (VHS), 1982.

Classic Artists: Yes: The Definitive Fully Authorized Story (DVD) Image Entertainment. Inc., 2006

Yessongs: The 1973 Concert Video of the Original Yes (VHS). VidAmerica, Inc., 1984.

Yesyears: A Retrospective (VHS). Atco Video, 1991.

Other Documents and Sources

Anderson Bruford Wakeman Howe official tour program, 1989.

Asia tour program, 1983.

Notes From the Edge: Alan White and the Beatles, NFTE #247. Interviewer Mike Tiano.

The Parish of St. Andrew, Kingsbury Weekly Bulletin (for the week beginning Sunday, July 5, 2015)

Press release: "YES Cancels 40th Anniversary Tour." Issued by Press Here Publicity, Wednesday, June 4, 2008, 3:15 p.m.

"Taggants in Explosives." NTIS order #PB80-192719. Congress of the United States, Office of Technology Assessment, Washington. D.C., April 1980.

Yes copyright contract from 1969.

Yes North American Tour program, 1984.

Yes transfer of copyrights from mid-1970s (estimated date: 1975).

University Archives

Bethany College
Bowling Green University
Brown University
Duke University
Gannon University
Gettysburg College
Kent State University
Lakeland University
Princeton University
Southern Illinois University Edwardsville
Stetson University
Stony Brook University
SUNY Plattsburgh
University of Akron
University of Notre Dame
University of Waterloo
University of Vermont

Websites

www.americanradiohistory.com
www.asia.si.edu
www.bbc.com
www.catholic.org
www.cbsnews.com
http://content.time.com
www.dictionary.com
www.dos.ny.gov/corps/bus_entity_search.html
http://forgotten-yesterdays.com
http://www.inthestudio.net/redbeards-blog/yes-close-edge-40th-anniversary/
www.metmuseum.org
www.mfa.org/
new.artsmia.org
www.Pantone.com
www.presidency.ucsb.edu
www.riaa.com
www.rockhall.com
http://www.soundandvision.com/content/steven-wilson-once-and-future-
    surround-king#F0ASzAFOMauRy2qt.97
www.yesmuseum.com (Lee Abrams interview with Jon Anderson)
yesworld.com
www.youtube.com/watch?v=5DinP93nW8Q

INDEX